Critical Issues in Educational Leadership Series
Joseph Murphy, Series Editor

Understanding and Assessing the Charter School Movement
JOSEPH MURPHY AND CATHERINE DUNN SHIFFMAN

School Choice in Urban America:
Magnet Schools and the Pursuit of Equity
CLAIRE SMREKAR AND ELLEN GOLDRING

Lessons from High-Performing Hispanic Schools:
Creating Learning Communities
PEDRO REYES, JAY D. SCRIBNER, AND ALICIA PAREDES SCRIBNER, EDS.

Schools for Sale:Why Free Market Policies
Won't Improve America's Schools, and What Will
ERNEST R. HOUSE

Reclaiming Educational Administration as a Caring Profession
LYNN G. BECK

Cognitive Perspectives on Educational Leadership
PHILIP HALLINGER, KENNETH LEITHWOOD, AND JOSEPH MURPHY, EDS.

D0792468

Understanding
AND
Assessing
THE
Charter School Movement

JOSEPH MURPHY
CATHERINE DUNN SHIFFMAN

Teachers College, Columbia University
New York and London

Published by Teachers College Press, 1234 Amsterdam Avenue, New York, NY
10027

Library of Congress Cataloging-in-Publication Data

Murphy, Joseph, 1949–
    Understanding and assessing the charter school movement / Joseph Murphy,
Catherine Dunn Shiffman.
        p.   cm. — (Critical issues in educational leadership series)
    Includes bibliographical references and index.
    ISBN 0-8077-4199-X (cloth : alk. paper) — ISBN 0-8077-4198-1 (pbk. : alk.
    paper)   1. Charter schools—United States.   2. Educational change—United
States.   I. Shiffman, Catherine Dunn.   II. Title.   III. Series.
LB2806.36 .M87   2002
371.01'—dc21   2001052285

ISBN 0-8077-4198-1 (paper)
ISBN 0-8077-4199-X (cloth)

Printed on acid-free paper
Manufactured in the United States of America

09   08   07   06   05   04   03   02   8   7   6   5   4   3   2   1

To the Doctor from Goose Lane Road
and
To John and my parents—with thanks

In short, charter schools are beginning to look
like a full-fledged, bipartisan educational movement.
(Buechler, 1996, p. 1)

Charter schools are the consummate
postmodern education reform.
(Wells, Lopez, Scott, & Holme, 1999, p. 181)

Contents

1. **Introduction. Laying the Foundations**   1

   Why a Book on Charter Schools?   1
   What Is a Charter School?   3
   Where Do Charter Schools Fit in the Struggle
   *   to Reform Schooling?*   5
   Why Are Charters So Popular?   11
   Why a Metanarrative Is Difficult to Construct   16
   Summary   20

2. **History of Charter Schools**   22

   Development of the Charter School Concept   22
   The First Charter School State—Minnesota   27
   Growth and Popularity of Charter Schools   29
   Evolving Opposition to and Support of
   *   Charter Schools*   36
   Factors Influencing State Approaches to
   *   Charter Legislation*   43
   Summary   47

3. **Exploring the Charter School Architecture**   48

   Dimensions of All Charter Schools   48
   The Charter Landscape. A Descriptive Snapshot   71
   Educational Program   91
   Summary   99

4. **The Supporting Climate for Charter Schools**   **101**

    A Supportive Environment for Reform Via Charters   *101*
    Continued Concerns about the Effectiveness
        of Schooling   *114*
    Conclusion   *124*

5. **The Embedded Logic of Charter Schools**   **125**

    The Reform Engine   *126*
    The Reform Dynamics   *136*
    Summary   *146*

6. ***Expected Benefits and Possible Costs***   ***149***

    Quality   *150*
    Efficiency   *153*
    Equity   *157*
    Impact on Employees   *165*
    Summary   *168*

7. **Charter School Effects**   **169**

    Setting the Stage   *169*
    Individual School Effects   *173*
    System-Wide Impact   *205*
    Summary   *216*

References   **219**

Index   **241**

About the Authors   **255**

CHAPTER 1

Introduction: Laying the Foundations

Because of the uncertainties about charter school initiation and survival, no one knows whether to expect charter schools to remain mar-
ginal phenomena . . . or to lead to a profound change in the way
American public schools are governed. (Hill, Pierce, & Guthrie, 1997,
p. 121)

For the better part of the last quarter century, vigorous efforts have been
underway to reform American public education. Well into maturity, this reform movement gave birth to a new change strategy, a hybrid form known as
charter schools. Drawing on earlier streams of reform energy while pushing
the change envelope, charter schools have become extremely popular. They
have experienced tremendous growth and, in the process, have helped to recast the definition of public education and to reframe our understanding of
school improvement.

In this introductory chapter, we begin the process of exploring what is
known about charter schools. We start with an explanation of the need for a
metanarrative on charter schools. The bulk of the chapter is then devoted to
answering three basic questions: What are charter schools? Where do they fit
on the landscape of school reform? And why did they emerge on the reform
scene with such vigor, (i.e., why is the charter concept so popular)? We conclude by returning to the topic of the charter school metanarrative, reviewing
reasons why constructing this story line is such a difficult task.

WHY A BOOK ON CHARTER SCHOOLS?

The charter school movement is the most radical challenge ever to
the existing system. (Sarason, 1998, p. 52)

As chroniclers of the comprehensive reform movement in the United
States, now seems a particularly good time to us to have an in-depth exploration of charter schools. To begin with, as Caudell (1997b) and others have

observed, "Charter schools have moved to center stage in the key debates facing schooling in America" (Rofes, 1995, p. 2). "A term unheard of just a few years ago has now become part of state and local educational reform debates across the nation" (Bierlein & Mulholland, 1993, p. 10). For an assortment of reasons we detail throughout the book, charter schools have risen to the apex of the educational reform agenda (Molnar, 1996). They are "beginning to look like a significant education movement" (Buechler, 1996, p. vii). And, as Vanourek and his colleagues have observed, "With swelling numbers and rising expectations comes intensifying curiosity" (Vanourek, Manno, Finn, & Bierlein, 1997b, p. 1). Also, because there are "many different opinions and strong feelings" (Sautter, 1993, p. 1) about the charter concept, stocktaking work that might inform the charter debate is clearly in order.

More important, charters are a special type of change in terms of robustness as a "tool for public education experimentation and change" (Sautter, 1993, p. 15). As Budde (1996) and other analysts have reported, charter schools introduce quite different and fairly radical elements into the school reform mosaic. For example, Sarason (1998) has concluded that charters are "the most radical educational reform effort in the post World War II era" (p. vii). They are "intended to open up the possibility of fundamental change in public education—in who makes decisions about public schools, in what forms public education may take, and, ultimately, in what students will learn" (Buechler, 1996, p. 37). As such "they are at the epicenter of America's most powerful educational reform earthquake" (Finn, Manno, & Vanourek, 2000, p. 219). Because the charter idea offers such a profound challenge to the existing system of public education, especially in the ways schools are organized and governed, "there is a growing need for understanding of the idea itself and where it fits in the national discussion about strategy" (Kolderie, 1994, p. 103).

Concomitantly, a review of the evolution of the charter school concept itself suggests that this is a propitious time for a thoughtful analysis of the movement. A good deal of ground has been covered in the decade since the first charter school opened its doors. Given the emergence of the charter movement into early adolescence, now is a ripe opportunity (Sarason, 1998) for a "searching reexamination of the sector's history, context, and role in reform efforts" (Rofes, 1995, p. 4). As Hassel (1997) has observed, as the charter movement has aged, we are uncovering increasingly good information about an array of critical issues such as implementation challenges. We would extend this conclusion, maintaining that the first round of studies which have begun to tease out the impact of charters lends additional impetus for the type of synthetic analysis we undertake in this volume.

The central question according to Bierlein and Bateman (1995) is "whether the charter school concept is powerful enough medicine to become meaningful reform, or will it become just another watered-down cure" (p. 48).

While we are still some distance away from crafting a definitive answer to this inquiry, we are able for the first time to make some preliminary assessments of the claims and counterclaims that fill the pages of the charter school literature. Is "the charter idea a seed that is spreading, changing the schooling and lives of thousands and thousands of youngsters," as Nathan (1996a, p. 71) avers—a reform that holds "the promise of bringing out the best in public school classrooms" (Prielipp, 1997, p. 1)? Or is it simply another reform de jure (Fusarelli, 1999), or, worse yet, a story of "waste and chicanery" (Little Hoover Commission, 1996, p. 86)—the pathway leading to the abandonment or dismantling of the American system of public education?

While, to be sure, the overall significance of the charter movement is yet to be determined, "some important questions about charter schools are starting to be answered" (Buechler, 1996, p. xi). We know considerably more now than we did even three years ago about consequences both intended and unintended (Becker, Nakagawa, & Corwin, 1997). Now is a good time then to stand back and see where the charter school movement has brought us in terms of school reform.

WHAT IS A CHARTER SCHOOL?

Legislation makes charter schools different from state to state, but charters still share key characteristics. (Loveless & Jasin, 1998, p. 11)

Throughout this volume, we attempt to provide a comprehensive answer to the question, "What is a charter school?" To do so, we explore the concept in a variety of different ways, including exposing the conceptual and theoretical scaffolding on which the charter school movement has been constructed; investigating what charter schools mean to the adults who work there, to the students who are educated there, and to the parents who send their youngsters to charter schools; analyzing the component parts of charters; cataloging the intended effects of charter schools; and examining what charters look like in action.

We acknowledge at the outset that there is no "quick and easy definition of the term 'charter school'" (Northeast and Islands Regional Educational Laboratory, 1999, p. 2), that there are nearly as "many definitions of charter schools as there are pieces of charter school legislation" (Buechler, 1996, p. 14), and that this variety "militates against one simple definition of a charter school" (National Education Association [NEA], n.d., p. 1). At the microlevel of the individual school, the plethora of educational philosophies and approaches in play only adds to this variety (Lane, 1998). In short, this "single policy concept" (Bulkley, 1998, p. 37) not only has "different meanings across states but multiple meanings within a state" (p. 37). Our intention at this point in the volume is simply to provide a brief definition from which we can build. Discussions of the complexity and diversity in the charter school movement are delayed to the final section of this chapter. The focus here is on the key characteristics that charters share.

Charter schools have been defined by nearly everyone who writes on the topic. A sample of those definitions is provided below:

> A charter school is an autonomous, results-oriented, publicly funded school of choice that is designed and run by teachers or others under contract with a public sponsor. (Buechler, 1996, p. 4)

> A workable starting definition is that a charter school is an "independent public school of choice, freed from rules but accountable for results." (Finn, Manno, & Vanourek, 2000, p. 14)

> Public charter schools are nonsectarian public schools open to all interested students. Legislation prohibits charter schools from charging tuition, and in most states they receive 80 to 100% of district per-pupil funding. Charter schools are held accountable for student outcomes and risk school closure if established performance standards are not met. Depending on state legislation, charter schools can be free-standing or operate under the jurisdiction of a local district. As public schools, they must comply with civil rights, health, safety, public disclosure, and other federal and state regulations. (Northwest Regional Educational Laboratory, 1998, p. 1)

> Charter schools are commonly defined as publicly funded, nonsectarian public schools that operate free of the many regulations, restrictions, and mandates of traditional public schools. These schools are chartered or contracted as separate legal entities. As defined in the contract, they are accountable for their results at the end of the contract period—usually 3 to 5 years. (Fulford, 1997, p. 2)

> Charter schools are publicly funded schools of choice operating free of state regulation and independent of local school districts. (Loveless & Jasin, 1998, p. 9)

> Charter schools are public schools that are granted a specific amount of autonomy, determined by state law and/or the specific charter, to make decisions concerning the organizational structure, curriculum, and educational emphasis of their school. Charter schools are granted waivers from certain regulations that typically bind public schools. In return for this additional autonomy, charter schools are held accountable for the academic achievement of the students in the charter school, and the school faces suspension or closure if accepted performance standards are not met. (Lane, 1998, p. 2)

> Charter schools are essentially deregulated, site-based managed schools of choice. (Corwin, Carlos, Lagomarsino, & Scott, 1996, p. 6)

> Charter schools are (mostly) independent public schools of choice accountable for the results of student achievement. (Manno, Finn, Bierlein, & Vanourek, 1998a, p. 537)

> Charter Schools are sponsor-created and administered, outcome-based public schools that operate under a contract between the school and the local board or the state. (Sautter, 1993, p. 2)

Core dimensions of charters include: (1) freedom for parents on the demand side of choice and, by opening up delivery, freedom for potential providers on the supply side of choice; (2) accountability realized by unleashing market forces (i.e., competition) and by fulfilling the charter contract—as opposed to accountability through regulation; and (3) decentralization of control to the local unit of operation, (i.e., the individual school). As such, charter schools are first and foremost an "institutional reform" (Rosenblum Brigham Associates, 1998, p. 27) or "an institutional innovation" (Kolderie, n.d., p. 1), a "state strategy for system change" (p. 2) that facilitates local school improvement. How these key characteristics—choice, deregulation, decentralization, and competition—play out in actual schools depends a good deal on the state and local contexts. We explore these context issues throughout the volume.

WHERE DO CHARTER SCHOOLS FIT IN THE STRUGGLE TO REFORM SCHOOLING?

> Today's charter-school initiatives are rooted in the educational reforms of the 1980s and 1990s, from state mandates to improve instruction, to school-based management, school restructuring, and private/public-choice initiatives. (Hadderman, 1998, p. 1)

Roots and Patterns

Much of the charter school literature pays insufficient attention to the place of charters in the larger history of school reform. The literature, as Rofes (1998b) has observed, reveals both "a lack of awareness of historical precedents for charter schools . . . and a failure to understand how charters are situated in the reform debate of the past twenty years" (p. 43). The reader is often left with the impression that charters simply appeared on the scene whole cloth, both unconnected to earlier reforms and borrowing little of the intellectual capital provided by analysts over the last two decades. This is unfortunate because it limits analyses that might enhance the capacity of the charter concept to improve public education. It is also inaccurate. Much of the charter schools tapestry was woven from reform ideas that emerged during the 1980s and early 1990s (Bulkley, 1998; Hassel, 1999a; McGree, 1995b). While the charter school movement greatly reinforced many of these policy strands (e.g., deregulation) and spun them together in ways unseen in earlier eras of reform, the fact remains that charter schools have their roots in earlier change initiatives and grow from "ideas that have been evolving among policy-makers, practitioners, and researches for the past 25 years" (Bomotti, Ginsberg, & Cobb, 1999, p. 5).

Equally important, as Nathan (1996a), Rofes (1998b), and others have discerned, charter schools are part of the long tradition of educational discourse about the role of education in a capitalist-democratic state. Their roots are quite deep. The entire concept is, according to Nathan, "an outgrowth of the 200-year effort in this country to expand educational opportunity" (p. 180).

In examining educational reform over the last 20 years—say from the release of *A Nation at Risk* (The National Commission on Excellence in Education, 1983)—distinct patterns emerge. Perhaps the most dominant has been the cycle of reform. In this recurring drama, problems with American public schools, both actual and manufactured, are exposed. Reform ideas are then generated to address these deficiencies. Subsequent analyses reveal that these initiatives have proven insufficient—they have not provided "an acceptable cure for the nation's public schools. . . . As a nation, we continue to be disappointed" (Bierlein & Bateman, 1995, p. 48). Receptivity to new ideas increases (Garn, 1998), especially to ideas that would have been viewed as "implausible" if it were not for the supposed failure of earlier reforms (Hill, Pierce, & Guthrie, 1997, p. vii). New models of change are then forged. It is through such a process that we arrived at the charter school model of school reform, cast, as noted below, with many of the reform elements from earlier times in reconfigured form.

The relevant question, then, is what components from earlier reforms were welded together to form the infrastructure of the charter school concept. To answer that question, we need to step back a bit and illuminate reforms of the last 20 years.

Reform 1980–2000

One can bundle reforms for analysis in myriad ways (Murphy & Adams, 1998). We find three methods to be especially helpful: by time or phase of reform, especially the broad sweeps of change (see Murphy, 1990); by level of the system affected, that is, core technology, management, or institution (see Murphy, 1991); and by the dominant mechanism or governance system emphasized: government, profession, citizens, or market (Murphy, 1999, 2000). Below, we employ two of these frameworks, examining U.S. educational reforms of the last 20 years in terms of three distinctive eras and four mechanisms of reform.

The Intensification Era (1980–1987)

Early action on the problems with education was almost entirely located in the government sector. There was a widespread feeling that, while seriously impaired, the educational system could be repaired by strong medicine. Because the government was the dominant player in the educational enterprise, reformers expected the state to develop and administer appropriate remedies. The philosophical infrastructure of early suggestions to repair this situation was highly mechanistic, comprised mainly of centralized controls and standards. This approach assumed that conditions of schooling contributing to poor student outcomes were attributable to poor quality of workers, low expectations and effort, and inadequate tools. Reformers viewed these conditions as subject to revision through mandated top-down initiatives, especially those from the state. In those early reform efforts, using a government model to institute improvement proposals led to an emphasis on policy mechanisms such as prescriptions, tightly specified resource allocations, and performance components that focused on repairing parts of the system (such as writing better textbooks); raising the quality of the workforce by telling employees how to work, for example, specifying instructional models; and mandating higher expectations by increasing graduation requirements and legislating success in the classroom as a prerequisite for participation in extracurricular activities.

The Restructuring Era (1986–1995)

Given the chain of reform activity outlined above, the reader will not be surprised to learn that initial government reform strategies quickly came under attack on philosophical and practical grounds. Critics questioned whether continued reliance on an increasingly discredited reform engine—government—would ever work. Even those who were not hostile to government raised serious doubts about the appropriateness of reforms mandated from the top. On practical grounds, critics made two points: that reforms did not seem to be producing desired outcomes and that reforms were never likely to do so because they were not designed to get to the heart of the problem.

Judging the intensification movement as inadequate at best and wrongheaded at worst, reformers clamored for fundamental revisions in the ways schools were organized and governed. Reformers in the late 1980s and early 1990s argued that continued repairs of the old system were not only unlikely to alleviate problems but likely to be counterproductive.

The philosophical foundation of the restructuring movement is that educational improvement is contingent upon empowering teachers to work more effectively with students. A less well-ingrained but still persistent theme is that real change also depends on empowering parents. The major policy mechanism employed in those reforms was "power distribution." Unlike the strategy employed in the intensification era, reformers designed the restructuring model to capitalize on the energy and creativity of individuals at the school site level.

Underlying almost all restructuring proposals was the assumption that problems in education could be ascribed to the structure of schooling, "that the highest impediment to progress is the nature of the system itself" (Carnegie Forum on Education and the Economy, 1986, p. 40). The bureaucratic infrastructure of education was subjected to close scrutiny and found to be failing. It is not surprising that the focus of improvement in this era of reform was on the professionals who populated schools and the conditions they required to work effectively, including basic changes in the organizational arrangements of schooling. Restructuring would require a shift from mechanistic, structure-reinforcing strategies to a professional approach to reform and from "regulation and compliance monitoring to mobilization of institutional capacity" (Timar & Kirp, 1988, p. 75). Nor is it surprising that reformers who considered the basic structure of schools as the root of education's problems should also propose more far-reaching and radical solutions than their predecessors who believed that the current system could be repaired.

Two broad content areas dominated the portfolio of reformers in the restructuring movement—decentralization/site-based management (SBM) and initial forays into school choice (Murphy & Beck, 1995). The tracks of this administrative or organizational decentralization are visible across the reform landscape of the late 1980s and early 1990s. Decentralization or SBM under a professional model occurs when influence shifts from school administrators to teachers. Legislation establishing structures for such power sharing was central to the restructuring agenda. In contrast to the professionally driven model of SBM, citizen control "shifts power from professionals and the central board to community groups not previously involved in school governance. Thus lay persons, not the professional hierarchy, are in control and accountability is directed outward toward the community" (Wohlstetter, 1990, p. 6).

At the same time that administrative, professional, and community decentralization initiatives were sweeping over the educational landscape, the restructuring era witnessed efforts to introduce the underpinnings of the market philosophy into schools, especially market-sensitive measures of accountability. Controlled choice plans were introduced. These plans permitted parents to select among traditionally defined public schools. While limited in scope, these early choice initiatives brought "the market" into the reform equation in a systematic fashion for the first time and with it new ways of thinking about educational improvement, ones built on sensitivity and responsiveness to customer needs and interests.

The Reformation Era (1992–Present)

While the dividing line between intensification and restructuring reform eras is fairly clear, the demarcation between the reforms of the restructuring era (roughly 1986–1995) and the subsequent reformation era is much less obvious. Still, enough information is available to indicate that in the early 1990s, the United States entered a stage of reform that is distinct from the improvement efforts of the restructuring period.

The reform infrastructure of the reformation era parallels the basic dynamic noted above—the feeling that prior change efforts did not produce the improvements for which advocates had hoped. In important ways, however, the reformation period is different from earlier eras of reform. To begin with, for the first time in the history of American educational reform, all four reform mechanisms fully share center stage. In particular, the legitimacy of citizen and consumer reform strategies are acknowledged in ways that had been impossible to imagine only a decade earlier. Part of this sanctioning can be traced to new analyses of the vitality of these reform strategies, while some can be attributed to continued, vehement attacks on the government-professional cartel in education. In addition, for the first time since its development, the very viability of the system of public education was thrown into question.

Early reform initiatives of this era indicate that the government reform portfolio is dominated by efforts to develop standards and accountability mechanisms. Reforms that privilege the profession look less to nurturing shared governance at the school site than they do to ways of strengthening the teaching profession. Key initiatives include the creation of professional standards for individual educators and for the institutions that prepare them. These standards support more effective systems of licensure and bring advanced certification to life for the first time.

Citizen-based reforms of the reformation era are designed to build on gains made in the restructuring era in enhancing parental voice. While this picture remains somewhat cloudy, reforms in this domain might best be grouped together under the heading of "parents' rights." Such initiatives allow parents to form their own schools and to participate more in the operation of the schools they select for their children. Such initiatives often blend with the market-grounded reforms discussed below.

In the restructuring era, market influences began to work their way into reform designs. In the reformation era, marketization has become a central reform ideology in its own right, one that is used at times to jar public schools from their perceived complacency and at other times to provide alternatives to public provision of educational services. The central strategies here are best captured under the concept of privatization (Murphy, 1996; Murphy, Gilmer, Weise, & Page, 1998).

Situating Charters

In Chapters 4 and 5, we explore the conceptual scaffolding of charter schools as well as theories of action that are driving the charter school movement. Here we simply describe the five strands from the earlier reform efforts that have become key threads in the charter school tapestry (see also Buechler, 1996; Bulkley, 1998; Hassel, 1997, 1999a). At the top of the list is a very robust notion of school choice, one that draws material from both the restructuring and reform eras but adds considerable additional firepower as well, thus "placing charter schools at the forefront of the school choice movement" (Cobb & Glass, 1999, p. 2). Choice in charter schools is designed first and foremost to open up the provision of educational services. This is a powerful addition to the reform algorithm, for opening up opportunities for consumers on the demand side of the choice equation means little in the absence of multiple providers on the supply side of that equation.

Deregulation and decentralization are the second and third major elements of the charter school movement. If choice provides autonomy for consumers and providers, deregulation and decentralization combine to create "operational, programmatic, and financial autonomy" (Finn, Manno, & Vanourek, 2000, p. 228) (i.e., local control) for individual schools—"the freedom to conceptualize the outcomes to be obtained and the practices to be used to accomplish goals" (Wohlstetter, Wenning, & Briggs, 1995, p. 334). Again, we underscore the fact that charters build from earlier reform initiatives, especially from school-based management and shared decision making on the ideology of decentralization, and considerably strengthen the notion of local autonomy as well, laying out what McGree (1995b) labels "the first real model for true decentralization and autonomy within the public schools" (p. 10). Underlying all three of the components described so far—choice, deregulation, and decentralization—is "the principle of 'subsidarity,' which states that problems should be solved as close to home as possible" (Finn, Manno, & Vanourek, 2000, p. 228), the "idea that increased school-level autonomy is a necessary, if not a sufficient condition, for improved educational practice" (Bulkley, 1998, p. 29), and an acknowledgment that "autonomy is essentially the underlying principle of charter schools" (Finn et al., 2000, p. 242).

Additionally, charter schools represent a maturing of the infusion of market forces into public education over the last 15 years. At the center of this trend toward the development of what Kolderie (1994) has labeled a "social market" (p. 107) has been the infusion of competition into the education system, the demands of which, in turn, have reinforced the need for local autonomy (McGree, 1995a).

Closely linked with competition and marketization, but with roots in all three of the eras of reform described above, is the fifth component of the charter school model: double-edged support composed of accountability and standards. In particular, the charter movement spotlights and merges two forms of accountability largely conspicuous by their absence before 1980 (Murphy, 1992; Weick, 1976)—outcome-based accountability and consumer-based accountability.

WHY ARE CHARTERS SO POPULAR?

Charter schools could easily be called the "all things to all people" reform. Free-market conservatives see them as a way to enhance competition in education and a step in the direction of vouchers. . . . Cultural conservatives hope that they will increase parental control over the values taught in schools their children attend, while those interested in restructuring schools see them as a way to further their goals. Charter advocates include a "strange bedfellows" combination of political actors and policymakers who are at odds on many other educational issues. (Bulkley, 1998, p. 1)

Indices

While charter schools are not without their critics, especially analysts who find some of the ideology on which they are built to be problematic, they are a hugely popular instrument of school reform. While appeal can be measured in multiple ways, we focus on two at this stage of our discussion—the growth of charter schools throughout the nation and their ability to harbor a collection of often quite disparate reform advocates and policy actors under the charter school banner. While we track the growth of charter schools in detail in a subsequent chapter, we simply note here that in 1990 there were no charter schools in the United States. Less than a decade later, there were over 1,700. During that same time period, 35 states adopted charter school laws.

The allure of charter schools for a wide array of actors in the reform drama unfolding in the United States has been nothing short of remarkable. As the authors of the UCLA Charter School Study (n.d.) concluded, "Unlike most partisan reform efforts, the charter school concept has been embraced by diverse groups of policy makers, educators, parents, and activists" (p. 8). Molnar has stated, "Everyone, it seems, loves charter schools" (1996, p. 9). On one front, this appeal can be seen in the "evidence of strong bipartisan support for charter schools" (Wohlstetter & Griffin, 1997a, p. 2). Indeed, the charter school movement is often referred to "as a bipartisan reform effort" (Wells, Grutzik, Carnochan, Slayton, & Vasudeva, 1999, p. 513) that draws political support across party lines (Manno, Finn, Bierlein, & Vanourek, 1998b).

In addition, this widespread attraction can be discerned in the assortment of ideological viewpoints and "the diverse political perspectives" (Rofes, 1998b, p. 52) that the charter school movement contains within its camp (Finn, Manno, & Vanourek, 2000). Charter schools appeal to and are supported by "advocates as dissimilar as conservative free market economists, religious fundamentalists, moderate Democrats, civil rights leaders, . . . so-called 'progressives' or child-centered educators" (UCLA Charter School Study, n.d., p. 9), "advocates of poor peoples' communities, and organizations championing youth of color" (Rofes, 1998b, p. 52); and appeal to reformers "who want to improve public education as well as [to] those who want to dismantle it" (American Federation of Teachers [AFT], 1996, p. 7).

Finally, popularity can be seen in the array of groups that are rushing to embrace charter schools (Bulkley, 1998), including political parties, civic associations, and business groups (Garn, 1998). And as Fulford (1997) has astutely noted, "the charter school concept appeals to different groups for different reasons and for some of the same reasons" (p. 1).

Explanations

At the most basic level, there are four reasons why the charter idea occupies such hallowed ground in the pantheon of reform strategies: (1) its portrait allows reformers to discern multiple images—it can mean many different things; (2) it contains something for nearly everyone—multiple actors can pursue this strategy to reach cherished ends, even ends that have historically been thought to be incompatible; (3) it emerges at a most opportune moment in the evolution of powerful political, social, and economic trends that define the larger environment in which the education industry is nested; and (4) it provides the calculus to capture, strengthen, and weld together seemingly unconnected, if not antagonistic, elements of the school reform movement of the last quarter century, while at the same time providing common ground to help resolve intractable differences.

Multiple Meanings

To begin with, to borrow a well-known metaphor from organizational theory, charter schools are the "garbage can" of school reform. This reform system allows for the presence of a large number of actors and a large variety of ideologies, problems, and solutions. All of these elements exist simultaneously under the charter school banner. Which of the diverse elements surface at any given time has as much to do with context, energy, and timing as with the ingredients themselves. In a similar vein, Wells and her colleagues (Wells, Lopez, Scott, & Holme, 1999) have referred to charter schools as the "empty vessel" of school reform. Berman and other members of the U.S. Department of Education's National Study of Charter Schools team have revealed how the charter concept creates "an opportunity space" into which different ideas can be bundled depending on the particular context, including "the political environment, the history of educational reform in the state, the role of the state education agency, the relationship between the state and the districts, and many other factors" (Berman, Nelson, Perry, Silverman, Soloman, & Kamprath, 1999, p. 2). Because charter schools "prescribe nothing" (Traub, 1999, p. 30), they can thus take on a variety of meanings and shapes, or as Bulkley (1998) has observed, there are "multiple constructions of the charter school idea" (p. 4) with, as we discuss below, "various themes appealing to different actors" (p. 4).

This openness, or ambiguity if you prefer, makes charter schools "a politically attractive response" (Contreras, 1995, p. 219) for many policymakers, permitting the development of a single policy construct that can be used to attack a host of problems and to address "various policy goals, and with different underlying theories of change" (Bulkley, 1998, p. 236). Quite naturally, therefore, this open space allows for the charter school construct to have different meanings and for various actors to see the meanings that have allure for them. For example, some who examine the landscape see charter schools as a vehicle to dismantle public schooling, and as the pathway to privatization. Others view the charter school movement as a new form of schooling, but one that is inherently public. Still others simply view charters as another arrow in the quiver of school reform strategies (Wells, Grutzik, Carnochan, Slayton, & Vasudeva, 1999; Wells, Lopez, et al., 1999). This opportunity space also provides fertile ground for the forging of coalitions (Bulkley, 1998). On the action front at the school level, the lack of prescription nurtures the development of a wide variety of schools serving the interests of an ideologically diverse set of actors.

Multiple Ends

Second, while not every group will be advantaged by charter schools, the movement gains much of its popularity by communicating to a great diversity of actors that the path to their desired aims passes through the charter house door. The core of this attraction is the capacity of charter schools simultaneously to connect to the four foundational educational values—quality, efficiency, liberty, and equity—and to appeal to many of those who prize any given value most highly. To craft a policy that can hit four valued targets at once, or simply to convince those who subscribe to them that it is possible, is a remarkable accomplishment. Charter schools provide freedom and choice to parents and school communities; they promise to help solve the intractable problems of schools that consistently have failed to educate well those children who are from low-income homes; they stand on the vanguard in the quest for excellence; and they assure us that they can meet those goals while dismantling "the conventional wisdom that improvement requires more money" (Kolderie, 1992, p. 28)—either by being revenue neutral or by actually promoting enhanced efficiencies or, at least, reduced costs (Szabo & Gerber, 1996).

At the same time, charter schools appeal to actors who historically have been on the sidelines of the public school reform debates, thereby augmenting the growing pool of interest in the charter idea. Charters energize efforts of entrepreneurs from the private sector who view them as a strategy for capturing a slice of the educational market (Molnar, 1996). Equally important, they engage some of the existing private sector providers, both secular and religious, who find charters a promising avenue to expand their delivery capabilities (Fulford, Raack, & Sunderman, 1997).

Environmental Fit

Third, charters are attractive because the ideology on which they rest matches up exceedingly well with shifts in the larger environment in which the educational enterprise resides. As we note more fully in Chapter 4, powerful new economic, political, and social dynamics were put in play at the dawn of the postindustrial world. On the larger political landscape, for example, the following trends are evident: the expanding importance of decentralization and local control; a growing preference for market-anchored as opposed to government-based solutions to public needs; and an enhanced interest in localism, with a concomitant focus on developing small communities emphasizing homogenous clusters of values—or, looking at the phenomenon from another angle, a diminution in our penchant for large-scale, collective action (for reviews, see Murphy, 1999; 2000).

Framework to Attract Diverse Viewpoints

Finally, there are a number of elements of charters as school reform that makes the movement quite appealing (Little Hoover Commission, 1996). Its dual focus on promoting systemwide change in the American educational enterprise as well as improvements in individual schools (Northeast and Islands Regional Educational Laboratory, 1999) energizes those who attend to macro-level policy reform as well as those who are primarily concerned with improvements in their neighborhood schools. Catering to both interests has expanded the lineup of supporters, thus enhancing the popularity of this reform mechanism.

For others, the charter concept looks like the preferred strategy to reach a long-standing but quite elusive goal of "creat[ing] new or distinctive types of schools within American public education" (Bulkley, 1998, p. 31), thus bringing hope to those educators who have worked for decades in the alternative schools movement.

More important still in explaining the attraction of charters is the fact that they add robustness to, or complete, elements of earlier eras of reform (e.g., choice) and weave into a comprehensive strategy elements that historically have not rested well together. As such, they mark:

> The culmination of efforts to reform America's schools. Borrowing from both the first and second waves of reform, the charter school concept embodies the values most central to school improvement in the last decade—accountability, school-based change, teacher professionalism, and choice. (McGree, 1995b, p. 11)

Not surprisingly, therefore, reformers increasingly are coming to view charters as an especially effective model of school reform. Or, as Hassel (1999a) has observed, "charter schools may hold special promise as an educational reform" (p. 13)—the movement promises to accomplish what previous reforms have failed to do (Kolderie, 1992).

In addition, the unique capacity of charter schools "to reflect both sides of some of the major current debates in education" (Bulkley, 1998, p. 7) has helped swell the ranks of its supporters. For example, as we explore in detail later, charter schools resolve the debate about which concept of accountability should undergird reform by calling for the use of both market and government mechanisms, thus appealing to a much broader audience than if one accountability measure had been privileged. In a similar vein, charters are seen as a tool to create a more professional workforce (e.g., by empowering teachers at the school site) and a strategy to dismantle professionalism (by undercutting traditional pillars of the profession, such as licensure/certification) (American Federation of Teachers [AFT], 1996).

Perhaps nowhere is this capacity to draw support by appealing to those on both sides of the street more apparent than in the area of privatization. For a number of policymakers and educational reformers, charter schools represent "an appropriate step toward a market-driven education system" (Contreras, 1995, p. 214) as well as "the first step toward privatization of the public school system" (Northeast and Islands Regional Educational Laboratory, 1999, p. 3), particularly in "opening the door for vouchers" (Bulkley, 1998, p. 102; see also Mahtesian, 1998) and private school choice (Schnaiberg, 1999b).

Different analysts, however, report that charters are expected to form the bulwark against privatization (Heubert, 1997; Nathan, 1996a; Wohlstetter, Wenning, & Briggs, 1995), where charters are seen "as the savior of the public school system" (Wells, Grutzik, et al., 1999, p. 526). They describe ways in which it is believed that charters "protect public education as an institution"

(Molnar, 1996, p. 1), especially by establishing alternatives to vouchers (Hadderman, 1998; Hill, Pierce, & Guthrie, 1997) or by providing an "escape valve" (Wells, Grutzik, et al., 1999, p. 526) to minimize demands to establish a voucher system.

Finally, some chroniclers of the charter school narrative maintain that charters provide a compromise between the need to infuse market forces into schools and the need to protect the core dimensions of public education (Szabo & Gerber, 1996; Caudell, 1997a, 1997b; Loveless & Jasin, 1998). Here, charters emerge as a "middle-of-the-road policy, creating more autonomous 'public' schools of choice that are purported to be free from state regulations and district oversight but still held accountable for student achievement" (Wells, Grutzik, et al., 1999, p. 515)—"a middle way between traditional public education and the proposals for private education" (Kolderie, 1992, p. 28).

> In short, a charter school is a hybrid, resembling a private school in some ways and a public school in others. Like a private school, a charter school is relatively autonomous. It can operate free from most education laws and rules, free from district oversight, and in control of its own curriculum, budget, and personnel. Also, it must attract and keep students, or it will fail. Like a public school, a charter school is funded by taxpayer dollars. It must accept all who enroll, free of charge. It cannot have a religious focus. And it is held accountable, through the charter, by a school district or some other public entity. (Buechler, 1996, p. 4)

Charters can also represent a political compromise, either from those who are unable to successfully pass voucher legislation and thus settle for the next best alternative—that is, charters (Rothstein, 1998a)—or from those who "fear the excesses of a full-blown choice regime" (Hassel, 1999a, p. 36) and reluctantly support a less offensive alternative—that is, charters.

WHY A METANARRATIVE IS DIFFICULT TO CONSTRUCT

> Despite some common threads, charter school laws across the country differ from one another so greatly that they appear to have been cut from different fabrics altogether. (Hassel, 1997, p. 19)

> Indeed, charter schools' diversity, as well as the many differences in the laws authorizing them, make generalizing about them difficult. (U.S. General Accounting Office, 1995b, p. 4)

While developing a charter school metanarrative is an important task, it is, nonetheless, a difficult one. The heart of the problem is that quite "different meanings [are] attached to this single policy idea" (Bulkley, 1998, p. 239). Because of this, "the 'charter school movement' cannot be viewed as a single entity" (Garn, 1998, p. 50). This means, as we noted earlier, that "there is considerable ambiguity as to the meaning of the charter school idea" (Bulkley, 1998, p. iv) and that as a reform, the charter concept "defies universalistic definitions" (Wells, Lopez, et al., 1999, p. 172), and thus charters are "extremely difficult to understand and research" (p. 182). It also means that "general statements about charter schools must therefore be drawn with care" (RPP International and the University of Minnesota [RPP], 1997, p. 12) or we run the risk of portraying "an increasingly diverse and difficult to define educational entity . . . in a simplified and homogenized form" (Rofes, 1995, p. 2).

Varying State Context

A major theme running through this volume is that charter schools are built from quite varied and often competing ideologies, a factor that accounts for much of the variation "in the practical meaning of the term" (Molnar, 1996, p. 2). Understanding the charter idea is further complicated because charters "are asked to serve many purposes" (Rosenblum Brigham Associates, 1998, p. 1) and roles (Wells, Grutzik, et al., 1999) and to meet the agendas of different actors (Lane, n.d.).

To begin with, "states play a primary role in defining the possibilities of charter schools, and states may vary greatly in their approaches" (RPP, 1997, p. 1). Not surprisingly, then, charter school legislation differs significantly across the states (AFT, 1996; Berman, Nelson, Perry, Silverman, Solomon, & Kamprath, 1999). Analysts have been fairly consistent in showing how "diverse and confusing collection[s] of values, motives, beliefs, and assumptions" (Lane, n.d., p. 1) mix with key aspects of the policymaking process and the policy context (Bomotti, Ginsberg, & Cobb, 1999) to produce "multiple constructions of the charter school idea" (Bulkley, 1998, p. 37). The work of Bulkley (1998) and Hassel (1997, 1999a) is especially helpful in observing how "the dynamics of the [charter school] debate change with every state context" (Garn, 1998, p. 48) and in viewing how charters are "socially constructed" (Bulkley, 1998, p. 196) differently in each context. Hassel (1997, 1999) describes three sources of variation in the policymaking process: (1) the larger legislative reform context in which the debate about charters unfolds, (2) "the role of partisan control of the legislature" (1997, p. 106), and (3) the key actors in the political process, especially the governor and the teachers' unions. Bulkley (1998) explains variance in charter laws "by providing a model that relies on four contextual causal factors: external forces, structural and historical variables, policy discourse, and politics and timing" (p. 44).

Varying Local Context

Building an integrated story line for charter schools is complicated by the fact that the diversity uncovered in the construction of charter frameworks at the state level is magnified at the local level. Because "charter school legislation varies tremendously from state to state . . . the result has been a set of schools that are as different from each other as they are similar" (McGree, 1995a, p. 3). At some fundamental level, all reform is local. This is especially true for charter schools. The "opportunity space" (Berman, Nelson, Ericson, Perry, & Silverman, 1998, p. 2) that charters provide means that "these schools are breathtakingly diverse" (Finn, Manno, & Vanourek, 2000, p. 23). To begin with, "each charter school is a unique and separate organization" (Rosenblum Brigham Associates, 1998, p. 6). By design, "the charter school title or 'banner' empowers people to do things differently" (Wells, Lopez, et al., 1999, p. 195). Izu, Carlos, Yamashiro, Picus, Tushnet, and Wohlstetter (1998) capture this idea nicely as follows:

> Granting schools greater flexibility is not a discrete policy lever that will yield similar results with similar schools. By virtue of having been granted the regulatory and decision-making flexibility to create and implement alternative structures and practices, schools will, by definition, be unique in their design. (p. 4)

Second, "each charter school operates in a unique context" (p. 3). As we saw at the state level, diversity of contexts produces considerable variety in types. For example, it makes a good deal of difference if a charter is a start-from-scratch organization or a conversion of a preexisting school (Lane, 1998; Nelson, Berman, Ericson, Kamprath, Perry, Silverman, & Soloman, 2000), or, if a conversion school, whether it is private or public—conclusions amply documented by the U.S. Department of Education's National Study of Charter Schools: "Newly created, pre-existing public, and pre-existing private school conversions differ greatly in terms of school size, grade levels, the reasons that charter schools were started, the difficulties they encounter during implementation, and their autonomy" (Berman, et al., 1999, p. 15).

The outcome of all of this is that "there is no typical charter school; they are extraordinarily diverse" (RPP, 1997, p. 3); "they are started for different reasons, they serve various types of students, and they promote multiple learning and teaching strategies" (Lane, n.d., p. 4); and "they encompass a wide variety of instructional and organizational models" (McGree, 1995a, p. 3). The variety in charter schools can be seen "both in their diverse education programs and missions, and in their array of approaches to management, governance, finance, parent involvement, and personnel policies" (RPP, 1997, p. 3). The overall outcome is that "what exists is a set of different schools, and not some monolith known as charter schools" (Rosenblum Brigham Associates, 1998, p. 6). Because these charter schools "take so many forms . . . it is difficult to convey the meaning of the term" (Public Agenda, 1999, p. 11).

A Moving Target

Developing a comprehensive and nuanced understanding of the charter school phenomenon is made more perplexing by three factors. First, the charter idea is exceptionally complicated, encompassing a wide array of reform elements that are complex in their own right (e.g., choice). Second, "charter schools are still a relatively new phenomenon" (Bomotti, Ginsberg, & Cobb, 1999, p. 4), both as a movement (Mickelson, 1997) and as individual organizations (Rosenblum Brigham Associates, 1998). The absence of a track record makes it difficult to conduct the thoughtful assessments from which much of the charter school narrative needs to be built (Goenner, 1996; Hassel, 1997). Finally, related to the freshness of the concept is the fact that the charter idea is evolving (Berman, Nelson, Ericson, Perry, & Silverman, 1998; 1999), both as it spreads (Kolderie, 1994) and as it loops back upon itself through "post-adoption politics" (Hassel, 1997, p. 127), creating what Wells, Lopez, and their colleagues (1999) describe as "a moving mosaic" (p. 183).

Reliability Problems

Compounding our task is the reality of a shortage of material from which to craft a narrative, and the fact that what resources are available are not always of the highest quality. To reinforce what we noted above, because charter schools are relatively new and because their complexity makes them difficult to study, there is not an abundance of available research. For example, Bomotti, Ginsberg, and Cobb (1999) have determined that "significant research on charter schools is just beginning to emerge" (p. 4). Some of the research that is available is less than objective, driven as much by values as by canons of scholarship (Arsen, Plank, & Sykes, n.d.). In their work, Hart and Burr (1996):

> . . . have noted a predilection among researchers to approach scholarship with a noticeable bias. Some hostile university researchers believe that charter schools are inherently unfair or are just a subtle attempt to undermine public education. On the other end of the spectrum, conservative think tanks, looking to validate

any kind of free market venture, bring a positive bias to any research on charter schools. (p. 40)

The effect of these two dynamics is that "the expert debate [on charter schools] has all the earmarks of a highly evolved discussion in which each side has made up its mind and hopes to rally the public to its position" (Public Agenda, 1999, p. 9). The inability or unwillingness of analysts "to draw on research-based literature leads opponents and advocates alike to rely on suppositions which may not be true, make wild claims which are not based in reality, and make charter schools into either a miracle cure for current school failure or an exaggerated demon aiming to destroy public education" (Rofes, 1998b, p. 43), to engage in what Molnar (1996) has labeled "a war of educational anecdotes and misleading statistics" (p. 7). This is hardly the raw material from which one feels comfortable constructing a thoughtful model of charter schools.

Even when we transcend these difficulties, the existing research base on charter schools leaves something to be desired. As the American Federation of Teachers (1996), Michelsen (1997), and others have uncovered, "Many of the national reports and evaluations lack the sophistication and rigor necessary to draw valid conclusions" (Cobb & Glass, 1999, p. 5) about important dimensions of charter schools, such as its potential segregating effects. Measurement problems are particularly difficult to crack, especially on issues such as sampling (Michelsen, 1997) and locating comparable data sets (Corwin, Carlos, Lagomarsino, & Scott, 1996). Given the complexity of the charter concept and other reform activity underway in nearly all states and localities, attributing changes to charters is an especially nettlesome task (Rofes, 1998b; Rosenblum Brigham Associates, 1998).

Earlier we argued that there is a need for a well-developed metanarrative on charter schools. Here we have underscored the fact that the creation of that story line will not be easy. The danger of providing a biased tale is quite real. So too is the opportunity for what Rofes (1995) terms "reductionism" (p. 19)—the potential to "picture charter schools as a single, well-defined entity which share similar origins, polities, educational philosophies, governing structures, and relationships to preexisting systems" (p. 19). At the same time, to affirm that a task is difficult, does not mean that it cannot be accomplished. We provided the analysis in this section not to fuel pessimism but as a cautionary backdrop for us as we develop the charter school story and for readers as they assess our efforts.

SUMMARY

We began this volume by examining charter schools from a variety of angles and with multiple lenses. We continue that work throughout the remainder of the book. Our goal is to provide sufficient overlapping pictures of the charter schools phenomenon that the reader will be left with a thoughtful understanding of this major element of the school reform movement unfolding throughout the United States.

We started the construction of our story line by reviewing the need for such a narrative, a rationale for the book itself, if you will. In the ending section, we revealed why the comprehensive development task at hand, never an easy one to begin with, is complicated by the complexity, diversity, and freshness of the charter concept. In between these two sections, we answered questions about the nature and growth of charter schools. We provided a beginning definition of the charter concept and explained why charters enjoy such widespread, bipartisan support. We also situated charters in the larger school reform movement of the last quarter century.

In Chapter 2, we analyze the history and development of charter schools. In Chapter 3, we parse out and examine each of the key dimensions of charters. Chapter 4 provides the intellectual infrastructure on which charter schools are built, while Chapter 5 exposes the theories of action that underlie their development. The final two chapters deepen our narrative by investigating charters in action. Chapter 6 explores implementation issues with which charter schools must grapple, both in getting started and in nurturing healthy growth. Employing the material from Chapter 5, Chapter 7 examines what we know about the impact of charter schools, by looking at school improvement at the local level and at reform at the system level. We move now to illuminate the history of charter schools.

CHAPTER 2

History of Charter Schools

> The charter school movement seems a quintessentially American enterprise, one that would not have surprised Alexis de Tocqueville when he visited America in the 1830s. (Gardner, 2000, p. 45)

In this chapter, we trace the history of the charter school movement in the United States from its conceptual origins, through early legislative initiatives, to the establishment of the first schools. We also review the subsequent growth and popularity of charter schools. We explore the rationales of groups that tend to oppose charter schools as well as the logic of those who have been staunch advocates. We close by investigating some of the factors that have contributed to the formation of different charter school models among the states.

DEVELOPMENT OF THE CHARTER SCHOOL CONCEPT

Ray Budde is widely credited with coining the term "charter" (Bulkley, 1998; Little Hoover Commission, 1996). Then, as the story goes, American Federation of Teachers (AFT) President Al Shanker introduced the word into the American vernacular in the late 1980s. However, the legislation and diverse array of charter schools comprising the movement today go far beyond Budde's original vision of a contract between a school board and teachers to devise new instructional programs. Instead, a wide range of ideas, both from this country and abroad, have informed and shaped this complex phenomenon. The infusion of these ideas and the influence of social, political, and economic forces on the evolving charter school movement are explored in greater depth in the Introduction and in Chapter 4. In this section, we will touch on some precursors to the charter school model, discuss the role of Budde and Shanker in bringing the "charter" idea into the education dialogue, and explore other dynamics that have informed and shaped the charter school movement into what it is today.

Precursors to the Charter School Model

Charter schools do not represent the first attempt in American history to release public school teachers from a bureaucracy perceived to stifle innovation and to thwart new instructional techniques. Indeed, attempts to alter the bureaucratic delivery of education have appeared throughout the nation's history (Rofes, 1998b). Three school models from recent decades, in particular, lay the foundation for the charter school prototype: innovative schools, magnet schools, and alternative schools (Nathan, 1996a). Innovative schools were created with teacher, parent, and community input and collaboration. These schools "gave public school teachers the chance to create the kinds of schools they thought made sense to a variety of students" (p. 56). A second empowerment model, the magnet school, emerged in the mid-1970s as a tool to further integration in targeted school districts. Armed with significant additional funding, these schools used the incentives of "specialized curricular themes or instructional methods" (Smrekar & Goldring, 1999, p. 6) to attract parents and students. Unlike the innovative schools, magnet schools were crafted by school district administrators with little input from parents, teachers, or community members (Nathan, 1996a). Alternative schools were designed by school districts to serve specific populations of pupils who were not well-served in their zoned schools, such as youngsters with behavioral problems and students at risk of dropping out (Bulkley, 1998; Nathan, 1996a).

The Budde-Shanker Charter Model

> The time has come for teachers, both individually and in what I call "charter teams," to accept full responsibility for the function of instruction. I would do this by having teachers receive three-to-five-year mandates (and funds) for instruction directly from the school board—with no one between the teachers and the school board, not me as superintendent, nor your principal nor a K–12 curriculum director. (Budde, 1988, p. 29)

In *Education by Charter: Restructuring School Districts* (1988), Ray Budde outlined a model for improving instruction and changing school organization. This prototype was based on a written agreement, or charter, between teachers and school districts to establish instructional programs. Like famous charters in history, such as the Magna Carta in 1215 and Henry Hudson's charter with the East India Company to explore the Arctic, these educational contracts would provide teachers with the authority to explore and develop new approaches to educating children with public funds but with minimal state intervention. The instructional programs that emerged from these agreements were expected to serve as models for restructuring school districts. Through "education by charter," the logic held, four dynamics are introduced:

> (1) The roles of teachers and administrators are redefined; (2) the operation of school boards changes; (3) a continuing cycle of curriculum improvement and

renewal is set in motion; [and] (4) all parties face the challenge of identifying the knowledge base for the entire school curriculum. (Budde, 1989, p. 520)

Budde (1996) envisioned chartering academic departments or programs rather than entire schools.

Under Budde's model, teachers were the central players in the process. "A superintendent, principal, or curriculum director could be a participant on charter teams providing they taught on a regular basis in the area of their expertise" (Budde, 1988, p. 29). Parents and community members could "join the teachers to form a discussion group" (Budde, 1989, p. 519) during the initial, idea-generation phase of developing an educational charter. However, under Budde's model, parents and community members were advisors, without the significant decision-making power found in many charter schools today.

Although Budde had written about charters since 1975, it was not until Al Shanker described the idea during a National Press Club speech on March 31, 1988, that the concept generated much attention (Nathan, 1996a). Shanker outlined the charter school concept in two subsequent, weekly Sunday advertisements in the *New York Times* during the summer of 1988 (Shanker, 1988c; 1988d). In July, the idea was "overwhelmingly endorsed by the 70th convention of the American Federation of Teachers" (Shanker, 1988e, p. 72).

For Shanker and the AFT, Budde's teacher-driven charter school model could further the aims of the so-called second reform movement, which focused on the 80% of students who were not adequately reached by the traditional structure of schooling (American Federation of Teachers, 1988; Shanker, 1988b). Key characteristics of the movement were trust in the "professional judgment and experience of teachers" (American Federation of Teachers, 1988, p. 56) and a continual commitment "to inquiry and development, to a search for solutions" (p. 56). Shanker believed that charter schools could provide "a regular policy mechanism that would make innovation an ongoing and valued part of the school community" (Shanker, 1988c, E7). He likened this mechanism to the special teams and task forces that private companies established to develop a new product or service (Shanker, 1988c).

In charter schools, Shanker and the American Federation of Teachers saw a way to circumvent an education system seemingly impervious to meaningful change. Frustrated educators did not need to wait for "near-ideal conditions" (American Federation of Teachers, 1988, p. 57) to expand the efforts of the second reform movement. Furthermore, they argued that a new innovation need not meet the greatly compromised fate of reforms adopted by the entire system: "If you try to change a whole system at once, you won't do it, or you'll water it down so much it's meaningless. You can't even change a whole school at once" (Shanker, 1988b, p. 19).

In Shanker's charter school framework, teachers unions played a decisive role. Districts established joint school board-union panels to review and support proposals. These panels were charged with issuing charters and waiving regulations that "legitimately stand in the way of implementing [a] proposal, if the faculty so argue" (Shanker, 1988a, p. 98).

Under the Shanker model, teachers were provided funds based on district per-pupil allotments and received the space and resources that they would have if employed in neighborhood schools. Shanker extended Budde's idea to chartering entire schools or autonomous schools within a school, rather than academic programs or departments (Contreras, 1995). Shanker and Budde both emphasized the need for a substantial, but *defined*, time period to allow initiatives to evolve and flourish. Budde (1988) proposed 3 to 5 years. Shanker (1988e) suggested 5 to 10 years.

Other Antecedents of the Charter School Movement

While some of the charter schools that have emerged reflect Budde's and the American Federation of Teachers' models of teacher-driven schools and programs, several other ideas were more prominently reflected in these schools and in the ideological blueprints from which they were built. Wells, Grutzik, Carnochan, Slayton, and Vasudeva (1999) place charter schools squarely in a "larger, global phenomenon of deregulating, privatizing, and marketing public education and a distinctly American phenomenon of the recurring demand for local and community control of schools" (p. 514). As we discuss in later chapters, a number of movements came together to forge the charter school concept: (1) choice for students, (2) competition to break public schools' monopoly, (3) school-based management, (4) deregulation to remove rules and policies seen as constraining the ability of educators to provide instruction, and (5) accountability for results.

Many credit Minnesotan Ted Kolderie with bringing these ideas together as he advocated for charter school legislation in his home state and, later, nationally. The contract system advocated by Kolderie contains several important elements, including: (1) a wide variety of groups, not just teachers, are given the authority to organize charter schools; (2) multiple entities can award contracts; (3) accountability is addressed in two ways—by the chartering agency through the contract and by families through the exercise of choice; (4) the school is designated the legal entity; (5) all students are eligible to attend the school, that is, open enrollment; (6) distribution of information about the school is widespread; (7) requirements placed on the school beyond those of civil rights, student rights, and health and safety are minimized; and (8) schools have the ability to determine for themselves how to structure the organization and how to provide instruction (Kolderie, 1990).

Researchers often cite two additional models that helped shape the American charter school: Great Britain's grant-maintained schools and Philadelphia's school restructuring efforts (Hart & Burr, 1996; Hassel, 1999a; Nathan, 1998). Under the Education Reform Act of 1988, Parliament gave British schools the "choice of 'opting out' of local control and being funded directly by grants from the national government" (Wohlstetter & Anderson, 1994, p. 486). These schools are known as "grant-maintained schools." Former California state senator Gary Hart and Sue Burr (1996) researched this model as they prepared charter school legislation for California. Loveless and Jasin (1998) believe the British grant-maintained schools and the writings of Ted Kolderie are "more fitting forebearers of charters" (p. 10) than the Budde and Shanker models, which are "better understood as site-based management schemes" (p. 10).

The chartering system developed by the Philadelphia Schools Collaborative to restructure the city's 22 comprehensive high schools provided another early model for charter schools. Philadelphia's charters are essentially schools-within-a-school. Each charter is composed of a heterogeneous group of students and core teachers who function as a unit throughout the 4 years of high school. The teachers work together to instruct students and to develop the curriculum and the assessment measures. Multiple charters exist in each school (Fine, 1994).

The development of the charter school concept has not been linear. In the same way that pinpointing an exact birthplace or tracing all the streams that flow into the concept is next to impossible, charting the evolution of the charter school concept once state legislatures began to draft and adopt laws becomes increasingly difficult. The term "charter school" now takes on multiple meanings defined in political debates, statutory language, and implementation strategies. Wells and colleagues (1999) describe charter school legislation as "less a clear consensus of views on education [than a] fragile compromise between policymakers and local activists with different intended outcomes and goals" (p. 533). As noted in Chapter 1, like a chameleon, the charter school concept takes on the tone, color, and fabric of each state and local community. Part of the appeal of charter schools to such a broad cross section of society is the looseness of its meaning—its ability to serve multiple aims and to be defined quite differently in different venues.

In the following section we discuss how the ideas advocated by Budde, Shanker, Kolderie, and others were adapted to meet the concerns and political environment in the first state to pass a charter school law, Minnesota. We also examine the early schools that emerged from this legislation.

THE FIRST CHARTER SCHOOL STATE—MINNESOTA

Most recent efforts at education reform throughout the nation are based on requiring the same system to meet tougher new standards. Minnesota, in contrast, has taken an incentives-and-opportunities approach, giving schools a reason and a way to become better. (Citizens League, 1988, p. i)

Legislation

In 1991, Minnesota became the first state in the United States to pass a charter school law. Since the 1980s, the state had attracted national attention for its pioneering use of public school choice legislation to address educational needs in the state (Sautter, 1993). As Mazzoni and Sullivan (1990) noted at the time, "Nowhere has choice among public schools been more prominent as a policy issue than in Minnesota; nowhere have there been more choice statutes put on the books" (p. 149). These initiatives in the 1980s laid the groundwork for charter school legislation in the state (Citizens League, 1988; Nathan, 1996a).

In 1985, Democratic Governor Rudy Perpich introduced several school choice proposals to the state legislature. He actively advanced these proposals during his tenure and was able to garner support from groups as diverse as the Minnesota PTA, the Minnesota Business Partnership, and school administrators (Mazzoni & Sullivan, 1990; Nathan, 1996a). The 1985 Postsecondary Enrollment Options Act allowed public high school students to take courses in colleges and universities with state funds. In 1987, three more choice initiatives were signed into law. The K–12 Enrollment Options Program established a voluntary open-enrollment program. The Area Learning Centers and the High School Graduation Incentive Program gave dropouts and at-risk students the opportunity to finish high school in regular public schools, postsecondary institutions, or other alternative programs outside of their residential districts (Mazzoni & Sullivan, 1990).

While controversial during the legislative process, these three initiatives gained popularity after implementation (Nathan, 1996a). With growing acceptance, however, a new problem emerged: the demand for choice programs exceeded available options for parents, students, and educators seeking alternatives to neighborhood schools (Sautter, 1993). The Citizens League (1988), a Minneapolis-based research group drafted to study charter schools for the state legislature, argued that educators needed to provide a fuller range of instructional possibilities. They reasoned that "without such options, choice is meaningless" (p. 3). Concerned by the limited choices available, State Senator Ember Reichgott worked closely with several Minnesota legislators and citizens, including Ted Kolderie and Joe Nathan, to develop and pass charter school legislation. Reichgott's 1990 charter school bill was accepted by the Senate but rejected by the House. In the fall of 1990, the charter school proposal suffered another setback when it became clear that the newly elected governor and his commissioner of education did not share Perpich's enthusiasm for charter schools. However, after much political log rolling, the bill did pass both the Senate and House in 1991. Teachers union officials played an influential role in the debates and negotiated several changes including mandatory certification for all charter school teachers, and a cap on the number of charter schools allowed in the state (Nathan, 1996a).

The resulting law "called for up to eight teacher-created and -operated, outcome-based charter schools across the state that would be free of most state laws and state and local education rules. Renewable Minnesota charters would be granted for three years" (Sautter, 1993, p. 7). To operate, a charter school would need the permission of both the local school board and the state school board. Each charter would have its own board, and teachers had to be a majority of the membership (Nathan, 1996a).

Like charter school legislation in many states, the Minnesota law has been expanded and revised since its first incarnation. As a result of a 1993 amendment, the local school board's permission was no longer required for charter approval. Applications rejected by the local school board but with minority approval could be appealed to the state board of education, which could sponsor the school (Jennings, Premack, Adelmann, & Solomon, n.d.; Sautter, 1993). In 1997, the legislature removed the cap, thus allowing an unlimited number of charter schools to operate in the state. The sponsorship of charter schools was changed as well. Public and private 4-year and community colleges could sponsor charter schools in addition to local school boards (Jennings, Premack, Adelmann, & Solomon, n.d.).

Minnesota's Early Charter Schools

In September 1992, the City Academy Charter School in St. Paul, Minnesota became the first operational charter school in the United States (Sautter, 1993). The school was designed to serve out-of-school youth, a population that had been the focus of two of the state's earlier choice initiatives. The school's founders were a businesswoman with an education background, and a teacher. Based on their experience with alternative programs, they crafted a school that addressed problems, such as the lack of personalization and individual attention, which they believed confronted at-risk students in larger schools (Cutter, 1996). In its first year, 35 inner-city high school dropouts attended the school, located at a recreational center in a low-income, racially diverse area of St. Paul (Nathan, 1996a; Sautter, 1993). State education funds provided two thirds of the school's budget; the other third was supported through grants (Cutter, 1996). At City Academy, teachers focused on developing foundation skills in traditional subjects, emphasizing individual attention in a small setting (Sautter, 1993). In 1995, City Academy's charter was extended, making it the first such school in the country to have its contract renewed (Cutter, 1996).

More than 20 proposals for charter schools were submitted by the spring of 1993. The remaining seven slots allowed by Minnesota law were filled by a Montessori elementary school, a school for the deaf, a pre-K–12 school for at-risk students, a school focused on vocational and technical skills with backing from the Teamsters Service Bureau, and three schools with alternative instructional techniques (Sautter, 1993).

GROWTH AND POPULARITY OF CHARTER SCHOOLS

Charter schools—an educational innovation that seemed radical only a few years ago—are now an accepted part of the public education system in many parts of the country. (Berman et al., 1998, p. 1)

The growth of the charter school movement in the 1990s was nothing less than phenomenal. From a single state law in 1991, by 1998 charter school legislation had proliferated to two-thirds of the states. (Hassel, 1999a, p. 147)

As we illustrate below, the charter school movement has quickly evolved and expanded over the course of a single decade from the somewhat radical— although now relatively conservative in scope—legislation of one state to the legislation of 38 states, with roughly 2,000 schools serving half a million students (Center for Education Reform, 2000b). Perhaps more significant, the charter concept has captured the attention of politicians, analysts, the media, educators, and families across the political spectrum, though the movement is still small relative to the entire population of students and the total number of public schools. For example, slightly less than 1% of all public school students in the 27 states with operating charter schools during the 1998–99 academic year were enrolled in charter institutions (B. Nelson et al., 2000).

Yet throughout its short lifetime, the charter school movement has been consistently characterized by expansion. In this section we examine four areas of expansion: an increase in the number of states with charter school laws, a broadening of statutes to allow for more charter schools and for greater flexibility for existing institutions, an increase in the number of charter schools, and growth in student enrollments.

Increasing Number of States with Charter Laws

Since 1991, some version of the charter school model has been considered by most state legislatures across the country. As of November 2000, 36 states, the District of Columbia, and Puerto Rico had a charter school statute on the books (Center for Education Reform, 2000b; WestEd & U.S. Department of Education, 2000a). As Table 2.1 indicates, the number of states with a charter school law increased steadily between 1993 and 1999, with no fewer than three states passing a law each year. These states represent all geographic regions of the country.

As of October 2000, 14 states did not have a charter school law: Alabama, Iowa, Indiana, Kentucky, Maine, Maryland, Montana, North Dakota, Nebraska, South Dakota, Tennessee, Vermont, Washington, and West Virginia (WestEd & U.S. Department of Education, 2000a). However, charter schools were not absent from the policy agenda in those states. Either legislation had been introduced or groups had actively advocated for a law in nearly all of these states (Berman et al., 1998). For example, in 1998 charter school bills were considered, but not adopted, by seven state legislatures: Indiana, Iowa, Oklahoma, South Dakota, Tennessee, Vermont, and Washington (U.S. Department of Education, 1998a). The following year, eight state legislatures considered and ultimately rejected charter legislation: Indiana, Iowa, Maine, Maryland, Montana, Nebraska, Tennessee, and Washington (Schnaiberg,

Table 2.1
States with Charter School Laws by Year Passed as of December 2000

Year	States
1991	Minnesota
1992	California
1993	Colorado, Georgia, Massachusetts, Michigan, New Mexico, Wisconsin
1994	Arizona, Hawaii, Kansas
1995	Alaska, Arkansas, Delaware, New Hampshire, Louisiana, Rhode Island, Wyoming
1996	Connecticut, District of Columbia, Florida, Illinois, New Jersey, North Carolina, South Carolina, Texas
1997	Mississippi, Nevada, Ohio, Pennsylvania
1998	Idaho, Missouri, Utah, Virginia
1999	New York, Oklahoma, Oregon
2000	—

Source: Nelson et al., 2000; WestEd & U.S. Department of Education, 2000a

1999b). Again in 2000, eight state legislatures considered but failed to adopt a charter school law: Indiana, Iowa, Maine, Maryland, Nebraska, Tennessee, Vermont, and Washington (Education Commission of the States, 2000). Between 1998 and 2000 charter school bills have been introduced repeatedly in legislative sessions in several states. In Indiana, the legislature has considered a charter school law during the past five legislative sessions (Center for Education Reform, 2000c). Tennessee, in 1991, was one of the early states to consider charter school legislation. Reintroduced in 1997, some form of the Tennessee bill has been rejected in each of the past four legislative sessions (WestEd & U.S. Department of Education, 2000b). State lawmakers have also convened studies to explore the issue. For example, Maryland and Maine created task forces to advise their legislatures on charter laws in 1998. South Dakota, Nebraska, and Tennessee commissioned interim study committees during the same year (U.S. Department of Education, 1998a).

The rate of adopting charter school legislation appears to be slowing. During 2000, no new state passed a law. School choice analyst DeSchryver believes the states with "strong grassroots movements and political support for charters have passed laws by now" (quoted in Schnaiberg, 1999a, p. 20). National Conference of State Legislatures analyst Eric Hirsch believes that states with unsuccessful attempts to adopt charter legislation are now waiting to analyze the results in other states (Schnaiberg, 1999a). At the same time, however, the battle over expansion may have shifted to efforts to make existing charter laws more robust. Here, the evidence suggests active growth as we describe below.

Expansion of Charter Laws to Allow Greater Flexibility

It is important to remember that "charter schools are not static" (Berman, Nelson, Perry, Silverman, Solomon, & Kamprath, 1999). During their year 2000 legislative sessions, 28 states considered amendments to existing charter school laws (Education Commission of the States, 2000). During the 1998 legislative session alone, seven states made significant changes (Berman et al., 1999). In 1997, five states made major revisions to their charter school laws (Berman et al., 1998).

States are now focusing on "fine-tuning" existing laws to address "second generation" (Schnaiberg, 1999b, p. 20) issues such as facilities financing, clarifying accountability, and oversight. The general trend among states is to "increase the avenues available to charter applicants and the resources for charter school operators" (National Conference of State Legislatures, n.d., p. 3). Common changes to the laws have been to increase or remove limits on the number of charter schools in a state and caps on student enrollment and to terminate sunset provisions in the laws. Other areas of expansion in the laws have included allowing additional sponsoring entities for charter schools, such as sponsoring by private colleges in Minnesota, and allowing new "start-up" charter schools in addition to schools that have been converted from traditional neighborhood schools (National Conference of State Legislatures, n.d.), as did legislatures in Arkansas, Hawaii, and New Mexico, which passed amendments in 1999 allowing start-up schools (Schnaiberg, 1999b). New Mexico raised its cap, and more funding was allotted in Arizona, Colorado, Louisiana, Minnesota, and New Mexico through legislative changes (National Conference of State Legislatures, n.d.; Schnaiberg, 1999b).

Increasing Number of Charter Schools and Expanding Enrollments

Charter schools were operating in 34 states, the District of Columbia, and Puerto Rico as of the end of 2000 (Center for Education Reform, 2000b; WestEd & U.S. Department of Education, 2000c). The authors of the U.S. Department of Education study estimated that 1,605 charter schools were in operation in September 1999. During the 1998–99 academic year 252,009 students were enrolled in charter schools (Nelson, Muir, Drown, & To, 2000). The Center for Education Reform, a charter school advocacy group, tallied 2,036 operating charter schools serving 503,230 children as of January 2001 (Center for Education Reform, 2000b).

The number of charter schools has increased exponentially since the City Academy opened its doors in 1992. During the 1993–94 school year, 34 charter schools opened. The number doubled in 1994–95 and then again in 1995–96. By fall 1997, 693 charter schools were in operation (Berman et al., 1998). In September 1998, an additional 361 charter schools opened, bringing the total to a little over 1,000 such schools (Berman et al., 1999).

As seen in Table 2.2, the distribution of charter schools across the country is quite uneven. Over half of the nation's charter schools are concentrated in five states: Arizona, California, Florida, Michigan, and Texas (Center for Education Reform, 2000b; B. Nelson et al., 2000). On the other end of the continuum, New Hampshire and Wyoming have had a law on the books since 1995 but still do not have an operating school (Center for Education Reform, 2000b). Prior to its 1999 amendment, Arkansas had no operating charter schools despite having a law since 1995.

As the number of new charter schools increases yearly, the number of charter schools that have closed remains relatively small. Only 59 schools, or 4% of all charter schools ever opened, had closed as of September 1999. Twenty-seven of those schools were closed during the 1998–99 school year (B. Nelson et al., 2000). Analysis of the 19 charter schools that ceased operating as of September 1997 reveals multiple reasons for closure. Four schools had

Table 2.2
Operating Charter Schools and Enrollment by State, as of January 2001

State	Operating charter schools	Enrollment
Alaska	17	1,400
Arizona	417	55,000
Arkansas	4	800
California	274	123,000
Colorado	79	21,000
Connecticut	16	2,300
Delaware	7	2,800
Washington, D.C.	36	12,000
Florida	152	29,000
Georgia	38	23,000
Hawaii	6	2,500
Idaho	9	1,100
Illinois	22	5,200
Kansas	15	1,900
Louisiana	23	4,000
Massachusetts	41	13,000
Michigan	184	54,000
Minnesota	68	9,600
Mississippi	1	400
Missouri	21	5,900
Nevada	7	1,300
New Jersey	55	15,000
New Mexico	11	1,600
New York	23	7,200
North Carolina	90	20,000
Ohio	70	19,000
Oklahoma	6	1,600
Oregon	12	700
Pennsylvania	65	22,000
Rhode Island	3	600
South Carolina	8	700
Texas	159	38,000
Utah	8	300
Virginia	2	30
Wisconsin	87	7,300
National Total	**2,036**	**503,230**

Source: "Charter Schools 2000–2001," by Center for Education Reform, 2001.
Copyright © 2001 by Center for Education Reform. Reprinted with permission.

their charters revoked, two schools rescinded their charters, five schools closed voluntarily, and one school's charter was suspended by the state but planned to reopen the following year. The remaining seven schools continued to operate, although two merged with other charter schools and five cancelled their charters, that is, they withdrew their charter status (Berman et al., 1998).

National charter school enrollment is heavily concentrated in three states: Arizona, California, and Michigan accounted for 46% of charter school enrollment as of January 2001 (Center for Education Reform, 2000b).

Charter school enrollment as a percentage of total public school enrollment provides evidence of the impact that charter schools are having in individual states. Arizona has both the most charter schools in a single state and the largest percent of students enrolled in charter schools—4% (B. Nelson et al., 2000). Enrollment in the other 25 states with operating charter schools ranges between 0.1% and 2.0% of enrollment in all public schools in that state (Nelson et al., 2000). Demand for charter schools is high. In 1997–98 and 1998–99, seven out of ten charter schools had a waiting list (B. Nelson et al., 2000).

Federal Government as an Agent of Expansion

The federal government has not sat on the sidelines of this local and state-based movement. Both President Clinton and Congress have supported charter schools despite an often contentious, partisan relationship. Federal support for charter schools has taken the forms of funding for start-up efforts, research and dissemination; and the relaxing of federal laws and regulations to accommodate charter schools.

In 1993, the Clinton administration proposed that a charter schools grant program be included in the reauthorization of the Elementary and Secondary Education Act (ESEA). The Democratic-led Congress authorized $15 million for the Public Charter Schools Program as part of the 1994 reauthorization. The federal money supports a program of grants to states with charter school legislation. The money is then competitively distributed by states to new charter schools for the purposes of planning and of funding start-up costs (Pitsch, 1995). Additional provisions in ESEA gave the U.S. Secretary of Education the authority to waive many federal laws and regulations when requested to do so by individual charter schools (Dunkle, Dunn, & Rentner, 1997). With the support of President Clinton, the Republican-led Congress passed the Charter Schools Expansion Act of 1998, increasing the authorized funding level from $15 million to $100 million for fiscal year 1999 (McQueen, 1998).

The dramatic increase in federal funding from 1995 to 2001 for charter schools, despite an often contentious relationship between the Republican Congress and the Democratic White House during those years, provides a telling example of charter schools' bipartisan appeal. As seen in Figure 2.1,

Figure 2.1
Federal Appropriations for Charter Schools

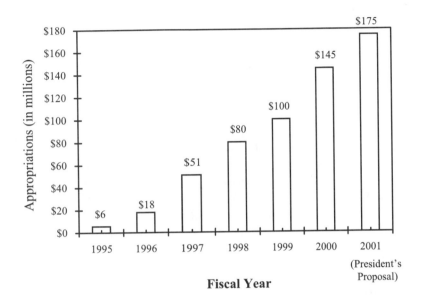

Source. Final fiscal 1999 education appropriations, 1998; Final fiscal 1997 education appropriations, 1996; Pitsch, 1995; President Clinton visits nation's first public charter school, announces new steps to support charter schools, 2000

federal financial support increased from $6 million in 1995 to $145 million in fiscal year 2000. During his 1997 State of the Union Address, President Clinton called for 3,000 charter schools by the year 2000 (WestEd & U.S. Department of Education, n.d.).

In addition to start-up grants, the federal government has been engaged in research and dissemination efforts on charter schools. The Department of Education is authorized to spend up to 10% of funding for the Public Charter Schools Program on research and dissemination (Hoff, 1996). In 1997, the Department of Education contracted for a $2.1 million, multiyear evaluation of charter schools (Harrington-Lueker, 1997). The Department of Education also maintains a website with WestEd and holds national conferences. Former President Clinton has spoken at this conference (WestEd & U.S. Department of Education, n.d.). Congress has held hearings and the Congressional Research Service and U.S. General Accounting Office have studied charter schools' experiences with the federal government in accessing funds and meeting federal regulations (Finn, Manno, Bierlein, & Vanourek, 1997b).

The federal role in the charter school movement will be discussed in greater detail in Chapter 3.

EVOLVING OPPOSITION TO AND SUPPORT OF CHARTER SCHOOLS

It is not surprising that a reform model like the charter school, which fundamentally alters structural relationships, would encounter both strong resistance and support. In Chapter 5 we will examine many of the arguments for and against charter schools held by proponents and opponents. In this section, however, we identify the groups that have been prominent in the charter school debate. We discuss why these groups have opposed or advocated charter schools and then describe how they have furthered their agendas in the charter school movement. In the final section, we explore the impact supporters and opponents of charter schools have had on legislation as part of a broader discussion of forces influencing the shape of charter school laws across the country.

Opposition

> The passage of charter school legislation is rarely a foregone conclusion in any state, because of intense opposition it is likely to face from educational interest groups. (Hassel, 1997, p. 14)

> We contend that it is too early to determine if charter schools will succeed, but we are not overly optimistic. Our opinion is based on the belief that although charter schools have already accomplished a great deal and hold promise for shaking up the current system, many status quo groups are finding charter schools a bitter pill to swallow. Powerful interests have mobilized to defeat this reform effort. (Bierlein & Bateman, 1997, p. 110)

Groups

Teacher unions, school boards, and school and district administrators are frequently cited as opponents of charter schools (Finn et al., 1997a, 1997b; Hadderman, 1998; Nathan, 1996a). These groups, threatened by the shifting power relations and associated funding implicit in the charter school model, are accused of fighting to maintain the status quo.

Teachers' Unions. Teachers' unions are frequently cited as the chief opponent of the charter school movement, both at the state and national levels (Caudell, 1997b; Hassel, 1997). Unions are viewed as a threat at the legislative formation stage and again during implementation. On the surface, it is somewhat ironic that the unions, as embodied by Shanker and the AFT, shifted their position from charter school promoters to opponents so quickly. However, the explanation for this change in attitude is found in the manner in which the charter school movement evolved. The current environment in which multiple charter school models coexist is quite different from the single prototype envisioned by Shanker, who saw a system of charter schools overseen by school district-union panels (Shanker, 1988b). As they have emerged, the "starting point for charter schools is simply to discard education laws and regulations that teacher unions have spent generations setting in place to enhance their members' interests" (Fuller, Elmore, & Orfield, 1996, p. 17), such as rules surrounding certification and employment rights (Hassel, 1997). Furthermore, these schools can be interpreted to be outside the scope of union contracts, such as collective bargaining agreements (Hassel, 1997). In addition to waiving laws and regulations, the charter school reform may reduce member demand for unions by empowering charter teachers to form their own bargaining units (Nathan, 1996a). Authority over charter schools may also be granted to parents, community groups, and businesses, thus further diluting the influence of the unions.

While analysts and charter school advocates attribute union opposition to concerns over lost power and diminished funding, statements from the National Education Association (NEA) and American Federation of Teachers (AFT) offer slightly different explanations for the skepticism. The issues they raise address more lofty educational concerns. They argue that there is mixed evidence, at best, linking charter schools to increased student achievement. Both groups are concerned that students are not equitably enrolled in charter schools. Oversight and accountability measures for charter schools are not uniformly effective, they argue. Both groups express concern about the role of for-profit companies in charter schools. Specifically, the NEA argues teachers in for-profit schools are less experienced and receive lower salaries. The AFT is critical of the standardized curriculum used by many privately managed charter schools (American Federation of Teachers, n.d.; Sund, 2000).

School Boards and Educational Administrators. Other frequently cited opponents of charter schools include school board associations, superintendents' groups, and other individuals representing the public education establishment (Center for Education Reform, n.d.d; Finn et al., 1997a, 1997b). Like the teacher unions, these groups are believed to fear the loss of both power and funding if charter schools are permitted.

School boards may view charter schools as competitors for scarce resources (Harrington-Lueker, 1997; Hill, Pierce, & Guthrie, 1997; Lieber,
1997). Another source of concern is the additional administrative time and
resources a charter school may require from a host school district (Rofes,
1998a). For example, local school board members in Minnesota cited concerns
about lost funding, time required of district administrators to work with charter schools, and equity (Poland, 1996).

Like the NEA and AFT, the National School Boards Association (NSBA)
(2000) "recognizes charter schools as one of several mechanisms available to
local school boards" (p. 6). However, like the teachers unions, the NSBA outlines conditions under which the association will accept charter schools—a
situation which is problematic for charter school advocates. The NSBA argues
that school boards must have "sole authority to approve, evaluate, and decer-
tify charters" (National School Boards Association, n.d., p. 1). Under the
NSBA scenario, a school board has the authority to hold charter schools accountable for raising achievement and ensuring equal access for students. The
NSBA (2000) also "opposes federal and state efforts to mandate public school
choice" (p. 5), including diverting or conditioning funding from existing federal and state programs.

Other education establishment groups, including the American Association of School Administrators (AASA), the National Association of Elementary
School Principals (NAESP), and the National Association of Secondary School
Principals (NASSP), outline criteria that protect member interests and support the concerns of teachers unions and school boards. The AASA (2000)
believes charter schools should operate under the "auspices of local public
school boards" (p. 9). The NAESP (2000) believes charter school principals
and their staff should be certified. The NASSP (2000) maintains that charter
schools should be required to follow the same licensing and certification requirements of professional staff that is required of other public schools in the
state. As in the other association platforms, the NASSP believes that charter
schools should be held to the same accountability standards as other public
schools. Not surprisingly, both principals groups believe that funding should
not be diverted from other public schools to support charter schools.

Efforts by the Education Establishment to Influence
the Charter School Movement

Concerns, both stated and inferred, held by the teacher unions, school boards,
and educational administrators are complementary and overlapping. Of the
education establishment groups, the teacher unions appear to have played
the most active role in opposing or influencing charter school legislation and
implementation across the states. Perhaps this is not surprising given the fi-

nancial and political resources and the organizational forces that unions are able to wield in a state.

Initially, the teachers unions' political muscle was viewed as a significant threat to the fledgling charter movement (Bierlein & Bateman, 1997). The unions fought charter school legislation passage both at the state and the national levels in the early years. Each of the first 11 states with a charter law encountered controversy during the process of developing the legislation—and most of the opposition came from teacher unions (Wohlstetter, Wenning, & Briggs, 1995). Teachers unions have been blamed for preventing the passage of legislation in Indiana, Nevada, Vermont, Virginia, and Washington (Nathan, 1996a). Teachers unions have been accused of using scare tactics with voters and leaning on state politicians who need their support in order to fight charter school bills (Nathan, 1996a). The Michigan Education Association's (MEA) alleged action offers an example of the extent to which a state union has been willing to go to stop legislation. The MEA is purported to have spent $2 million to defeat the charter school bill and attack its major advocate, Governor John Engler (Wohlstetter et al., 1995).

At the national level as well, the unions have tried to influence charter school policy. In 1992, the NEA sent a letter to U.S. senators stating their opposition to charter schools (Nathan, 1996a). By 1995, the NEA had spent over $12 million and the AFT had committed over $3 million to defeat charter school legislation (Bierlein & Bateman, 1997).

The charter school movement gained momentum by garnering broad, bipartisan support among policymakers, citizens, individual educators, and businesses in the early 1990s. In this atmosphere friendly to the notion of public schools run by entities outside traditional channels, opponents in the education establishment altered their approach to the charter school movement. They grew increasingly sophisticated in their tactics (Bierlein & Bateman, 1997; Nathan, 1996a). Rather than stonewall legislation, these groups, particularly the unions, began to enter into state discussions on drafting charter school bills. This strategy served three functions. First, the unions were better able to hold off the greater perceived threat to the educational establishment posed by vouchers. Second, the unions could influence legislation and thus help shape elements that they viewed as problematic. Third, the unions minimized the risk of poor public relations.

The national offices of both the NEA and AFT deny that they oppose charter schools. However, the organizations have specific detailed conditions under which charter school legislation meets with their approval. Many of these elements are problematic for charter school advocates. The AFT (n.d.) offers six criteria for "good charter school legislation which embody the standards all public schools should meet" (p. 1). However, no current state meets all six conditions. Charter school legislation acceptable to the AFT must:

(1) demand high academic standards, (2) have students take the same tests that all students in the state or district must take, (3) require teachers to be certified, (4) ensure that employees are covered by the collective bargaining agreement, (5) compel schools to have the approval of the local school district, and (6) obligate charter schools to make information available to the public.

Charter school advocates have labeled unions and other establishment groups as "false friends" (Finn et al., 1997b, p. 3) of charter schools. Advocates allege that while unions voice support for legislation, they undermine the autonomy of charter schools by rejecting elements of the charter school model deemed by supporters to be essential for its viability (Finn et al., 1997b). Nathan blames union activity in Arkansas, California, Delaware, and Louisiana for successfully weakening legislation (1996a).

Once legislation has been adopted in states, opponents often maneuver to block expansion of laws and to undermine implementation. In some states, opponents have used the court system to fight charter schools. For example, the Michigan Education Association brought a suit claiming that charter schools were not eligible for state funding (Berman et al., 1998; Goenner, 1996).

Opposition to charter schools also surfaces in the local arena. When a law restricts charter school sponsorship to local school boards, charter applicants must lobby these entities for the right to exist. Charter applicants have invested "immense amounts of time and energy in trying to convince local school boards to approve their proposals" (Finn, Bierlein, & Manno, 1996, p. 7). School boards in California and Colorado have been particularly difficult. Universities in Michigan and Minnesota, endowed with the statutory authority to sponsor charter schools, have been intimidated by union officials. For example, the Michigan Education Association sent a letter to Saginaw Valley State University (SVSU) threatening to discourage members from hiring SVSU graduates for teaching positions and from making alumni contributions. They also threatened to undermine collaboration between the school district and the university (Nathan, 1996a).

National education groups continue to play a role in the charter school movement through studies and pilot projects. The NEA has underwritten a 5-year Charter Schools Initiative project to study "the efficacy of charter schools as a model for improving student achievement, enhancing professional development for teachers, and strengthening the ties between public schools and their communities" (National Education Association, n.d.d., p. 1) as well as to help interested members take advantage of charter school laws. As part of this project, six charter schools were established in six states to reflect current research on student achievement, teacher development, and community outreach. The NEA hired a research team from the University of California at Los Angeles to study these schools. The NEA has prepared guidance for policy developers, parents and communities, and association members who are considering starting charter schools. Finally, the NEA, AFT, and NSBA publish occasional studies and other papers on the topic.

Support

> Because these schools can and do take so many different forms, charter schools appeal to a broad base of public school critics, including those who want to improve public education as well as those who want to dismantle it. (American Federation of Teachers, 1996, p. 7)

As noted in Chapter 1, charter supporters form an eclectic group comprised of both liberal and conservative individuals and associations. The nature of the charter school reform as "an empty vessel" has drawn seemingly disparate groups and individuals to the movement, with divergent and sometimes competing goals and theoretical assumptions. In this section we highlight some of the groups and individuals who are advocates of charter schools. We briefly examine the capacity of the charter movement to encompass different goals and assumptions. We also briefly review the actions proponents have taken to promote this reform.

Groups and Individuals Supporting Charter Schools

The constituency representing charter schools is not clearly defined because it embodies "a blend of ideas and often has appeal across party lines" (Bierlein & Bateman, 1997, p. 122). The movement has been characterized by this diversity since its inception (Wells et al., 1999). Efforts to identify advocates by institutional affiliations are less consistent in describing the universe of supporters than are related attempts to categorize opponents. One analyst included "right-wing conservatives[,] . . . progressive educators[,] . . . Christian fundamentalists[,] . . . [and] civil rights groups" (Learning Matters, 1999, pp. 7–8) in the pool of charter advocates. Garn (1998) included teacher organizations, business groups, and parent associations in the league of supporters. In 1995, Tom Watkins, director of the Detroit Center for Charter Schools, clustered advocates into three groups: *zealots*, who favor market-oriented solutions to public schooling; *entrepreneurs*, who hope to profit from the entry of private enterprise into the realm of public schooling; and *reformers*, who wish to expand opportunities within public schooling (Molnar, 1996). Rofes (1998b) argued that while charter school advocates have been quickly aligned with conservative interest groups, a "rich mix of voluntary associations" (p. 52) with diverse political views "make[s] up the vast masses of charter advocates" (p. 52). Indeed, liberal education leaders, like Al Shanker, are credited with introducing the charter school reform to Americans. Progressive educators from the alternative schools movement, like Ray Budde, have been staunch advocates as well (Rofes, 1998b; Wells et al., 1999). Charter school supporters have also included advocates for the poor and organizations that focus on students of color (Rofes, 1998b).

Multiple Ideological Frameworks Underpin Charter School Support

Advocates' arguments supporting charter schools are not uniform and do not necessarily complement each other in the same manner that do opponents' concerns about charter schools. Rather, there is a "continuum of political themes" (Wells et al., 1999, p. 520) embraced by charter school advocates that ranges from viewing charter schools as the beginning of the end of public schools to an antidote for revitalizing public education. The open nature of this reform may allow these rationales to coexist under the rubric of charter schools while clouding the serious differences in models advocated by charter supporters. Voucher discussions provide an example of the charter school reform's ability to support two competing goals. Conservatives may view charter schools as a step toward vouchers, whereas opponents of vouchers have viewed charter schools as a way to "appease voucher proponents" (Mintrom & Vergari, 1997, p. 8) while halting further consideration of the more radical reform.

Actions Taken by Supporters to Promote Charter Schools

Bierlein and Bateman (1997) voiced concern that advocates for the charter school movement often lack the resources and organization to fight the movement's opposition effectively. Charter school funding that is available is earmarked for specific schools, start-up costs, and technical assistance rather than for promotion of the concept. However, policy entrepreneurs—defined as "individuals from government, interest groups, or other policy-related organizations who promote a particular policy solution, and help link this solution to existing problems" (Bulkley, 1998, p. 20)—have worked to influence state legislatures in their consideration, drafting, and adoption of charter laws. Like opponents in the educational establishment, policy entrepreneurs who were pro-charter have provided guidance to legislators and published papers that advanced the cause of charter schools.

FACTORS INFLUENCING STATE APPROACHES
TO CHARTER LEGISLATION

In this section, we examine factors that influence the approaches state legislatures have taken toward the charter school movement. Some states have passed laws quickly while others have revisited the subject in repeated legislative sessions. The laws that have been adopted vary significantly "along a continuum of autonomy" (Wohlstetter, Wenning, & Briggs, 1995, p. 352). Some legislation has been so expansive or permissive that few restrictions were placed on the establishment, administration, and oversight of charter schools. Other state laws have been so confining that few if any charter schools have actually been established. At least six broad categories help explain these differences: (1) regional, economic, and social factors; (2) the condition of education; (3) partisan control of the state government; (4) opposition forces; (5) influential policy entrepreneurs; and (6) political context.

Regional, Economic, and Social Factors

At first blush one might hypothesize that geography has played a role in the shape and texture of charter laws. Several of the 14 states that do not have a charter school law are largely rural (Schnaiberg, 1999b). Between 1991 and 1995, almost twice as many states characterized as urban (close to 70% of the population residing in an urban area) adopted a charter law than did those described as less urban. Of the ten states with strong charter laws, nine can be described as more urban (Hassel, 1997).

Hassel hypothesized that the "innovativeness" of a state may influence its propensity for adopting charter school legislation. States considered to be more "modern" would be more likely to pass innovative legislation. Using income and urbanization as indicators of modernity, Hassel (1997) concluded that charter school laws, and expansive laws in particular, were more likely to be adopted in wealthier and more urban states. He found that 17 of the 30 states classified as above the median on at least one of these two indicators had a charter law. In contrast, only 3 out of 20 states with both indicators below the median had passed a charter law.

Condition of Education

Analysts have suggested that when a state's education system is perceived to be in crisis, policymakers are more apt to consider charter schools. Evidence thus far is mixed. Mintrom and Vergari's (1997) survey-based study found that states with low scores on the National Assessment of Educational Progress

(NAEP) relative to other states provided charter school supporters with strong ammunition for introducing a charter school bill to legislatures. In addition, a low rank on the NAEP increased the likelihood that a charter school law would be adopted (Mintrom & Vergari, 1997). In contrast, another quantitative analysis of state activity during essentially the same time period did not find a statistically significant difference between high and low performing states on the NAEP or the Scholastic Aptitude Test and the likelihood of adopting a charter school law (Hassel, 1997). The inconsistent conclusions drawn by the two studies may indicate that test scores do not provide the most useful evidence of the condition of education in a state.

Partisan Control in State Government

A common perception is that charter schools are closely aligned with Republican ideology, emphasizing limited government, consumer choice, and the power of market forces to address social problems. Yet, as discussed throughout this volume, charter schools are receiving wide bipartisan support. Systematic analyses of party control over the executive and legislative branches provide a more accurate picture of the partisan environment in which charter school bills have been considered. While "both Democrats and Republicans served as policy champions" (Wohlstetter, Wenning, & Briggs, 1995, pp. 334–335), research analyses have shown that single-party control of the state legislature and governor's office did play a role both in the passage of a law and in the degree of permissiveness within the law. Mintrom and Vergari (1997) found that charter school legislation was more likely to be considered in states where both houses were controlled by Republicans. In his analysis of 50 state legislatures and governors, Hassel (1997) found that two thirds of the states in which both houses were Republican-controlled passed charter school laws (six out of nine). Only 15% of state legislatures controlled by Democrats passed a charter school law during the same time period. The party affiliation of the governor did not appear to have an impact on the passage of a charter school law. Both Democratic and Republican governors have passed charter school laws in relatively equal numbers (Hassel, 1997).

The scope of the charter school laws, however, has been influenced by the partisan makeup of the legislature and the governor's office. No state with Democratic control of the legislature and the governor's office had passed a strong charter school law as of early 1996 (Hassel, 1997). In case studies of Colorado, Georgia, Massachusetts, and Michigan, Hassel found that the partisan balance influenced the degree of compromise incorporated in the bill (Hassel, 1997). Bulkley (1998) reached a similar conclusion in her analysis of charter school legislation in Georgia, Michigan, and Arizona. She concluded that the "most significant structural variable" (p. 205) influencing the way in which charter schools were politically constructed in a state was party control of the legislature and governor's office.

Opposition Forces

Research on the influence of opposition forces on charter school legislation has focused largely on teachers unions. In an analysis of all 50 states, evidence does not support the hypothesis that states with powerful unions, as measured by membership in labor unions, are less likely to pass charter school legislation, and strong legislation in particular (Hassel, 1997). A closer examination of Colorado, Georgia, Massachusetts, and Michigan cases led Hassel (1997) to conclude that union power was "almost entirely contingent . . . on the political context, gubernatorial leadership, and the partisan configuration of the state government" (p. 108). Bulkley (1998) concurs with this assessment. To illustrate her point, she offers the case of Michigan, in which the Michigan Education Association, one of the "strongest teacher unions in the country" (p. 209) is closely aligned with the Democrats. At the time charter school legislation was under consideration, however, Republicans dominated the state government. Therefore, the MEA's influence was constrained. In contrast, Bulkley found that the unions in Georgia, while historically weak, were able to exert greater influence over charter school legislation in the Democratic-led government (1998).

Mintrom and Vergari's (1997) findings were consistent with criticisms lobbed at unions as "false friends" (Finn et al., 1997b, p. 3). Union support increased the likelihood of adopting a law if that law was restrictive. This support "served as a mixed blessing, because that support appears to have come at the cost of compromising important elements of the charter school concept" (Mintrom & Vergari, 1997, p. 26).

Policy Entrepreneurs

Policy entrepreneurs play an influential role in state policy discussions of charter schools (Bulkley, 1998; Mintrom & Vergari, 1997). These groups and individuals serve as catalysts for consideration of legislation (Mintrom & Vergari, 1997). Bulkley (1998) questioned whether charter school laws would have passed in Arizona, Georgia, and Michigan without the advocacy of a few select state-based policy entrepreneurs. However, their impact was contingent upon the match between their ideas and the state legislative context and support from "key political actors" (p. 219).

Contact with policy entrepreneurs influences the scope of charter legislation as well. As contact between state policymakers and national policy entrepreneurs increases, the state is more likely to pass a charter law and it is more likely to be permissive in nature (Mintrom & Vergari, 1997).

Political Context

The previous five influences shape the environment in which state legislatures consider the charter school reform. Additional variation can be accounted for by other legislation and policies under consideration at the time, the broader political culture and organization in a state, and the ways in which charter school laws are proposed and formulated.

The broader legislative context informing debate is a significant influence on the contours of charters. Other policies under consideration at the same time as charter schools can distract opponents and influence the compromises that policymakers are willing to make. For example, in Michigan and Massachusetts charter school bills were introduced in the context of other large-scale reforms, which included proposals to revamp school finance to ensure a more equitable distribution of resources. Threats to the educational establishment were also present in policy discussions in these states and in Arizona. Proposals to shut down school districts, abolish tenure, institute a statewide system of inter-district school choice, and provide vouchers are some examples. The other reform measures under consideration consumed considerable resources of charter school opponents, thus facilitating passage of relatively strong charter laws in those three states. In contrast, charter legislation was not debated in the context of other large-scale education debates in Colorado and Georgia. These two state laws are characterized as weak (Bulkley, 1998; Hassel, 1997).

The presence of vouchers on the legislative agenda is frequently cited as a motivating force behind compromises centered on charter schools. In several states, charter school legislation represented a compromise between voucher proponents and opponents. Indeed, charter schools have emerged as a "middle-of-the-road policy" (Wells et al., 1999, p. 515) between these two positions.

The political culture of the state also plays a significant role in shaping charter school debate. Bulkley (1998) found the "construction of charter schools was consistent with the state's political culture" (p. 201) in Arizona, Georgia, and Michigan. Arizona and Georgia, traditionalistic political cultures, were concerned with maintaining power elites. In Georgia, the power elites included Democratic Party leaders and local school officials. In contrast, Arizona power elites were found in the business community, and, therefore, the educational establishment did not hold as much influence (Bulkley, 1998). The resulting laws reflect this degree of autonomy, respectively: Georgia's law is considered to be weak while Arizona's is characterized to be extremely permissive.

Of the first 11 states to pass charter school laws, only Massachusetts and Wisconsin passed legislation as part of broader bills that included other substantive reforms. The other nine states passed "stand-alone reforms" (Wohlstetter, Wenning, & Briggs, 1995, p. 335). "The catalyst for charter school reform was typically the governor or the chair of an education committee in the state legislature" (p. 334). The other states' laws and the models that policymakers studied and used in the drafting of charter school legislation for their home state were an important source of variation. When policymakers used models characterized as permissive, the bill was more likely to be permissive. Similarly, when more restrictive models were used, policymakers drafted legislation that was weaker (Mintrom & Vergari, 1997).

SUMMARY

In this chapter we traced the history of the American charter school movement to the beginning of the new millennium. The charter school movement emerged from multiple sources and has grown increasingly complex as it has been adapted to state and local contexts. The state charter school laws are, at their heart, a compromise that involves the input of often competing parties with varying degrees of influence. We identified both opponents and supporters of the charter school movement and examined their roles. In the final section of the chapter, we discussed the sources of influence that shape the way that legislatures handle charter school reform.

CHAPTER 3

Exploring the Charter School Architecture

Individual charter schools have many differences in the students they attract and their curricula and approaches to learning. Some would be considered conservative; others are liberal. Some defy easy philosophical description. But despite these differences at the individual level, it is possible to define what the charter school movement is and what it is not. (Nathan, 1996a, p. 1)

In this chapter, we undertake the task of describing the charter school movement utilizing three strategies. We begin by examining the statutory, fiscal, and relational dimensions of charter schools. These dimensions shape the manner in which charter schools negotiate the task of educating children in a complex web of public and private obligations. Second, we review available descriptive data about charter school buildings and their inhabitants—students, teachers, school administrators, and parents. Where possible, we note underlying trends suggested by the data. In the final section, we explore the education program of charter schools.

DIMENSIONS OF ALL CHARTER SCHOOLS

Simply passing a law does not guarantee that charter schools will blossom in a given state. The specific provisions in each law help determine how many charter schools actually will open and how independent they actually will be, according to the opportunities or barriers established by legislation. In addition, the attitude (support, neutrality, or opposition) of key actors in the existing local and state education system toward charter schools can also have a significant effect on actual charter school activity and autonomy. (Center for Education Reform, n.d.c, p. 1)

In order to make sense of the descriptive data that policymakers, analysts, and citizens mine for evidence of the charter school movement's success or failure, we must first understand the environment in which charter schools operate. This is shaped by legal parameters, fiscal issues, and the relationships charter schools hold with the public and private entities that share responsibility for the provision of education to charter school students.

Legal Foundations

The "starting point for charter schools is state charter school legislation" (Berman et al., 1998, p. 2). These state laws and "the formal and informal regulations that implement the legislation" (p. 2) have a profound effect on "the charter development process, the charter granting process, and ultimately the ways in which charter schools operate and relate to their sponsors" (p. 2). Because the range of possibilities of a charter school is hinged to the legal apparatus upon which it is based, we will begin our exploration of the charter school architecture by looking at components found in most laws.

Analysts, critics, and proponents evaluate charter school programs based on a relatively common set of components that are either specified in the law or left for individual schools to negotiate. RPP International and the University of Minnesota (1997) identified legal and policy components to examine in the 4-year U.S. Department of Education study, including (1) charter development; (2) school status; (3) fiscal issues; (4) students; (5) staffing and labor relations; (6) instruction; and (7) accountability. The Center for Education Reform (n.d.c), an advocacy group, has ranked existing charter school laws as strong or weak based on similar components. The ten key areas used by the Center for Education Reform include: (1) the number of charter schools allowed; (2) the number of entities with charter-granting authority; (3) which individuals and entities may apply to operate a charter school; (4) whether new schools may be newly started or converted; (5) whether charter applicants must provide evidence of local support; (6) the range of waivers allowed from state and district laws and regulations; (7) legal and operational autonomy; (8) fiscal autonomy; (9) guaranteed per pupil funding; and (10) exemptions from collective bargaining agreement/district work rules. The series of questions and answers prepared by the National Education Association to evaluate state legislation is quite similar (National Education Association, n.d.b.). Wohlstetter, Wenning, and Briggs (1995) divided charter school laws into three clusters of autonomy: (1) the autonomy of the school from the district and the state; (2) the autonomy within the charter school; and (3) the autonomy of parents and students to choose schools. Within each dimension are many of the same components noted by the Center for Education Reform.

Statutes that are perceived to grant the charter school more degrees of freedom in the areas outlined above have been described as "strong," "live," "permissive," "effective," and "progressive" (Center for Education Reform, n.d.c; Hassel, 1999a). Laws that are perceived to restrict a charter school's autonomy are frequently termed "weak," "dead," "restrictive" and "ineffective" (Center for Education Reform, n.d.c). Critics and proponents of charter schools tend to agree on the categorization, if not the terms, applied to different categories.

To discuss the legal dimensions of the charter school movement, we have grouped important components of a state charter program into four categories: (1) the components that define the school's organizational identity; (2) the mechanisms that operationalize the "freedom for accountability exchange tenet" of the charter school model; (3) the chartering process; and (4) the elements that shape the roles and makeup of the workforce. A word of caution should be injected here. In the following sections, we often note the number of states that address a particular component in a similar way. For example, we count how many state laws limit the number of charter schools that may operate in a state. The tallies we provide suggest trends, but the numbers themselves are constantly changing as each legislative session yields new amendments.

Organizational Identity

Public, Nonsectarian Schools. We begin by discussing what all charter schools have in common with traditional public schools. As public entities, they are tuition-free and nonsectarian. These schools must abide by federal civil rights legislation. They cannot discriminate on the basis of gender, race, ethnicity, or religion in their admissions process (RPP International & University of Minnesota, 1997). They must also abide by health and safety laws.

Even at this elemental level, there are some aspects of charter schools in which they have the *potential* to differ from conventional schools. For example, while charter schools are "nonsectarian in their programs, admissions policy, employment practices, and all other operations, and are not affiliated with a sectarian school or a religious institution" (RPP International & University of Minnesota, 1997, p. 2), there is a "fairly wide net" (Schnaiberg, 1999a, p. 11) regarding who can apply to start a charter school. The laws do not provide guidelines for an application submitted by a religious group or leader.

Types of Charter Schools. Charter schools can be classified by their origins. Researchers have noted that charter schools with different roots have diverse characteristics and face unique challenges. A charter school may trace its origins to one of three blueprints. The first type is the brand-new school, frequently referred to as a start-up, newly formed, newly created, or new start school. These schools came into existence with the charter agreement. A second type of charter school is one that operated as a public school prior to gaining charter status. These schools are referred to as preexisting public schools or public conversion schools because their status was converted from that of a traditional public school to that of a charter school. The third type of charter school operated as a private school prior to gaining charter status. These schools are referred to as preexisting private schools or private conversion schools.

State legislation defines the types of charter schools that may operate. All states with charter school laws allow preexisting public schools to convert to charter schools (Nelson, Berman, Ericson, Kamprath, Perry, Silverman, & Solomon, 2000). All of them except Mississippi allow start-up charter schools. The District of Columbia and nine states allow preexisting private schools to convert to charter schools directly—Arizona, Michigan, Minnesota, Missouri, North Carolina, Pennsylvania, South Carolina, Texas, and Wisconsin. An additional three states allow private schools to convert under certain conditions.

The majority of charter schools are newly created and this percentage is increasing. The Department of Education study estimated that 72% of charter schools were newly created in the 1998–99 school year (B. Nelson et al., 2000). That same year, only 19% were converted from public schools, and 11% were converted from private schools. The newly created schools, as a percentage of charter schools that open in a given year, increasingly outnumber the other types of charters. For example, of the charters that first opened their doors during the 1994–95 school year, approximately half were newly created (Berman et al., 1999). By 1997–98, 84% of the schools beginning operation that year were start-ups.

Researchers have looked for and found differences based on the charter school's origins in most aspects of charter school operations, including size, enrollment patterns, types of teachers employed, reasons for founding a charter school, implementation challenges, and levels of autonomy. Also, the resource needs differ for these types of charters. In later sections, we will discuss these differences in some detail.

For-Profit Management of Charter Schools. The "most contentious charter school issue" (Mahtesian, 1998, p. 26), according to some, is the provision that allows for-profit companies to manage or operate these entities. The majority of states do not allow for-profit companies to directly manage and operate charter schools. However, a sizeable proportion of charter school laws (20) either allow the charter holder to subcontract the management of charters to for-profit companies or do not explicitly prohibit the charter holder from doing so (Center for Education Reform, 2000a). In 1998, one tenth of the 700 operating charter schools were run by for-profit companies (National Education Association, 1998b). These schools were operating in nine states.

Arsen, Plank, and Sykes (n.d.) believe that "charter schools present a set of conditions that are especially favorable for the entry and growth" (p. 54) of education management organizations (EMOs). The authors document a rapidly expanding presence of EMOs in Michigan's charter schools, known as Public School Academies (PSAs). During the 1998–99 school year, 70% of PSAs in the state contracted out services to EMOs. "By some estimates, Michigan has more PSAs run by for-profit firms than any other state" (p. 53). In the 1995–96 school year, 28% of Arizona's charters were operated by for-profit companies (McKinney, 1996).

The Freedom for Accountability Trade-Off

Proponents assert that the "whole rationale for charter schools hinges on the red tape-accountability tradeoff: maximum operational and instructional freedom in exchange for strict accountability for student outcomes" (Caudell, 1997b, p. 4). Here we will examine the mechanisms in state laws that operationalize freedom and accountability. The rationale behind this freedom for accountability exchange and its role in the reform engine will be discussed in greater depth in Chapter 5.

Legal Status. The legal status that is granted to charter schools has significant implications for the level of autonomy that the charter school is able to exert. Berman et al. (1998) grouped state charter laws into three categories based on the type of legal status bestowed. Under one scenario, charter schools are designated as independent legal entities. These bodies can take several forms depending on the law, including corporate organizations such as "business cooperatives" (Buechler, 1996, p. 41), nonprofit organizations, and independent governmental organizations, essentially a one-school school district. As independent legal entities, charter schools can "own property, sue and be sued, incur debt, control budget and personnel, and contract for services" (Center for Education Reform, n.d.c, p. 4). Not surprisingly, charter advocates maintain that independent legal status is essential to the viability of charter schools (Finn et al., 1997b; Kolderie, 1990; Nathan, 1996a). In 19 states, charter schools are independent legal entities (Berman et al., 1998).

A second category of state laws retains the charter school's legal status as part of the local school district. In their 1998 report, Berman and his colleagues found that nine states fell into this category. A charter school in this group has significantly less control over its activities. The school district remains legally liable for the charter's actions. Educational groups such as the National Education Association (n.d.b, n.d.c) favor this more limited level of autonomy for charters. They contend that autonomous charters will not encourage systemic change because these schools operate in a different world from traditional schools in a district.

A final category of statutes leaves the charter school's legal status unclear. In 1998, the legislation was not explicit on this topic in two states (Berman et al., 1998).

Freedom from Laws and Regulations. A key feature of the charter school model is the ability of these schools to receive exemptions from state and local laws and regulations. Sarason (1998) notes that while "all states in principle agree that these schools should be radically free to depart from rules and regulations of all other schools" (p. 13), there is a large amount of variation in the freedom granted to charter schools across the states.

Berman and his team (1998) identified three approaches states are taking to allow exemptions from state and local regulations. They found that the majority of states (18) at the time gave charter schools automatic waivers of "all or most of the state education code" (p. 18) with the exception of regulations pertaining to health and safety, civil rights, nondiscrimination, disability, and requirements to remain nonsectarian. A large group of states (10) require charters to apply for waivers on a case-by-case basis. In two states, charters must abide by most of the state education laws.

Despite the importance placed on this feature in the early stages of the charter movement, it may, in fact, prove less critical to a school's autonomy than other legal provisions such as establishing charter schools as independent legal entities and providing for nonlocal charter-granting agencies (Hassel, 1999a). Furthermore, the states that grant independent legal status to charter schools also tend to be the states that provide these schools with "a 'blanket' exemption from all state and local codes" (McGree, 1995a, p. 5).

Accountability. Charter school accountability has several dimensions that we explore in considerable detail in later chapters.

The Chartering Process

Chartering Agencies and Appeals. The statutory provisions that define which entities have the power to grant charters and the scope of their authority provide the foundation for a state's charter school program. There are three factors to consider when examining the degree of constriction present in a state charter school law. First, who has the authority to grant a charter? Second, are multiple agencies granted this authority? And finally, if one chartering agency rejects an application, is there an appeals process in which the application can be reconsidered? The answers to these questions have an important bearing on the school's autonomy. For example, if a state law allows one entity the authority to grant charters with no appeal to another agency, the charter program in the state will be shaped by the priorities and constraints of that entity. This can be a particularly constraining factor when the single entity is the local school board because "local boards often have their districts' interests to consider in approving a school and, as a result, may not be objective in their evaluation of an application" (Weiss, 1994, p. 11).

Most often, the chartering authority is a state or local school board. Other chartering entities include universities, state administrative offices, and specially created chartering boards (Manno et al., 1997b). Only local school boards may grant charters in 14 states. Of those, the school board has the final authority in 6 (Alaska, Kansas, Pennsylvania, Virginia, Wisconsin, and Wyoming) (B. Nelson et al., 2000). In the other 8 states (California, Colorado, Florida, Idaho, Illinois, New Hampshire, Oklahoma, and South Carolina), charter applicants may appeal a local school board's decision to another agency. A state agency—usually the state board of education—has the sole authority to grant charters in 7 states (Arkansas, Connecticut, Georgia, Hawaii, New Jersey, Rhode Island, and Utah). In 16 states multiple entities may grant charters. Usually these entities include the local school boards and a state agency. Five states that allow multiple charter agencies allow universities to grant charters (B. Nelson et al., 2000).

Length of Charter. Agreements between a chartering agency and a school are "limited-term contracts" (B. Nelson et al., 2000, p. 12), which are performance-based and must be renewed to continue operation. The duration of these contracts is stipulated by law and varies across the states. The majority of states (31) allow charters to operate from 3 to 5 years before seeking renewal. Arizona and the District of Columbia have the longest agreements—15 years; however, a review is required after 5 years. Texas law does not mandate a time limit; rather, the length of the charter is stated in the charter agreement (B. Nelson et al., 2000).

Caps on Charter Schools. Most of the original state charter school laws included a cap on the number of charter schools that could operate in the state. As the charter school model has evolved in the different states, however, some laws have been changed to either increase caps or do away with them altogether. Caps can be placed on the total number of charter schools allowed to operate in the state, the number that can operate in a school district, or the number that are approved in a given year. Also, caps may vary based on the types of charter schools in existence; for example, newly created charter schools versus conversion schools. Caps can be linked to the educational focus or student populations served. For example, Texas law allows an unlimited number of charter schools that target at-risk children (B. Nelson et al., 2000). All other charter schools in the state operate under a cap. Charter advocates argue that caps emasculate choice and stifle competition with public schools, thus undermining the infrastructure of charter schools.

An unlimited number of charter schools may operate in 13 states (B. Nelson et al., 2000). An additional two states limit the number of charter schools but provide exemptions for schools that serve at-risk students. The other 22 states have caps either on the total number of charter schools allowed in the state, the number allowed in a district, or the number allowed in a given year. Mississippi and Utah allow the least number of charter schools to operate—six for Mississippi and eight for Utah.

Employment Conditions

Bierlein and Mulholland (1993) describe resolving employment-related issues as "one of the most politically-charged components of a charter school program" (p. 19). Finn, Bierlein, and Manno (1996) argue that "compromise in this arena is the surest way to strangle an infant charter school program in its cradle" (p. 11). We explore three personnel-related factors that are generally specified in the legislation. First, we examine who is the employer of charter school teachers. Second, we discuss personnel issues related to collective bargaining, job security, and benefits. Finally, we investigate qualification requirements for charter school teachers.

Employers of Charter School Teachers. Charter school employers vary. One set of state laws makes teachers employees of the charter school. In a second group of states, charter school staff are employed by the school district. Under a third scenario, the employer varies depending on the status of the school. Staff of newly created charter schools or schools converted from private schools are employed by the charter school, while staff of charter schools converted from public schools remain employees of the district (Berman et al., 1998). Control over personnel decisions has major implications for the level of autonomy a school enjoys. Wohlstetter and her colleagues (1995) characterized laws that allow charter schools to make their own personnel policies as having a high degree of autonomy. In contrast, laws that require hiring and termination decisions to be made within the context of district policies and union agreements provide much lower degrees of autonomy to schools. Charter schools advocates unequivocally assert that charter schools should have the power to select staff (Finn, Bierlein, & Manno, 1996).

Employee Benefits and Union Relations. The participation of charter schools in collective bargaining agreements made between local school districts and teacher unions to establish teacher salaries, working conditions, and hours varies across the states (Berman et al., 1998). A charter school's flexibility and operations are affected by whether its employees are included in the district's collective bargaining agreements (Northeast and Islands Regional Educational Laboratory, 1999)—a condition denounced by charter advocates. Other analysts, however, are concerned that freeing charter schools from collective bargaining agreements will result in "an unfair system of wage and benefit distribution within the public school system" (p. 19).

The U.S. Department of Education study identified four state approaches to labor relations (Berman et al., 1998). In the majority of states (19), charter schools must abide by state collective bargaining laws. Some of these states require charter school employees to remain part of the school district's bargaining unit, while other states allow these employees to form their own bargaining unit, independent of the district. A second approach, found in 4 state laws, is not to address charter school participation in collective bargaining agreements. In a third scenario, the state does not have collective bargaining laws (6 states). Finally, California requires charter schools to address collective bargaining in their charters.

Another issue facing charter school teachers is the status of their tenure and retirement benefits. Nathan (1996a) argues that states should allow teachers to take a leave of absence from their public school and retain their seniority. Additionally, Nathan argues, the state should allow continued participation in local or state retirement programs for these teachers. The American Federation of Teachers (1996) concurs, exclaiming that states need to provide retirement benefits.

Teacher Qualifications. Certification is a contentious issue between charter school advocates and teacher unions. Close to one third of states require charter teachers to be certified (Center for Education Reform, 2000a). In another third of the states, a charter must have a specified percentage of certified teachers in the school. In another third of the states, while certification is required, there are exemptions. Finally, four states do not require any charter teachers to be certified.

By removing the certification requirement, charter schools can draw from a larger pool of applicants, including professors and retired professionals (Bierlein & Bateman, 1995). Proponents argue that the focus shifts from inputs—that is, teachers who have completed appropriate collegiate coursework and training—to results. They assert that "individuals with subject matter expertise and experience working with young people" (Buechler, 1996, p. 41) should not be rejected as potential teachers because they lack the necessary certification. The American Federation of Teachers (1996) counters that "teacher professionalization is not enhanced by charter school laws that encourage the hiring of uncertified people to teach" (p. 53). They acknowledge that while the input of certification does not guarantee a good teacher in every classroom, "it does ensure that a minimum level of competency has been demonstrated" (p. 53). Furthermore, they argue that pedagogical skills and knowledge in designing, teaching, and evaluating learning are as important as subject matter expertise in defining a good teacher.

Finance

A guiding principle of charter school finance systems is that "resources should follow children from school districts to charter schools" (Nelson, Muir, Drown, & To, 2000, p. 30). Full per-pupil funding is "essential to the financial viability of charter schools . . . and is the primary mechanism through which charter schools can have an impact on regular public schools" (Hassel, 1999a, p. 151). However, given the myriad of funding sources and mechanisms for dispensing revenue as well as the differing costs faced by charter schools and traditional public schools, unpacking the term "resources" to assess whether this revenue transfer does in fact take place proves to be a complex task. Charter schools have different relationships with revenue sources and different capacities for garnering resources. At the same time, the costs charters face are similar to school districts in some instances; in other cases, the costs are experienced in different degrees; and finally, some costs are unique to charters—particularly the newly created entities. Some argue that the relatively higher financial burden charter schools face is somewhat offset by some exemptions from costly regulations such as hiring unionized staff, providing transportation, or adhering to public school building codes (U.S. General Accounting Office, 2000). As is a recurrent theme in this chapter, the what and how of charter school funding is characterized by variation both in terms of revenues and expenditures.

In the first two subsections, we unpack the core funding for charter schools—a calculated per-pupil amount supplied by the state and supplemented by state and federal categorical funds. Next, we turn to charter school expenditures, looking in particular at the costs that charter schools find most challenging to cover. As part of this discussion, we explore alternative revenue sources used by charter schools to meet these expenses.

Per-Pupil Base Funding

The "heart of charter school funding systems" (H. Nelson et al., 2000, p. 1) is the per-pupil-based funding. Like school districts, this per-pupil amount finances day-to-day operations. In the National Charter School Finance Study, Howard Nelson and his colleagues found that states take one of three approaches to calculating this foundation funding for charter schools in the 24 states they studied. The amount is based on (1) a school district's average per-pupil amount, (2) the state average per-pupil amount, or (3) a formula determined by the school district that charters the school.

The majority of states employ the first approach. In this scenario, the funding is based on either the per-pupil average of the school district in which the charter is located or the average of the district in which the student resides. Charter schools "inherit funding generated by the wealth, tax effort, and geographic characteristics" (p. 30) of the school district or of the students enrolled. There is further variation with regard to how the per-pupil amount is calculated based on whether the average income or expenditure is used. Ten states base charter school funding on the school district's average per-pupil income. Under this revenue-based model, the amount a charter school receives is influenced by the "grade-level, special needs or low-income characteristics" (p. 30) of enrolled students. Eight states base this per-pupil amount on the school district's average per-pupil expenditure. Under the expenditure-based approach, charter school funding is based on the student characteristics of the school district. If the charter school has different student characteristics from the school district, it will receive either more or less funding. The calculation is further complicated in several states because "school districts have some control over the amount of funding that charter schools receive, or the funding is subject to negotiations between school districts and charter schools" (p. 31).

In their study, H. Nelson and his team (2000) found that a minority of states calculate charter school foundation funding using methods two and three noted above. Two states base charter school funding on the state's average per-pupil amount. In six states, charter school funding decisions are left to the school districts that charter them. Bierlein and Bateman (1995) argue that when the amount is negotiated between the school districts and the charter schools, districts "are often not supportive since they see charter schools as taking *their* students and *their* funding" (p. 54).

There is some disagreement as to whether charter schools receive their full per-pupil cost. The National Charter School Finance Study authors concluded that "most or all per-pupil funding flows with students from school districts to charter schools in almost all states" (H. Nelson et al., 2000, p. 2). In 1996, Finn, Bierlein, and Manno argued that many charter schools had smaller operating budgets than traditional schools when compared pupil for pupil. Finn, Manno, Bierlein, and Vanourek (1997b) cite examples where the basic formula for funding charter schools is inequitable in the statute. In New Jersey, charter schools receive, by law, 90% of per-pupil operating expenses. In other instances, while full funding is guaranteed, in "reality [it] is eroded by other provisions" (p. 6). In Texas, 80% of the school district's "per-pupil funding follows the student to the charter school" (Fusarelli, 1998, p. 30). In

California, charter schools received less per-pupil funding because "funneling the money through the local districts allows for funding discrepancies for charter schools across and within school districts" (UCLA Charter School Study, n.d., p. 36).

The process used to count students has significant implications for a charter school's per-pupil funding. The majority of states count students based on an average daily membership. In California and Texas, average daily attendance is used. The use of attendance may put charters who target at-risk populations, such as dropouts, at a disadvantage (H. Nelson et al., 2000). Due to the small size of most charter schools, any changes in enrollment have "immediate effects on school income" (Hill, Pierce, & Guthrie, 1997, p. 116). The timing of student enrollment counts also can be problematic, particularly for charter schools that are expanding. For example, some charter schools' funds are calculated using the previous year's enrollment figures (Finn et al., 1997b).

Categorical Funding for Charter Schools

Categorical funds provide another source of revenue for both charter schools and school districts. These funds add "supplementary aid . . . for disadvantaged or disabled youngsters" (Finn et al., 1997b, p. 7) to other funds that reflect state or federal priorities. Like any public school, charter schools are obligated by law to serve all students regardless of ability. The high cost of educating students with special needs is not a unique challenge to charter schools. Here, we identify state and federal funding available for students with special needs, for transportation, and for other categorical programs. As part of our discussion, we examine the degree to which charter schools access these funding sources.

State Categorical Funding. In this section, we examine state assistance for students with disabilities, students at-risk, transportation costs, and other categorical programs that are available to charter schools.

Howard Nelson and his colleagues (2000) identified three strategies that states use to provide additional support for students with disabilities enrolled in charter schools. The majority of states studied provide additional revenue based on the disabilities of the students actually enrolled in the charter school. Using a second model, seven states base special education funding for charter schools on the school district's special education costs or revenue. This practice results in charter schools only receiving equal funding when the proportion of special education students enrolled in the school is the same as the proportion in the entire school district. Therefore, if a charter school enrolls fewer students with disabilities, the school will receive more money than other schools in the district. However, a disincentive exists for charter schools to enroll more students with disabilities than the district—appropriate funding will not be available. The third strategy is employed by four states. In this approach, special education funding amounts are negotiated between the school district and the charter schools.

Financing services to educate special needs students is a contentious issue. For special education advocates, the high cost of such students may lead to discrimination. For fledgling charter schools, these students pose an enormous fiscal challenge that could possibly "'break the budget' of small charter schools" (Bierlein & Fulton, n.d., p. 3). As we note in Chapter 7, some studies suggest that charters in Michigan and Massachusetts that are managed by for-profit companies may restrict services to special education students to save on costs (Dykgraaf & Lewis, 1998; Zollers & Ramanathan, 1998).

As with special education, additional support is typically available to provide services for at-risk students. Howard Nelson and his colleagues (2000) found that the majority of states "provide additional funding to charter schools for at-risk students either directly, or through school district negotiations" (p. 2). Seven states provide funds to support at-risk students that are based on school district averages, which, as noted above, serves as a disincentive for charter schools to serve at-risk students.

Transportation presents a large cost yet may raise "subtle issues of charter school selectivity" (H. Nelson et al., 2000, p. 48) when it is not provided. The availability of state funding for transportation for charter schools varies among the states. Of the 24 states in the Nelson study, "the responsibility (if any) for providing transportation services or funding rests with school districts in 12 states" (p. 49). In 8 states transportation was not required.

The National Charter School Finance Study authors (H. Nelson et al., 2000) found that charter school income does not include many categorical sources besides those that support special education, at-risk students, and transportation costs. In fact, only 4 states out of the 24 states studied supplied charter schools with over $50 per pupil in other state categorical funding. Charter schools encounter two issues here. First, the associated paperwork to apply for and document use of categorical funds is time-consuming and challenging for small staffs that often have little experience dealing with federal or state programs. Second, the program demands may reduce the school's freedom to operate or splinter its educational focus (Finn et al., 1997b).

Federal Categorical Funding. The U.S. General Accounting Office (1998b) found that two fifths of the charter schools in their survey received Title I funding for additional services for economically disadvantaged children and half of the schools received Individuals with Disabilities Education Act (IDEA) support. Most of the schools sampled that did not receive these funds did not apply for them. The authors of the Hudson Institute report voiced concern about the under-utilization of federal dollars by charter schools (Finn et al., 1997b). For example, in the 1996–97 school year, 16 out of the 24 state-sponsored charter schools in Massachusetts did not receive any Title I funds, and 20 did not receive any support from IDEA. The absence of enrollment and student eligibility data and lack of administrative experience, as well as the time and costs of the application process may explain some of the difficulties the charters face in accessing Title I and IDEA support (U.S. General Accounting Office, 1998b).

A source of disagreement between charter schools and school districts is the process of "divvying up federal funds, such as Title I or bilingual education funds" (Harrington-Lueker, 1997, p. 11). The U.S. General Accounting Office report (1998b) identified three methods states use to allocate Title I and IDEA funds: (1) directly to the charter school; (2) to the parent school district which then provides a share of the district amount to the charter; or (3) the pathway is dependent upon whether the charter school is legally independent of the school district, in which case the school receives funds directly from the state, or whether the school is a part of the district and federal funds flow through the district to them.

Charter School Expenditures

The expenditures of charter schools generally parallel those of their traditional public counterparts. However, there are some significant differences both in the relative scale of the cost to the school, as in the area of operations, and in the expenditures themselves. We begin by discussing the operational costs of charter schools. Then we explore capital and start-up costs charter schools face, as well as the schools' access to revenue for these expenditures.

Operational Costs. In general, the per-pupil base amount received from the state or school district is used to pay for the operational costs of running a charter school. A school district offers a wide range of services to schools within its jurisdiction, such as administrative, instructional, legal, and food services. Under the principle of economies of scale, this makes for an efficient delivery of services. The legal status or relationship of the charter school to the school district in which it resides has important implications for what operational costs the charter must assume. In cases where the charter is independent of the school district, the charter—usually a very small institution—must decide how to address a broad and varied range of expenditures. Many school districts offer "a menu of central-office services, such as transportation, payroll, and special education that charters can purchase" (Harrington-Lueker, 1997, p. 11).

Capital Costs. Capital costs pose a significant challenge to charter schools, particularly to the newly created entities. Securing a facility dominates any discussion of capital, but other items, such as "computers, furniture, textbooks, [and] playground equipment" (Finn et al., 1997a, p. 4), fall into this category as well. The problem charter schools face in financing capital projects is one of scale and access. A newly created charter school essentially has to start from scratch and undertake many one-time costly investments that an existing public school has already made. At the same time, charters' access to capital financing is limited. Although generally insufficient, some targeted capital funding is available to charter schools. In an inadequate fiscal environment, charter schools tend to devote large proportions of their operating funds to cover capital costs.

The cost of securing and maintaining a facility presents a major challenge for newly created charters. These new schools must purchase or rent a facility and must pay for renovations to meet building codes and for ongoing maintenance (Finn et al., 1997a). The costs of securing and maintaining a facility often represent a large portion of the school's budget. It is not unusual for facility costs to account for 20 to 25% of a charter school's expenditures (Hassel, 1999b). Two case studies revealed one charter school that spent over $400 per pupil to pay off a capital debt and another that paid approximately $1,360 per pupil in rent payments on loans for renovations (Anderson, 1998).

Charter schools are different fiscal entities than school districts. In general, charters have one budget, whereas school districts have separate capital and operating funding streams. School districts typically rely on "borrowing—usually via bonds that are sold to investors and . . . paid off with interest over a number of years" (Finn et al., 1997b, p. 4) and taxes to finance capital projects. Charter schools do not have access to either pool of resources. Furthermore, state laws are often ambiguous as to whether charter schools may "issue tax-exempt debt or whether public bodies . . . may issue tax-exempt bonds on behalf of charter schools" (U.S. General Accounting Office, 2000, p. 10). Without such tax advantages, a charter school is likely to pay more for a facility than a school that is part of the school district (Hassel, 1999). Some states are making changes to address this problem. For example, Colorado and North Carolina have legislation that allows the state bonding authority to sell bonds to finance charter school facilities (Hassel, 1999b; U.S. General Accounting Office, 2000).

Charter schools are generally considered to be "poor credit risks" (U.S. General Accounting Office, 2000, p. 14) by "private lenders, investors, and property owners" (Hassel, 1999b, p. 5). They are characterized by limited revenue that is tied to enrollment figures, little or no credit history, inexperienced management, and charters that often have shorter terms than lease agreements (Hassel, 1999b; U.S. General Accounting Office, 2000). Furthermore, without the ability to tax, charter schools "cannot pledge future tax payments as backing for financing" (Hassel, 1999b, p. 8).

In most states, charter schools are allowed to incur debt—20 out of 24 states in 1997–1998 (H. Nelson et al., 2000). Where charter schools can incur debt, the charter school corporation or board is usually responsible for the obligation. The school district is responsible for charter debt in Massachusetts's school district-initiated charter schools and in all Alaskan charters. In many cases, state laws are ambiguous concerning the ownership of charter school assets in the event of the school's closure. In ten states, the school's assets revert to the school district or state.

Some targeted facilities financing is available from states, the federal government, and private sources. Approximately half of the states "provide facilities as part of the conversion process or directly provide some facilities funding" (H. Nelson et al., 2000, p. 71). School districts that are allowed to share their facility funds with charter schools often do not because they are "struggling to meet their own facility needs" (U.S. General Accounting Office, 2000, p. 11). State funding for facilities is available in five states, ranging from $1,200 per pupil in Arizona to $260 in Massachusetts (Hassel, 1999b). A small amount of federal funding is available to finance charter facilities through two grant programs sponsored by agencies other than the Department of Education. Although important in specific cases, private donations are believed to be small. Finally, surplus public buildings are not often used (U.S. General Accounting Office, 2000).

The per-pupil base funding is often used to help pay facility costs, although this is generally considered to be an unsatisfactory solution (Bierlein & Fulton, n.d.). First, the amount is rarely enough to cover capital costs because charter schools often: (1) do not get their full allocation, (2) have small enrollments, thus a poor economy of scale, and (3) have their per-pupil allocations based on operating funds or costs rather than on facilities (U.S. General Accounting Office, 2000). A second problem is that when charter schools divert operating funds to cover facilities, it is done so at the expense of important operational activities—that is, instruction.

Start-Up Costs. Insufficient start-up funding is viewed as a significant barrier to establishing a charter school (H. Nelson et al., 2000). In general, "start-up costs are borne by school organizers" (Hill, Pierce, & Guthrie, 1997, p. 116). However, some state and federal assistance has been targeted to assist charter schools to begin operation. State start-up funding or assistance was available in 9 out of 24 states studied by the investigators in the Howard

Nelson study (2000). In 4 of those 9 states, start-up support took the form of assistance with "cash flow problems through loans and/or advance aid payments" (p. 56).

Federal funding is available to "assist with costs for opening and starting a charter school" (H. Nelson et al., 2000, p. 56). The state education agency applies to the federal government for the funds and then awards subgrants to charter school developers on a competitive basis. If a state education agency does not participate in this federal program, individual charters may apply directly to the U.S. Department of Education for these funds. The federal grants can be used for up to 3 years to cover "refinement of the desired educational results and the methods for measuring those results; implementation costs; informing the community about the charter school; and acquiring the necessary equipment, materials, supplies, and other operational needs that cannot be met from state and local revenues" (p. 57). Subgrants usually finance 1 year of planning and 2 years of implementation.

Of the 24 states studied in 1997–98, 20 states received federal start-up grants. The method of dispensing the subgrants varies across the states. Some states base the grants on a per-pupil amount. Other states give "equal-sized block grants" (H. Nelson et al., 2000, p. 57). In other states, the grant amount is determined on a case-by-case basis. There also is tremendous variation in the size of planning grants across the states, from $5,000 in Georgia and Louisiana to $115,000 in Massachusetts. Implementation grants vary as well—from $15,000 in South Carolina to approximately $200,000 in Wisconsin and Colorado (H. Nelson et al., 2000). Federal start-up money tends to be used for facilities if the charter is a newly created school or for operating costs such as salaries and rent if it is a conversion school (Anderson, 1998).

A corollary issue is the timing of government disbursements in general and for the first year in particular. Finn and his colleagues (1997b) voiced concern that public charter school funds did not reach these schools until the school opened and students were present. While school districts have mechanisms for covering costs between payments and their budgets are large enough to defer some costs, charter schools are again at a disadvantage (Bierlein & Fulton, n.d.). This presents major cash flow challenges for charter schools with limited or no credit to furnish schools with basic supplies for educating students. Case studies conducted for the Education Commission of the States found that "many founders borrowed money or used their own personal money to get through this period" (Anderson, 1998, p. 9). Approximately half of the states had some provisions in place for speeding up payments to charter schools in 1997–98 (H. Nelson et al., 2000). In another six states, advance payments were arranged in the charter agreement or at the discretion of the school district. The rapid growth of for-profit companies managing charter schools can, in part, be attributed to the challenge of start-up costs (H. Nelson et al., 2000).

Other Sources of Revenue. Loan pools provide another mechanism for charter schools to finance facilities. These pools have been established by private lenders and some school districts (Hassel, 1999). For example, the Chicago school district established a $2 million "low-interest loan pool" (p. 13). The Prudential Foundation established a $10 million revolving fund from which New Jersey incipient charters may borrow for start-up and operations costs (Finn et al., 1997b).

Relationships with Government Agencies and Other Entities

We now turn to the third dimension in our analysis of the charter school environment, that of relationships. In large part, the interactions that charter schools have forged with government, private entities, and each other are shaped by the financial and legal dimensions outlined above. In this section, we focus primarily on charter schools' relationships with local and state education agencies and the federal government. Then we conclude with a brief discussion of the relationships that charter schools hold with each other and with private entities.

Governmental Relations

Charter schools are neither typical schools nor a school district. While statutory and fiscal parameters provide a framework for interaction, it is often incomplete—as becomes evident in its implementation. As a new type of public institution, charters force government entities to interact with them in different ways. These relationships forged by charters and government at all levels are both evolutionary and context-specific. The context in which relationships develop is also shaped by the attitudes, needs, and priorities of government entities and of charter schools. For example, on the one hand, a school district may perceive a charter to be a threat due to lost resources, a perceived liability, or an implied criticism of the district's ability to educate students. On the other hand, the charter may help the district by providing an education that better meets the special needs of some groups of students. These charter-government relations are further complicated by potentially conflicting responsibilities for support and oversight.

The School District. Despite the hopes of some charters and school districts, the two entities can rarely remain entirely independent of each other because they share the task of educating students in a common community.

Regulatory and fiscal relationships specific to a particular state also bind the two entities together. In addition, charters may seek technical assistance and support from districts. For their part, local education agencies may rely on charters to educate students that their traditional schools have not served well.

While the bond between charters and districts is frequently depicted as adversarial, *Education Week* reporter Lynn Schnaiberg argues that district attitudes are "really all over the map" (Learning Matters, Inc., 1999, p. 31). Some districts have been very supportive while others have been quite threatened by charter schools. Similarly, some charters are critical of districts. For example, the National Charter School Study found that approximately 20% of newly created charter schools and public conversion schools identified "district resistance or regulations" (B. Nelson et al., 2000, p. 44) as a barrier to their implementation. Similarly, one fifth of the same types of schools identified state or local board opposition as a barrier as well.

The confusion and complexity of school district-charter school associations have been attributed to state laws that "do not outline a formal process for charter schools to interact with their local districts" (McGree, 1995a, p. 5), thus placing schools and districts in "the difficult and unfamiliar position of defining and redefining their relationship" (p. 5). And yet, no formula for interaction prescribed in state legislatures could entirely erase the kinks and unanticipated consequences associated with implementing a new policy and a new education model at the local level.

Particular issues that lie within the processes that authorize charter schools and define their autonomy "can have a divisive and polarizing effect" (McGree, 1995a, p. 5). These relationships can be particularly problematic when the school district is the chartering agency. The Little Hoover Commission (1996) found that in California the "relationship between charter schools and their sponsoring districts is often an uneasy one" (p. 65). Districts feel "caught between a law that says charter schools have absolute freedom and the belief that they maintain some liability for charter school actions" (p. 66). As a result, school boards are often "ambivalent about their responsibilities to monitor charter schools" (UCLA Charter School Study, n.d., p. 24) and thus "many are reluctant to become involved" (p. 25).

Support and the provision of services provide a frequent point of interaction between charters and school districts regardless of whether or not the school is "legally autonomous [or] semi-autonomous" (McGree, 1995a, p. 5). In addition to financial support discussed elsewhere in this chapter, charter schools need technical assistance, such as legal advice or guidance in completing paperwork to meet federal or state regulations. Due to their experience and similar clientele, the school district is a logical organization to turn to for advice. The UCLA Charter School Study team (n.d.) found that California charters often tapped the school district for assistance. Newly created schools needed the most support. In the case of California, school districts were not reimbursed for this technical assistance. The costs can be high. For example, the Los Angeles Unified School District created a 20-person working committee to facilitate charter implementation and designated an administrator to devote 65% of staff time to "coordinating responses to charter school issues" (Izu, Carlos, Yamashiro, Picus, Tushnet, & Wohlstetter, 1998, p. 11).

Charter schools also need services to support their daily operations, including transportation, payroll, food, and health services. While the school district is a likely provider, charters typically have the freedom to pick and choose service providers. The U.S. Department of Education study found that in 1998–99, only 26% acquired services solely from the school district (B. Nelson et al., 2000). Not surprisingly, research suggests that the degree to which a charter relies on the school district is influenced by the school's status as a newly created, private conversion, or public conversion school. Over half of public conversion schools received "payroll, accounting, purchasing, health, food programs, legal services, custodial, building maintenance, and transportation services from the district" (Berman et al., 1999, p. 9). In contrast, private conversion and new charters are more likely to provide the services themselves or to contract with an outside provider. Sometimes, the law may mandate that the district provide a service to the charter that proves unsatisfactory for both. For example, school districts are required to provide transportation in Minnesota. The outgrowth of this provision is that charter schools must "coordinate their calendar and school hours with the district's transportation schedule" (McGree, 1995a, p. 6), thus restricting the school's freedom to develop innovative scheduling. At the same time, communication about the number and location of students requiring transportation to the charter proves frustrating for districts. And transporting students from all over the district to the charter is costly and time consuming.

Support can also go the other way. Charters can relieve school districts of some pressure to serve students and their parents with unique needs or wants by operating niche schools (Rofes, 1998a). The schools that are the least threatening to school districts are those that serve special needs populations primarily or do not seek autonomy (McGree, 1995a).

State Education Agency. Like that of school districts, the state education agency's relationship with charter schools is multidimensional. It comprises interactions related to support and oversight, both as part of a new reform initiative and as a public entity. In addition to statutory provisions, a state's approach to charters is defined by "case law, regulatory context, and agency actions" (RPP International & University of Minnesota, 1997, p. 2).

The state education agency's identity as a chartering agency has implications for the relationship of the charter and the state. Conflicting purposes of these interactions may interfere with a sponsoring agency's ability to carry out each role. For example, a state sponsoring agency can be characterized as one of "both shepherd and executioner" (Loveless & Jasin, 1998, p. 26) because it must assist and nurture charter schools while also holding them accountable for results. In 1996, Finn, Bierlein, and Manno argued that no state had a "thoughtful and well-formed plan for evaluating its charter school program" (p. 9). The size of staff working on charter school issues has implications for the state education agency's role in holding charter schools accountable (U.S. Department of Education, 2000).

State support to charter schools takes the form of revenue (described elsewhere), technical assistance, and waivers of state laws and regulations. The amount of staff resources that state education agencies devote to charters ranges from "a very small percentage of one person's time to six full-time staff" (U.S. Department of Education, 2000, p. 123). States with a large number of charter schools tend to have a larger staff at the state level.

States also waive many statutory and regulatory provisions that may inhibit charter school functioning. Half of all states with charter laws "automatically grant waivers from many state laws, rules, and regulations" (U.S. Department of Education, 2000, p. 38). In general, however, charter schools are not exempt from "state budgeting and audit regulations or from student assessment requirements" (p. 40).

Federal Government. Like the state and local education agencies, the federal government's relationship with charter schools is evolving and is characterized both by compliance and by support. There are three forces that undergird the federal government-charter school relationship. First, because it has become a politically popular reform model, Congress and the Executive Branch have developed mechanisms for lending federal support to the growing, locally based movement. At the same time, charter schools "pose new challenges . . . in allocating funds, providing services, and assigning legal responsibility" (U.S. General Accounting Office, 1995b, p. 19) for a federal government accustomed to dealing with school districts as the "local point of federal program administration" (p. 19). Finally, there is an element of compliance in the federal-charter relationship in areas where federal law supercedes local practices, such as in the civil rights statutes.

Federal support for charter schools is manifested through planning and implementation grants discussed elsewhere in this chapter, research on the charter school movement, dissemination, technical assistance, and waivers. The majority of federal support comes from the Public Charter Schools Program, whose purpose is to expand the number of high-quality charter schools by providing financial assistance, an evaluation of the impact of charters, and dissemination of information about charter schools and about successful practices found in charter schools. The U.S. Department of Education has undertaken a wide range of research studies about the charter school phenomenon, including the 4-year National Study of Charter Schools that charts the entire movement from macrolevel descriptions to analyses of specific areas, such as accountability, finance, and students with disabilities. Federal funds also support collaborative efforts between charter schools and other public schools. Technical assistance funded by the U.S. government for charters includes leadership training, teacher fellowships, and demonstration projects. The Department of Education has also issued papers targeted to charters that outline their responsibilities concerning federal civil rights and disabilities legislation.

Waivers provide another avenue of support, although this strategy is underutilized (Finn et al., 1997b). Charter schools may seek waivers of "almost any requirement of federal education law or regulations that hinders the successful operation of schools" (Handel, Jehl, & Rentner, 2000, p. 38) and of federal statutory requirements that "charter schools must be public elementary or secondary schools that do not charge tuition" (p. 39). In states that are participating in the federal Public Charter Schools program, waivers for individual schools are submitted to the state education agency, which in turn submits the request to the U.S. Department of Education. In states that do not participate in the program, the individual charter school applies directly to the federal department of education. A school district or chartering agency may request a waiver as well. Waiver requests must include a description of relevant state and local laws and regulations that have also been waived.

Compliance is an important function of the federal government in terms of enforcing civil rights laws for all public schools. Research in this area has focused on the obligations of charter schools to adhere to the Individuals with Disabilities Education Act (IDEA). Charter schools are subject to the Americans with Disabilities Act (ADA), IDEA and the accompanying federal regulations. Yet compliance raises many challenges to the freedoms charter schools are promised, because IDEA can impact almost every area of school, including "pedagogy, classroom organization, curriculum, staffing, staff time, and resource allocation" (Heubert, 1997, p. 319). Furthermore, compliance with IDEA poses a larger burden on charter schools that are independent of school districts because the school has the "same legal obligations" (p. 346) as an entire district and because these schools must deal with the tension of being nondiscriminatory while offering "educationally distinctive" (p. 346) programs. In one well-publicized ruling, the U.S. Department of Education found that the Boston Renaissance charter school (run by a for-profit company) "violated federal law by neglecting to tell [a student's] family of his right to classroom interventions" (Farber, 1998, p. 508). The U.S. Department of Education has published a guide for charter schools that outlines their responsibilities under ADA and IDEA (Nathan, 1998).

Relationships with Private Organizations

A discussion of charter school relationships would be incomplete without acknowledging the substantial role that private entities often play in a charter school. The influence of private organizations is often greater because charters do not have the safety net that a traditional public school has in the school district. Due to the relative autonomy of these schools, charter operators may turn to private organizations for financial support, services, guidance, or evaluation.

Charter networks have sprung up across the country to spread information about charter schools. The first organizations to take the lead were the Center for School Change at the University of Minnesota and the Pioneer Institute in Massachusetts (Garn, 1999). Organizations such as the Charter Friends Network have compiled guidebooks on such topics as school reform models for charter school operators (Lane, 1998). Another group, the National Charter School Accountability Network, organized to help charters establish measurable benchmarks and improve accountability and oversight (Schnaiberg, 1999a). The Center for Education Reform is a frequently cited source for information on charter schools. In addition, national education reform networks typically provide assistance in curriculum and instruction (Wohlstetter & Griffin, 1997b).

Charter proponents "often operate charter school support organizations that provide a variety of services" (Wohlstetter & Griffin, 1997b, p. 7). Support may include "workshops; site visits; individual school assistance and assessments; opportunities for charter school staff members to share problems and practices; outreach to the corporate and foundation community; legal research; and policy education about charter school laws and implementation issues" (p. 7).

Additionally, the emergence of charter schools on the national scene has coincided with that of the Internet. Access to a voluminous amount of material on charter schools is now at the fingertips of any would-be charter school operator, parent, or analyst. This sort of electronic network reduces the isolation that might define these schools' independence by providing instant communication and access to advice.

Charters in Minnesota and Delaware provide examples of relationships with private entities. One Minnesota charter received financial assistance from the New American Schools project, the Southwestern Minnesota Initiative Fund, the Center for School Change, and a local business (Nathan, 1996b). When the Delaware charter law passed, "six of the state's major employers, including DuPont and Bell Atlantic, joined forces to sponsor a school with high standards" (Traub, 1999, p. 31).

THE CHARTER LANDSCAPE: A DESCRIPTIVE SNAPSHOT

In this section, we examine data on charter schools and their inhabitants. We also explore available information about charter school founders and governance structures. We rely on multistate data, where available, and use state-level sources to provide further illustrations. Also, where data is available, distinctions are made between newly created charter schools and those that have been converted from public or private schools. A potential source of bias present in our collection of information is the relatively high levels of autonomy granted in the laws of the states for which we have studies (as assessed by the Center for Education Reform [2000e]), with the exception of Connecticut.

School

> In virtually every instance, charter schools are small—even intimate—places where everyone knows the names and faces of everyone else. (Manno, Finn, Bierlein, & Vanourek, 1998b, p. 498)

Enrollments

Rofes (1995) speculated that the small scale of charter schools might be "one of the truly innovative aspects of the sector" (p. 32). Throughout their short history, charter schools have been consistently characterized by low enrollments coupled with frequent reports of waiting lists (Manno, Finn, Bierlein, & Vanourek, 1998b; B. Nelson et al., 2000). In the 1998–99 school year, 65% of charter schools enrolled fewer than 200 students in contrast to just 17% of all public schools (B. Nelson et al., 2000). These findings are consistent with the previous three reports of the U.S. Department of Education study. During the 1998–99 school year, the median enrollment in charter schools was 137 compared to 475 for all public schools. Smaller charter school enrollments are evident when one looks at individual states as well. During the 1995–96 school year, the average charter school enrollment in Colorado, Massachusetts, and Michigan was under 200 whereas the average public school enrollment in those states was well over 400 (Hassel, 1997). In California, where the state average is over 750, the average charter school enrollment is much lower—400 (Powell, Blackorby, Marsh, Finnegan, & Anderson, 1997).

Differences are found in enrollment levels based on the schools' origins. Charter schools that were converted from preexisting public schools tend to be larger than newly created or preexisting private schools. This is not surprising, given that preexisting public schools have preexisting enrollments as well. Public conversions have a median enrollment of 368 (B. Nelson et al., 2000).

In contrast, newly created charter schools have a median enrollment of 128 students. Preexisting private schools also have low enrollments, with a median of 159.

Grade Configurations

Only half of all charter schools are organized in typical elementary, middle, and high school grade breakdowns (B. Nelson et al., 2000). Patterns in grade configurations correlate with school type. For example, public conversion schools are more likely to be high schools.

Geographic Location

Based on available studies of Michigan, Texas, and California charter schools, we surmise that the geographic distribution of charter schools throughout a state varies across the states. In Michigan and Texas, the majority of charter schools are clustered in metropolitan areas. In Michigan, charter schools are overwhelmingly found in metropolitan areas (85%) (Arsen, Plank, & Sykes, n.d.). Of these charter schools, one half are located in the city and the other half are found in the suburbs. Metropolitan Detroit is the home to over 40% of all charters in the state. The majority of Texas's state-sponsored Open-Enrollment charter schools are found in urban areas (Fusarelli, 1998, p. 7). A 1997 study of California charter schools paints a different picture, one in which schools are more evenly distributed (Powell et al., 1997). Approximately one third of charter schools are based in small towns. Another third are found in suburban districts. A little less than 20% are based in a central city. And 13% are found in rural areas.

Facilities

Two multistate surveys provide differing evidence of the types of facilities used by charter schools. In the Center for Education Reform's 1996–97 survey (n.d.f) the largest group of respondents (30%) noted that their school was based in a district facility. A 1995 survey conducted by the Education Commission of the States and the Center for School Change reported that a little over 15% of respondents identified a district school as their home. The Center for Education Reform (n.d.f) found that another quarter of the respondents reported charter schools based in retail or commercial facilities. Another 12% of charter schools were said to be located in a nonprofit facility, a church facility, or another public facility. Two percent were located in an institution of higher education or a museum. Seventeen percent of the respondents reported another type of facility such as new buildings, private or residential buildings, closed private schools, daycares, and factories. The Education Commission of the States and the Center for School Change (1995) found the most frequently identified facilities used by charter schools were leased commercial space and leased space in a nonprofit facility—approximately one fifth of respondents identified each type.

Students

> Indeed, the charter school experiment will be valid only if charter schools serve the same student populations as do traditional public schools. (Heubert, 1997, p. 344)

> Our fieldworkers have been struck with the extremes of students—bright and struggling—that had become 'square pegs in round holes' in the public system. (Berman et al., 1998, p. 83)

In this section, we examine student demographic characteristics. Much interest is centered on the ethnic, economic, and linguistic makeup of charter school enrollment as well as the proportion of students with disabilities served by these schools. For many, it is a critical piece of arguments for and against charter schools as either equalizing or segregating agents (see Chapter 6). As with so many of the descriptive characteristics we explore in this section, there is variation. This variation is from state to state, and that which depends on the school's mandate and the school's geographic location. Some variation has been detected between for-profit charter schools and other charter schools. And finally, there is variation according to the school's prior status as a preexisting public school, a preexisting private school, or a new school (see also Chapter 7).

Racial-Ethnic Makeup of Student Populations

The predominant conclusion of national and state analyses is that charter schools have similar ethnic/racial compositions of students to that of *all* public schools in a state, or enroll a higher proportion of nonwhite students (Berman et al., 1998; B. Nelson et al., 2000; Vanourek, Manno, Finn, & Bierlein, 1997a). However, there are dissenters who question whether the fear that "charter schools would serve primarily white students" (B. Nelson et al., 2000, p. 30) can truly be put to rest. They argue that by employing different methodologies, evidence of ethnic segregation is present (Cobb & Glass, 1999; Good & Braden, 2000).

The 4-year Department of Education study and the Hudson Institute's *Charter Schools in Action* report estimate that approximately one half of all students enrolled in charter schools are white (Berman et al., 1998; Berman et al., 1999; B. Nelson et al., 2000; RPP International & University of Minnesota, 1997; Vanourek et al., 1997a). This percentage is consistent with estimates of white students in all public schools in states with charter schools. During both the 1996–97 and 1997–98 school years, white students comprised 52% of charter school enrollment compared to 56 and 59%, respectively, of enrollment in all public schools in those states with charter schools (Berman et al., 1998). In the 1998–99 school year, the percentage of white students enrolled in charter schools further decreased to 48%, compared to 59% in all public schools in the 27 states with operating charter schools (B. Nelson et al., 2000).

African American and Hispanic students represent the next largest racial/ethnic groups of students enrolled in charter schools and in all public schools. The Department of Education studies suggest that the percentage of African American students in charter schools has increased whereas the percentage of Hispanic students has decreased (Berman et al., 1998; Berman et. al., 1999; B. Nelson et al., 2000; RPP International and the University of Minnesota, 1997). For both groups, however, an equal or larger proportion are enrolled in charter schools than in all public schools. Close to 24% of charter school students were African American compared to 17% in all public schools in the 27 states with operating charter schools during the 1998–99 school year (B. Nelson et al., 2000). Similarly, 21% of charter school students were Hispanic compared to 18% in all public schools during the same year.

In addition to comparisons made by analyzing state averages, some analysts have contrasted student characteristics in charter schools with those in the surrounding school district. These comparisons between charter schools and surrounding districts also suggest that the majority of charter schools have similar or higher percentages of nonwhite students in charter schools. Close to 70% of charter schools were found to be within 20 percentage points of surrounding districts in terms of nonwhite enrollment (B. Nelson et al., 2000). Seventeen percent of charter schools had over 20% more nonwhite students than their surrounding districts.

Distinct trends are evident in particular states. For example, charter schools in Massachusetts, Michigan, Minnesota, New Jersey, Pennsylvania, and Texas enroll "at least 20% more nonwhite students than all public schools in those states" (B. Nelson et al., 2000, p. 32). The American Federation of Teachers (1996) partly attributes this to state legislation that "explicitly encourages or requires charter schools to be targeted on at-risk groups, where minority children tend to be over represented" (p. 49) and to sponsoring agencies that are "more likely to grant charters to schools designed to educate children who are at-risk of being unsuccessful in the current public schools" (p. 49).

Dissenting Views. Cobb and Glass (1999) caution that the methodologies employed in many of the national policy reports and evaluations "lack the sophistication and rigor necessary to draw valid conclusions about the possible segregating effects of charter schools" (p. 5). Three criticisms are leveled at these studies. First, they do not account for variation in state requirements that affect enrollment patterns. Second, data aggregated at the state and district levels "mask variation among schools" (p. 5). Finally, it is difficult to obtain accurate data on charter schools. These researchers found "evidence of substantial ethnic separation" (pp. 1–2) in almost half of the Arizona schools sampled when compared to public schools in close geographic proximity. In addition, charter schools with a majority of nonwhite students "tended to be either vocational secondary schools that do not lead to college or 'schools of last resort' for students being expelled from the traditional public schools" (p. 2). Good and Braden (2000) argue that the discrepancy among the findings of Department of Education and Hudson Institute findings; those of Cobb and Glass; that of a national survey conducted by Good, Braden, and Nichols; and the SRI International report are due to methodological choices made by the researchers—namely the unit of analysis. We return to this discussion in Chapter 7.

Low-Income Students

Between 33 and 40% of charter school students are estimated to be eligible for free or reduced-price lunch—a common indicator of low income (Berman et al., 1998; Berman et al., 1999; B. Nelson et al., 2000; RPP International & University of Minnesota, 1997; Vanourek et al., 1997a). This proportion is consistent with the number of students in all public schools in states with operating charter schools. In the 1998–99 school year, charter schools served a slightly higher percentage (39%) of students eligible for free or reduced-price lunch than the percentage (37% in 1994–95) of eligible students in all public schools in the 27 states with operating charter schools (B. Nelson et al., 2000). Berman and his colleagues (1998) found that on a national scale, approximately half of charter schools were not distinct from the district in terms of the percentage of low-income students served. The UCLA Charter School team (n.d.) reported that of schools receiving free or reduced-price lunch funding in their sample of California charter schools, half had percentages consistent with those of the district.

As in the case of ethnic/racial student composition, these national figures on low-income students mask wide variation in the states. The percentage of low-income children enrolled in charter schools ranges from only 4% in Alaska to 95% of charter school enrollment in South Carolina (B. Nelson et al., 2000). In 1998–99, charter schools served at least 10% fewer eligible students than all public schools in 6 states—Alaska, California, Colorado, Delaware, Georgia, and New Mexico. In that same year, charter schools served at least 10% more eligible students than all public schools in 11 states—Connecticut, Illinois, Louisiana, Massachusetts, Michigan, Minnesota, New Jersey, Ohio, Pennsylvania, South Carolina, and Texas.

Consistent with our investigation of the ethnic composition of charter schools, the unit of analysis employed may yield different conclusions. For example, fewer low-income students were enrolled in a sample of California charter schools than in comparison schools (rather than a district or state). However, the data do not "substantiate sensational claims that charter schools are either creaming the most able, privileged students, or skimming out those who have been underserved" (Corwin & Flaherty, 1995, p. 7).

Students with Disabilities

As we discuss in considerable detail in Chapter 7, there appears to be some evidence that fewer students requiring special education services as defined in the Individuals with Disabilities Education Act (IDEA) are found in charter schools than in regular public schools. Several factors discussed previously in this chapter may contribute to the difference in proportions of disabled students in charter schools and traditional public schools, including procedural and legal issues such as the decision to develop Individualized Education Plans (IEP) for these students and the financial costs of providing special educational services. Here we explore available enrollment data on special education students in charter schools and the variation found across and within states.

During the 1998–99 school year, 8% of charter school enrollment was comprised of students served by IDEA, in comparison with 11% found in all public schools in the 27 states with operating charter schools (B. Nelson et al., 2000). In each of the 4 years of the Department of Education study, the percentage of students with disabilities was slightly smaller in charter schools than in all public schools (Berman et al., 1998, 1999; B. Nelson et al., 2000; RPP International & University of Minnesota, 1997). The 1997 Hudson Institute study reached a different conclusion, arguing that "when it comes to disabled students, our sample indicates that charter schools are pulling their weight" (Vanourek et al., 1997a, p. 8). By employing a broader definition of students with disabilities, these researchers asserted that over 12% of charter school students have disabilities.

Enrollment of special education students in charter schools varies across states and among schools within states. At the state level, the number of special education students served in charter schools ranged from 5% in Delaware and Louisiana to 18% in Florida in the 1998–99 school year (B. Nelson et al., 2000). This represents a wider range than that found in all public schools in those 27 states—9% to 16%. A study of Arizona charter schools in 1995–96 found that 4% of students were "served as special education students" (McKinney, 1996, p. 22). Just over a third of operating charter schools reported that they served special education students in the same study. In a Massachusetts study, 10 out of 11 charter schools had special education enrollments of 3%—significantly lower than the normal percentage (10 to 13%) found in the state's public schools (Dykgraaf & Lewis, 1998). Variation within a state's charter schools was noted in Colorado and California studies. In Colorado, significant differences were found among the charter schools in terms of "how students with disabilities access the schools as well as how special education is provided" (McLaughlin & Henderson, 1998, p. 99). Two California studies found no or low percentages of special education students in newly created charter schools (Powell et al., 1997; UCLA Charter School Study [n.d.]). In Chapter 7 we explore the meaning of these data.

Limited English Proficiency

Limited English Proficient (LEP) students are estimated to comprise between 10 and 13% of charter school enrollment (Berman et al., 1998, 1999; B. Nelson et al., 2000; Vanourek et al., 1997a). This proportion is similar to the proportion of LEP students found in all public schools in states with charter schools (Berman et al., 1998, 1999; B. Nelson et. al., 2000; RPP International & University of Minnesota, 1997). Wide variation in the percentage of LEP students across the states exists in both charter schools and all public schools. B. Nelson and colleagues (2000) estimate that 17 states serve approximately the same number of LEP students as all public schools in the state. In two states with relatively large populations of LEP students—Alaska and Florida—the percentage of these children enrolled in charter schools was much smaller than in all public schools in the state. In contrast, a much higher percentage of LEP students was enrolled in charter schools than in public schools in Minnesota and Washington, D.C. in the 1998–99 school year.

Teachers

To date, relatively few studies have focused on charter school teachers (Bomotti, Ginsberg, & Cobb, 1999). However, some descriptive data can be extracted from state evaluations. In this section, we highlight the findings on professional backgrounds—including certification, formal education, and teaching experience; demographic data; and teachers' reasons for choosing to teach in a charter school. Where researchers have distinguished charter school teachers by their affiliation with a converted public school or a start-up, differences have been found in teacher characteristics.

Certification

Most charter school teachers are licensed to teach (Berman et al., 1999). Over 75% of respondents in a 10-state survey reported that they were certified, with close to 72% certified in the state in which they were teaching (Vanourek et al., 1997a). In 10 of the 14 states that require certification, charter schools employed certified teachers at rates comparable to public schools in the state (Berman et al., 1999). Charter schools in the other 4 states—Delaware, Louisiana, North Carolina, and Pennsylvania—hired over 10% fewer certified teachers than in all state public schools (Berman et al., 1999).

Berman and his colleagues (1999) found that another 10 out of the 24 states with operating charter schools *did not* explicitly mandate teacher certification. In 5 of those states—Arizona, Florida, Illinois, Massachusetts, Texas—and in Washington, D.C., at least 10% fewer certified teachers were employed in charter schools than in all public schools. For example, a 1998 state evaluation of Texas Open-Enrollment charter schools discovered that over half of the charter school teachers were not certified compared to just under 4% of teachers in all Texas public schools (Taebel et al., 1998). However, despite the fact that certification was not required of California charter school teachers until 1998, the percentage of certified charter school teachers has been consistently high in that state, a story line largely explained by the fact that the majority of these schools are conversions.

One rationale frequently cited in the support of hiring noncertified teachers focuses on the flexibility to hire an individual with experience in a particular field. Almost two thirds of respondents to a 1995 survey of charter schools in seven states reported that they employed uncertified teachers because they had expertise in domains valued by the institutions (Education Commission of the States & Center for School Change, 1995).

Education

No multistate data were identified on the educational backgrounds of charter school staff. Samples of individual state studies suggest variation in education levels of teachers. For example, in their Michigan sample, Horn and Miron (2000) found that 17.5% of teachers held a graduate degree. In contrast, a Connecticut study found that nearly 60% of such teachers had a graduate degree (The Evaluation Center, 1998). Over one third of California charter school teachers had an advanced degree (Corwin & Flaherty, 1995). Less than

28% of Colorado charter school teachers sampled had a masters degree in comparison with 47% of teachers in all Colorado public schools (Clayton Foundation, 1998). Only slight percentage differences were found in degrees held in Texas between Open-Enrollment charter school teachers and all public school teachers (Taebel et al., 1998).

Professional Experience

Multistate as well as individual state data collected thus far suggest that the majority of charter school teachers tend to have 6 or fewer years of experience. Results from the *Charter Schools In Action* (Vanourek et al., 1997a) multistate survey suggest low levels of teaching experience. Respondents who came from public schools had taught for an average of 5.6 years. Respondents who came from other types of schools, such as private schools, universities, or home schools, had less than 2 years of experience. In Colorado, charter school teachers have an average of 6 years of teaching experience compared to a 13-year average for all public school teachers in the state (Clayton Foundation, 1998). In Michigan, the teachers sampled had taught for an average of less than 5 years compared to the state average for public school teachers of 15 years (Khouri, Cleine, White, & Cummings, 1999). Similarly, 42% of California charter school teachers sampled had 5 or fewer years of experience prior to employment in the charter school (Corwin & Flaherty, 1995). In Connecticut, the average was 6 years (The Evaluation Center, 1998). In New Jersey, 54% of charter school teachers had taught for fewer than 3 years (Kane, 1998). Mulholland (1999) estimates that 20% of Arizona charter school teachers came to the job without prior teaching experience.

In their study of California charter schools, Corwin and Flaherty (1995) found several differences in teacher preparedness between conversion charter schools and new institutions. In new schools, 25% of teachers held preliminary credentials and 8% held emergency credentials. Teachers with the most academic training were clustered in converted schools. Over two thirds of the teachers in new schools had less than 5 years of experience. Only about one third of teachers in conversion schools had taught for less than 5 years.

Demographic Data

State-specific studies provide evidence of variation in the ethnicity and age of teachers by state. Charter school teachers in California, Colorado, Connecticut, and Michigan studies are predominantly white (Bomotti, Ginsberg, & Cobb, 1999; Powell et al., 1997; Khouri et al., 1999; The Evaluation Center, 1998). In the cases of California and Connecticut, the ethnic breakdown of teachers is consistent with the breakdown of all public school teachers in the state. However, when California teacher ethnicity data is disaggregated, staff in new charter schools are less likely to be ethnically diverse than staff in conversion schools (Powell et al., 1997). In contrast, greater ethnic diversity was found in Texas Open-Enrollment charter schools. There are fewer white teachers in these schools than in all state public schools. Thirteen percent of charter school teachers are African American and one fourth are Hispanic (Taebel et al., 1998).

In Michigan, Texas, and Colorado charter schools, the majority of teachers are under 40 years of age. Approximately half of Michigan charter school teachers are under 30 (Horn & Miron, 2000; Khouri et al., 1999). Another 24% are under 40. In Texas Open-Enrollment charter schools, the largest percentage of teachers (36%) is between the ages of 31 and 40 (Taebel et al., 1998). Bomotti and her colleagues (1999) found the average age of their sample of Colorado charter schools teachers (39.1) to be only slightly lower than the state average (42.1). In Connecticut, charter school teachers are evenly distributed across four age brackets—20s, 30s, 40s, and 50 years and older (The Evaluation Center, 1998).

Studies of Colorado, Connecticut, Michigan, and Texas indicate that charter school teachers are predominantly female (Bomotti, Ginsberg, & Cobb, 1999; The Evaluation Center, 1998; Khouri et al., 1999; Taebel et al., 1998). Researchers found the proportion of female teachers to be particularly high in Colorado (90%), Michigan (76%), and Connecticut (70%) (Bomotti, Ginsberg, & Cobb, 1999; The Evaluation Center, 1998; Khouri et al., 1999).

Reasons for Working in a Charter School

In their survey, Vanourek and his colleagues (1997a) asked charter school teachers why they chose to teach in their current charter school. The most important factors cited by respondents included the school's educational philosophy, the opportunity to teach in a new school, colleagues with shared concerns and priorities, good administrators, and small class size. Survey responses of teachers in individual states echo the findings of Vanourek and his team. In Michigan and Connecticut, the opportunity to work with like-minded educators was one of the most important reasons respondents gave for seeking employment in a charter school (The Evaluation Center, 1998; Horn & Miron, 2000). In 1996, Bierlein reported that teachers were drawn to charter schools by greater autonomy and flexibility, the learning environment, increased accountability and dedicated coworkers (Bomotti, Ginsberg, & Cobb, 1999). The top three factors cited by respondents from Texas Open-Enrollment charter schools as having impacted their decision to teach in a charter school were the school's educational philosophy, class size, and school size (Taebel et al., 1998). The top four reasons that Massachusetts teachers chose to teach at a charter school included the school's mission, control over curriculum and instruction, quality of the academic program, and a collaborative working environment (Massachusetts Department of Education, 1998).

Salaries

Data from Arizona, California, Massachusetts, Michigan, Colorado, and Texas offer conflicting evidence of teacher salaries in charter schools and traditional public schools. An Arizona study of charter schools in operation for 5 years or more found that most teacher salaries in charter schools "are competitive with the local school district" (Gifford, Phillips, & Ogle, 2000, p. 17). Similarly, California data suggest that the average starting teacher salary in charter schools (approximately $27,500) is similar to the state average ($25,500) (Powell et al., 1997). A 1998 Pioneer Institute survey found that Massachusetts charter school teachers had an average salary range of approximately $27,000 to $42,000 in comparison with the average state range of $26,500 to $50,000 (Massachusetts Department of Education, 1998).

In contrast, Michigan, Texas, and Colorado studies found low teacher salaries in charter schools. A Michigan sample of charter schools found that charter school teacher salaries were lower—under $30,000—compared to the state average of over $47,000 (Khouri et al., 1999). In Texas, 40% of teachers sampled from the state-sponsored charter schools reported that they "were making significantly less money than they otherwise might make" (Taebel et al., 1998, p. 72). Finally, the average Colorado teacher salary was approximately $26,500 in 1997 (Clayton Foundation, 1998).

Parents

In this section we spotlight general characteristics of the parents of charter school students. We begin by examining available demographic data on topics such as income and education levels. Then we explore the reasons parents provide when asked why they chose a charter school for their child. We also describe available data on how parents gathered information on charter schools. We return to parents as a subject in the final section of this chapter where we discuss parent involvement as part of the educational program in charter schools, and in Chapter 7 where we assess the degree of satisfaction these parents have with charter schools.

Demographics

In one multistate survey and three single state studies, between 25 and 40% of charter school parents were found to hold a college degree. The *Charter*

Schools in Action report (Vanourek et al., 1997a) found that 30% of charter school parents in their nine-state survey possessed a college degree, while another 30% of parents had no higher than a high school degree. Arizona provides a similar picture—approximately one third of charter school parents have a college degree. This percentage is higher than the percent of parents with college degrees throughout the state—22 (Gifford & Keller, 1996). A Massachusetts parent survey compared the education levels of charter school parents and of all parents in the corresponding school district. Fewer charter school parents (25%) held a college degree compared to the school district (31%) (Massachusetts Department of Education, 1998). A Connecticut survey found that 40% of charter school parents had a college degree (The Evaluation Center, 1998).

Annual family incomes reported in one multistate survey and two single state studies do not suggest that any single income bracket is overrepresented in charter schools. Vanourek and his colleagues (1997a) found that the largest proportion of parents—26%—reported incomes between $20,000 and $39,000. Thirteen percent of respondents reported family income that exceeded $60,000. Connecticut survey data also reveal variation in family incomes—28% reported incomes between $40,000 and $59,000. Close to 20% listed incomes over $60,000. A Massachusetts study compared the proportion of charter school families with income under $35,000 (39%) to the proportion of families with similar incomes in corresponding school districts (29%) (Massachusetts Department of Education, 1998).

A Texas state evaluation uncovered differences in the demographic characteristics of parents in charter schools that serve at-risk students and charter schools that do not specifically serve these students (Taebel et al., 1998). Parents of children in at-risk charter schools have less education, are less likely to be white, and have lower family incomes. For example, while only 10% of parents whose children attended at-risk schools had a college degree, close to half of parents in non-at-risk schools had a college degree. Furthermore, only 7.4% of parents of children in at-risk schools identified themselves as white, whereas 46% of parents with children in non-at-risk schools classified themselves as white. Over 66% of parents of students in at-risk schools identified themselves as Hispanic compared to only 11% in non-at-risk schools.

Reasons for Choosing a Charter School

Findings about parent rationales for selecting a charter school tend to be consistent across studies. The U.S. Department of Education study characterizes the conditions that prompt parents to enroll their children in charter schools as those factors that "pushed" (Berman et al., 1998, p. 83) parents away from traditional public schools and factors that "pulled" (p. 83) or drew parents toward charter schools. Factors that *pushed* parents and students away from regular public schools centered on low academic expectations, a school culture that alienated students or emphasized social aspects of school, an unacceptable level of safety, and an environment in which parents did not feel welcome. Pull factors mirror push factors. Factors that *pulled* parents and students toward charter schools included high academic expectations, a well-articulated value system, and a nurturing and safe environment.

A survey of charter school parents conducted in Arizona found that the main reason parents withdrew their child from a previous school was the curriculum. Large class size and the poor attitudes of teachers were two other reasons frequently cited. As in the Department of Education study, the reasons that led parents to reject their previous school are mirrored in their rationales for enrolling a child in a charter school (Gifford & Keller, 1996). A second study of Arizona charter school parents found that curriculum, safety, and teacher qualifications were the most important criteria when shopping for a school (Gifford & Ogle, 1998). Additional factors that were considered important included class and school size, communication, and administrator qualifications. The least important variables were facilities, geographic location, extracurricular programs, and teacher certification. In Texas, the three most cited reasons for parents of students in at-risk schools and non-at-risk schools to enroll their child were the same: educational quality, class size, and safety (Taebel et al., 1998). A Michigan study found educational quality and safety to be the most important determining factors in choices exercised by parents. The least important factors included convenient location and the child's special needs, which were not met at the previous school (Horn & Miron, 2000). Parents in a Connecticut survey identified the same issues of educational quality and safety as the most important determinants in enrolling their child in the charter school (The Evaluation Center, 1998).

Vanourek and his colleagues (1997b) disaggregated parental reasons for choosing a charter school by ethnicity and income. All ethnic groups cited small school or class size as very important. This sentiment was particularly strong among African American parents (63%) and Native American parents (71%). Perceptions that the child's previous school was unsafe were found most frequently among Hispanic (29%) and Asian (27%) parents. Approximately a quarter of white, African American, and Native American parents believed that their child's special needs were not met at the previous school. Less than 20% of the five identified ethnic groups cited their child's poor performance in the previous school as an important factor.

Vanourek and his team (1997b) note a "striking . . . consistency across income levels" (p. 3) that parents were looking for small schools and classes and believed their child's needs were not met in the previous school. Lower-income parents more frequently expressed concerns about safety and poor academics at the previous school.

How Parents Learn about Charter Schools

Our review of the literature uncovered limited information from California, Arizona, and Texas about the mechanisms by which parents learn about charter schools. Wells and her team (1998) contend that "charter schools have increased control over their enrollment" (p. 44), in part because they control the "publicity, information dissemination, and recruiting strategies" (p. 44) used to attract parents and students. In their study of California charter schools, these authors believe these "efforts were often targeted toward certain audiences" (p. 44). Studies from Arizona and Texas suggest that word of mouth is the most frequent pathway by which parents receive information about charters. In a survey of Arizona charter schools, almost half of all parents learned about charter schools through friends (Gifford & Keller, 1996). Close to 13% learned about these schools through the newspaper. In Texas, the majority of parents learned about the charter school from friends and relatives (Taebel et al., 1998). Non-at-risk parents were also likely to learn of the school through the media. At-risk parents were also likely to learn about the charter through the public school system.

Charter School Founders

Characteristics of Founders

The range of charter school founders is constrained by charter school legislation. The "strongest laws invite almost any citizen or organization, perhaps with the exception of religious organizations, to come forward with proposals. The weakest laws allow only existing public schools to apply for 'conversion' to charter status" (Hassel, 1997, p. 21). The Hudson Institute's *Charter Schools in Action* report (Manno, Finn, Bierlein, & Vanourek, 1997b) places charter school founders into three "loosely clustered" (p. 2) groups which are "not mutually exclusive" (p. 2)—educators, parents, and organizations. Educators include teachers and other "education professionals who are frustrated in their educational vision and goals by the bureaucracy, norms, or culture of conventional schools and want to do things differently" (p. 2). Parents who found charter schools are described as seeking "something different and better for their children and have not found satisfaction in their public school systems, yet, in many cases, cannot afford private schools" (p. 3). These parents hold diverse political views and educational priorities. Organizations that found charter schools range from nonprofit organizations to for-profit companies to government agencies to community groups such as the Urban League. Results of the 1996–97 Center for Education Reform Survey (n.d.f) found that 39% of respondents designated a nonprofit organization as the "applicant/operator" of the charter school (p. 3). The second most common applicant/operator identified was the public school (30%). Parents came in at 22%, teachers at 17%, and for-profit companies at 7%.

The first-year report of the U.S. Department of Education study offers a different approach to grouping founders (RPP International & University of Minnesota, 1997). These researchers identified two categories: "one or several individual leaders" (p. 1) and a "coalition of stakeholders" (p. 1). Seventy-five percent of the schools sampled fell into the first category. Half of these individuals were either a school principal or administrator. The majority of the remaining founders in this category were either "a few active teachers or parents" (p. 1). Not surprisingly, when an administrator leads the movement to start a charter, the school is likely to be a conversion school. When teachers or parents lead the movement, the school is more likely to be a new school. The remaining 25% of charters were founded by a coalition that included parents, teachers, school administrators, district administrators, business representatives, postsecondary institutions, advocacy groups, and other community groups. All of these institutions were newly created schools.

In their study of charter schools in ten California school districts, the UCLA Charter School Study team (n.d.) found that newly created schools were more likely to be established by individuals not currently working in the public school system such as "parents, entrepreneurs, and educators from the private sector or those who were leaving the public system" (p. 14). In contrast, founders of conversion schools tended to be a "combination of administrators, teachers, and parents at the existing public school" (p. 14).

Reasons for Founding a Charter School

In each year of the U.S. Department of Education's 4-year study, over half of survey respondents have cited "realizing a vision" as the most important reason for founding the school (Berman et al., 1998, 1999; B. Nelson et al., 2000; RPP International & University of Minnesota, 1997). This percentage has increased steadily from 51% in 1997 to 59% in 2000. In contrast, those leaders citing "autonomy/flexibility" as the most important rationale for founding a charter school has decreased from a high in 1997 of over 20% of respondents to under 9% in 2000. At the same time, the number of respondents citing "to serve a special population" as the most important reason has almost doubled from 12.6% in 1997 to over 22.8% in 2000. Other rationales offered in the survey—"financial reasons," (B. Nelson et al., 2000, p. 42) "parent involve-ment," (p. 42) and to "attract students" (p. 42)—have not been cited by many respondents (less than 6%) as the determining factor in founding a school in any of the 4 years of the study.

An earlier seven-state survey conducted by the Education Commission of the States and the Center for School Change (1995) revealed the most important reason for founding a charter school was "to provide better teaching and learning for all students" (p. 15). The next most frequent responses in-cluded to "run a school according to certain principles and/or philosophy" (p. 15), "innovation" (p. 15), and "more parental control" (p. 15).

Horn and Miron (2000) grouped motives of Michigan founders in two categories: profit-making motives and a mix of reasons that they contend can only be described on an individual basis but include a "desired focus of curric-ulum, dissatisfaction with the local public school, attractiveness of a stable base of resources for converted public schools, [and] expectations of a safe school environment" (p. 21). A second study of Michigan charter schools (Khouri et al., 1999) uncovered the following reasons for establishing a charter school among their sample: to provide high-quality education opportunities to inner-city minority students in a safe, clean, and effective learning environ-ment" (p. 38); to "prepare the students for specific careers" (p. 38), such as plastics manufacturing; to "serve a specific population" (p. 38); and to "put into practice specific education theories or apply a proven school model in a new setting" (p. 39).

Case studies of California charter schools (Powell et al., 1997) uncovered reasons for founding a charter school that included "a desire for innovation, alternatives to existing programs, a particular curricular focus, or more parent participation in the education program" (p. 3); however, the "particular moti-vation was often determined by the role and perspective of the petitioner" (p. 3). The Connecticut evaluation concurs with this characterization, stating that "each school is a story in itself" (The Evaluation Center, 1998, p. 11); how-ever, "the founders seemed to be looking for a situation where they could have a substantial impact on the focus, methods, and operations of the schools" (p. 11). A study of New Jersey charter schools in their first year of operation concluded that "the motivation for founding a school was dissatisfaction with the local public school system, particularly the failure to succeed with urban youth" (Kane, 1998, p. 21). An investigation of Minnesota charter schools identified seven categories of most important reasons for founding a charter school that are consistent with national findings. These were the opportunity to serve a special population, to implement an educational vision, to increase parent involvement, to provide more options for students, to establish a special learning environment, to achieve greater autonomy, and to access more finan-cial support (Lange, Lehr, Seppanen, & Sinclair, 1998).

When the U.S. Department of Education reports disaggregated results by the type of charter school—newly created, preexisting public, and preexisting private—some distinct patterns emerge. While the majority of founders of all three types of charter schools listed "to realize an alternative vision" (B. Nelson et al., 2000, p. 42) as the most important reason, a larger proportion of new charter schools (64%) cited this reason. In contrast, 44% of preexisting public schools and 39% of preexisting private schools identified an alternative vision as the primary motivation. The frequency with which other reasons were identified is dependent on the origins of the charter as well. Twenty-six percent of newly created schools were founded to serve a special population. Over a third of preexisting public schools cited the opportunity to gain autonomy as the most important reason. Only 11% of preexisting public schools identified "to serve a special population." Preexisting private schools identified serving a special population (21%), attracting students (19%), and financial reasons (16%).

Although founders are an eclectic mix, the majority express a strong sense of purpose in starting a school—either embodied in an educational vision or a mission to serve a special group of students. As we have noted, some variations exist in founders' rationales depending on the school's origins as a newly created, public conversion, or preexisting private school.

Leadership

> Charter schools employ numerous approaches to leadership and governance. Some are "out-sourced," in whole or in part, to non-profit or for-profit groups. Some are teacher-led without a conventional principal. Some have strong boards that make or approve nearly every decision. Others have charismatic principals whose fingerprints are visible all around the school. The traditional "principal, assistant principal" roles are relatively rare. Rather we have found a plethora of executive directors, chief educational officers, directors of instruction, etc. (Manno et al., 1997b, p. 6)

The majority of state laws do not impose requirements on charter school governance structures other than providing a description of such arrangements in the charter (Center for Education Reform, 2000a, 2000c, 2000d; Jennings, Premack, Adelmann, & Solomon, n.d.). Given that autonomy and flexibility are cornerstones of the charter school model, it is difficult to make generalizations about the manner in which governing systems are created and operate.

The most common governance blueprint features a charter school board and a chief administrator. While this structure is most often used to run charter schools, in almost all cases the roles and responsibilities need to be hammered out. For example, the process of defining the roles of the director and board and their respective scopes of responsibility often pose enormous challenges (The Evaluation Center, 1998; Fitzgerald, 2000). A second challenge frequently noted is the need for specific expertise in a charter's leadership, particularly legal and financial skills and experience.

Since limited data is available on a national scale on the leadership and governance arrangements in charter schools, we rely primarily on state-level studies to provide portraits of governance in this area.

Board of Directors

Responsibilities. Due to the autonomous nature of charter schools, the governance structure is, in large part, determined by the charter school applicants and operators, resulting in considerable variation. In general, based on available state-level data, charter school governing boards appear to exercise typical boardlike powers and responsibilities. For example, Colorado charter school governing bodies have authority over "curriculum, personnel, budget, and all other aspects of the school, under the terms and conditions of the charter contract" (Fitzgerald, 2000, p. 38). Minnesota legislation states that the board of directors will decide matters relating to school operations (Lange, Lehr, Seppanen, & Sinclair, 1998). New Jersey charter schools are run by a board of trustees that provides financial oversight, guides the director, and sets policy (Kane, 1998). Most of the Texas Open-Enrollment charter schools have passed by-laws, and approved operating policies and budgets (Taebel et al., 1998). Michigan law stipulates that there must be a governing board. In general, primary responsibilities of Michigan charter boards of directors include setting policies, establishing operational procedures for the school, approving contractual arrangements, and exercising oversight over the school's finances (Horn & Miron, 2000).

While almost all schools in a California sample had "some type of representative charter council or collection of committees with different areas of responsibility" (Powell et al., 1997, p. 12), there was a range of duties. Some of these boards were "strictly advisory to the sponsoring agency" (p. 12) which maintained control over the school. Other boards directed the school with little input from the sponsor.

Board Member Selection. Based on available state evidence, procedures for selecting board members appear to be primarily determined by the charter and more members are appointed than elected. Most Arizona charter school operators appoint members (Mulholland, 1999). This practice may serve the interests of the school but can restrict parent input. Most Michigan boards, as well, are appointed rather than elected. In fact, chartering agencies in Michigan request that applicants include a list of proposed board members and their qualifications in a charter request (Horn & Miron, 2000). Most Texas Open-Enrollment charter schools also appoint board members (Taebel et al., 1998). Minnesota charter schools offer an alternative model, in which board members must be elected. Boards in Minnesota include school staff and parents of enrolled children (Lange et al., 1998).

Composition. Some state laws place requirements on the composition of the governing board. For example, Alaska law mandates charter schools to be overseen by an academic policy committee which includes parents, students, teachers, and other school employees (Center for Education Reform, 2000a). Minnesota law used to require that the majority of the governing board be composed of certified teachers employed by the school. A waiver may now be requested on a case-by-case basis. In Michigan, the chartering agency establishes certain criteria for board members (Horn & Miron, 2000).

A premise of the charter school model is that multiple stakeholders, be they parents, teachers, or community members, will play a greater role in the school. Available state evidence provides some insight into how these stakeholders are represented on governing boards. Colorado governing boards are primarily comprised of parents, staff, and community members (38%); parents only (28%); or parents and school staff (21%) (Fitzgerald, 2000). In fact, parents are in the majority in close to three quarters of Colorado governing boards. Other state-level studies note parent membership on governing boards but not the force with which they are represented. For example, a large majority of California case study schools (88%) included parents on the governing board (Powell et al., 1997). Approximately half of Texas Open-Enrollment charter schools have parents on their governing boards (Taebel et al., 1998). However, parents appear to be in the minority—the average number of parents and teachers on a board was less than one in at-risk charter schools and under two for parents in non-at-risk schools. In the first year of operation, New Jersey charter school governance structures were found to reflect "an emphasis on parental membership and community involvement" (Kane, 1998, p. 16). Connecticut governing boards "include a broad range of the stakeholders in the schools as well as in the surrounding communities" (The Evaluation Center, 1998, p. 45).

Available board demographic data in Texas provides some information about the ethnic and gender composition of boards as well as the size of these entities (Taebel et al., 1998). Over 40% of the governing boards of open-enrollment charter schools were equally represented by two or more ethnic groups. In the other schools, one racial group dominated the board. The racial and ethnic makeup of the governing board tends to reflect the racial and ethnic makeup of students enrolled. The boards are diverse in terms of gender. Additionally, the size of governing boards range from 4 to 18 members, with an average of over 9 in at-risk charter schools and under 6 in non-at-risk charter schools.

School Directors

Charter schools have given their chief administrators numerous titles such as principal, director, dean, and chief executive officer. Despite evidence suggesting that "the day-to-day leadership of a charter school is [a] crucial component to charter reform" (UCLA Charter School Study, n.d., p. 39), little information is available about the kinds of professional and educational backgrounds that these chief administrators bring to the organization.

Responsibilities. We uncovered little information about the duties of charter school administrators in our review of the literature. A study of New Jersey charters concluded that with a minimal amount of administrative support, the chief administrator or director has a wide range of day-to-day responsibilities, which demands a diverse array of expertise and large time commitments (Kane, 1998). For example, during the first year of operation, over half of the New Jersey charter school directors taught classes.

Professional and Educational Backgrounds. There is variation across the states in terms of the number of charter school chief administrators who are certified. A 1995 seven-state survey found that 59% of charter schools reported that all their administrators were certified (Education Commission of the States, & Center for School Change, 1995). When these schools are disaggregated by state, clear majorities appear in most of the states. For example, a large majority of California, Michigan, and New Mexico respondents reported that all their administrators were certified. In Colorado, Massachusetts, and Minnesota, a large majority reported that all their administrators were *not* certified. In a Texas-based study, less than a third of open-enrollment charter schools required "mid-management certification" (Taebel et al., 1998, p. 29) for directors. An Arizona study found that close to half of survey respondents reported that their director had an education-related degree and/or certification (Center for Market-Based Education, 1999). This study also found that three quarters of the directors had a degree beyond a bachelor's.

Information about the prior experience of charter school directors was extracted from Arizona and Texas reports. An estimated 33% of Arizona charter school directors have no prior school administration experience (Mulholland, 1999). Over half of administrators have a background in business or education (Center for Market-Based Education, 1999). The majority of directors in open-enrollment charter schools in Texas have prior teaching experience in public and/or private schools (Taebel et al., 1998).

Salaries and tenure are frequent concerns of charter school critics. Again, available data are quite limited. A Center for Market-Based Education survey (1999) found that a majority of Arizona respondents reported annual salaries between $35,000 and $50,000 for charter school administrators. Approximately two thirds of administrators have a contract—a large majority of whom are employed for a one-year term. Turnover is reported to be low, mostly occurring in urban schools. A Colorado study uncovered a different story, one of high turnover among charter school directors. The average tenure for the chief administrator in the study was 2.2 years, with a median tenure of 1.67 years (Fitzgerald, 2000). Challenges include finding the "right balance of responsibilities between policy-making boards and on-site administrators" (p. 39). Another challenge is "making the transition of leadership from the charter school founders . . . to the professional staff" (p. 39).

The UCLA Charter School Study (n.d.) team raise the importance of personal attributes held by the chief administrator in assessing his or her ability to operate a charter school successfully. These attributes may be less associated with pedagogical skills than with other areas of strength. In their study of 17 California charter schools, strong leaders were characterized by their "ability to draw together diverse constituencies, such as parents, community members, and teachers, as well as to network outside the immediate school community" (p. 40). These strong leaders were also characterized as having a "high degree of business savvy" (p. 40). In sum, strong leaders "provided entrepreneurial leadership, in addition to or instead of instructional leadership" (p. 41). These researchers found different degrees of importance placed on skills depending on the school's identity as a newly created or preexisting school. For example, strong networking skills are particularly important for leaders of newly created charter schools.

EDUCATIONAL PROGRAM

It's impossible to say what charter schools look like. The Minnesota New Country School, in the farming town of Henderson resembles a Kinko's, with children at personalized work stations and teachers moving from child to child, guiding them on long-term projects. There are Afrocentric charter schools and Outward Bound-type charter schools. Colorado has five Core Knowledge charter schools, where children study a specified and rigorous curriculum. (Traub, 1999, p. 30)

In the U.S. Department of Education study, the majority of founders cited "to realize an alternative vision" (B. Nelson et al., 2000, p. 42) as the primary reason for starting a charter school. In this section, we explore how this alternative vision is manifested in charter schools' educational programs. We begin our analysis with attention to the educational focus or mission of charter schools. Then we turn to the student populations these schools are intended to serve and to the curriculum and instruction. We conclude with an examination of the role of parents in charter schools.

Core Educational Philosophy

The range of educational philosophies that guide charter schools reflects the capacity of this movement to encompass an enormous variation of goals and ideologies. What these schools do share despite diverse goals is the presence of an educational philosophy that is mutually owned by stakeholders and which provides critical guidance for the direction of the school (see also Chapter 5).

Broad Range of Educational Philosophies Encompassed by Movement

A wide array of educational missions exist simultaneously in the charter school movement, ones that encompass both conservative and progressive thought as well as "some interesting efforts to blend the two" (Finn et al., 1996, p. 3). As noted in our discussion of their historical roots in Chapter 2, charter schools draw on many of "the governance and cultural characteristics of alternative public schools" (Rofes, 1998b, p. 55). However, "the philosophical and pedagogical aims are broader and more diverse" (p. 55). Some progressive models that were advanced in the 1960s have reemerged in the educational philosophies of charters, such as open classrooms, multiage groupings, and child-centered instruction. At the same time, the more conservative trends of the mid-1970s, such as "back-to-basics curricula and conservative cultural norms" (p. 55), are also quite visible in the movement.

Studies of charter schools in individual states echo national conclusions that tremendous variation exists in core educational philosophies. Findings from the UCLA Charter School Study (n.d.) on California charter schools provide an illustration of the often antithetical forces that inspire individuals and groups to develop a charter school. These researchers found that charter operators who expressed dissatisfaction with the public schools included those who thought the public schools were *too* structured and those who thought they were *not structured enough*. Dissatisfaction was also expressed over the public schools' approach to diversity: some founders believed the public schools did not validate the history and culture of some minority groups while other individuals believed that multiculturalism receives too much attention in the current school system.

Unifying Force

Finn, Bierlein, and Manno (1996) argue that what distinguishes charter schools "is not the originality of their educational vision but that uncommon level of commitment to their educational approaches" (p. 3). As we describe in considerable detail in Chapters 5, 6, and 7, these philosophies about education are powerful in generating enthusiasm (Learning Matters, Inc., 1999). The potential of charter schools to be "more productive than regular public schools can be found in their commitment to a common educational vision or purpose" (Lutz, 1997, p. 3). This vision unifies the charter school both by binding together staff, parents, and students around a core understanding of the school and by bringing "an integration of many practices toward a single objective" (Rosenblum Brigham Associates, 1998, p. 6). For example, only teachers who buy into the vision are likely to work in the school. In their analysis of Massachusetts charter schools, Rosenblum Brigham Associates (1998) found that there was the presence of a strong sense of vision across charter schools despite a wide range of practices and beliefs advocated by the schools' operators.

Target Focus

Some charter schools are designed to serve a particular population of students. These schools are frequently termed "niche schools" and can be grouped into three categories: schools that serve minority groups, schools that target students with special needs, and schools that focus on students believed to be at risk. The majority of schools that serve a particular population are start-up charter schools (RPP International & University of Minnesota, 1997).

Estimates about the proportion of charter schools that are designed to address the needs of a particular population of students are inconsistent. The second U.S. Department of Education study (Berman et al., 1998) estimated that during the 1998–99 school year one fifth of charter schools served a particular student population including minorities, the economically disadvantaged, and students with disabilities. The Center for Education Reform (n.d.d.) reached a different conclusion based on its 1996–97 survey. In this study, only one third of the respondents reported that their school did *not* target a particular population of students. The largest number of schools (40%) served students described as at risk or dropouts. The needs of gifted and talented students were addressed by 22% of the schools.

State-level analyses in Colorado, Michigan, and Massachusetts support the Department of Education findings that most charters serve general populations of students. The majority of charter schools targeted the general population in Colorado, Massachusetts, and Michigan according to 1995–96 state data (Hassel, 1999a). No Colorado charter schools targeted ethnic minorities, while 13% of Massachusetts and 22% of Michigan schools did. Similarly, only 8% of Colorado charters targeted at-risk students, whereas 20% of Massachusetts charters and 15% of Michigan charters did. Of the three states, only Michigan had charter schools that targeted students with special needs (5%). By 1999, the proportion of Michigan charters that served special populations may have changed. Approximately half of the Michigan schools sampled had a "general curriculum targeted to the general population of students" (Khouri et al., 1999, p. 15); 36% of schools served a special student population or a specific career-oriented curriculum; and 13% provided an ethnocentric curriculum. In Texas, however, where incentives are in place, state-sponsored charter schools are *more* likely to serve at-risk students. Eleven out of 19 state-sponsored charters in operation served at-risk students (Taebel et al., 1998).

For some, the practice of tailoring a school to meet the needs of a specific population of students raises potentially troublesome equity issues (see also Chapter 6). Under a rationale for this practice, termed "group equity" (Lane, 1998, p. 16), groups that are culturally or ideologically different have "different learning requirements" (p. 16). In the context of group equity, charter schools can "provide various groups of ideologically and culturally distinct parents, teachers, and students the equal opportunity to choose, develop, and attend a high quality school specific to their cultural values and beliefs" (p. 16). However, when it is implemented, group equity "walks a fine line between group specialization as a means to enhance education and group specialization as a means to exclude the ideas of opposing groups" (p. 17).

Curriculum and Instruction

The freedom to develop alternative curricula and employ different instructional techniques is often a motivator for "going charter." Research indicates that a broad range of curriculum and instructional techniques are used in these schools. Many charters rely on national models. Some argue that while the techniques used are "familiar from other school reform initiatives" (Manno et al., 1998b, p. 493), they are "startlingly fresh in their contexts" (p. 493).

For some public conversion schools, changing the school's status to a charter is a way to "protect their educational programs" (Izu et al., 1998, p. 9). One California school system decided to charter the entire district to "withstand the controversial pendulum swings of teaching and learning that periodically rock the Golden State" (Harrington-Lueker, 1997, p. 7).

Colorado and Minnesota provide illustrations of the diversity of teaching methods and curriculum found in charters. For example, some Colorado charters offer a highly structured academic curriculum while others provide student-directed, discovery-based learning, and still other schools focus on a particular discipline (McLaughlin & Henderson, 1998). In Minnesota, teaching methods and curriculum found in charters reflect progressive and conservative thought (Lange et al., 1998). Lange and his colleagues found the similarity across charters was not in the approach but in the "strong common thread [that] is the commitment of the instructional staff to their chosen approach, and their efforts over the past few years to bring their collective visions to reality" (1998, p. 82).

Curriculum. A specific curricular focus is often "central to the purposes of these charter schools" (Wells et al., 1998, p. 22). The 1995 seven-state survey found that the three most frequently cited characterizations of the charter's academic focus were "integrated curriculum/interdisciplinary" (Education Commission of the States & Center for School Change, 1995, p. 13); "technology" (p. 13); and "back to basics" (p. 13). An analysis of charter school curricula in Colorado, Massachusetts, and Michigan charter schools revealed that 36% of schools had an alternative curriculum such as Montessori or Paideia (Hassel, 1997). Another 23% had a general curriculum, 16% had a basics approach, 9% were culture-centric, 10% were vocational, and 6% focused on a specific subject.

Over two thirds of respondents to the seven-state survey reported that their charter school's curriculum was based on a national school reform model (Education Commission of the States & Center for School Change, 1995). The most frequently cited reform models were Community Learning Centers and the Coalition of Essential Schools. Over 60 percent of Colorado charter schools "used a recognized national reform model as the foundation of their educational program" (Fitzgerald, 2000, p. 14). A sampling of major reform efforts with which California charters have networked include the Coalition of Essential Schools, the New American Schools Development Corporation, Accelerated Schools, and the state's Healthy Start program (Premack, 1996).

Core Knowledge and other back-to-basics approaches are frequently found among charter schools (Center for Education Reform, n.d.f). In Colorado, the majority of charters that do use a national reform model employ Core Knowledge (Fitzgerald, 2000).

Another type of charter school that is allowed in some states is one that does not have a campus—that is, a home school, a virtual school, or an "independent study approach" (Premack, 1996, p. 62). The 1995 Education Commission of the States and Center for School Change survey found that 24 out of 110 respondents across seven states served home-schooled students. The vast majority of these responses came from California. Fourteen of those 22 respondents reported that their charter school served students in their home as opposed to providing a home-schooled child with school-based services (Medler, 1996). Recent charter legislation in California has placed many limits on public charter funding for home schools.

Curriculum Development. Limited data suggest that the curricula are not set; rather, they are continually shifting. For example, a study of Arizona charter schools in operation for at least 5 years described the curricula as "diverse" and often "evolving" (Gifford, Phillips, & Ogle, 2000, p. 8). Similarly, the curriculum in Connecticut charters was characterized as "fluid" (The Evaluation Center, 1998, p. 15) during the first year of operation. But the authors note that changes were mainly in refining the existing curriculum rather than in large overhauls, lending further support to the hypothesis that the common feature of the educational programs in these schools is in the commitment to a vision.

Wohlstetter and Griffin (1997b) found a range of individuals responsible for curriculum decisions in charters. In some instances, curriculum was developed by "broad groups of stakeholders in committees, task forces, grade-level teams or subject-area teams" (p. 3). In the study of 5-year-old Arizona charters, most used a team approach to curriculum development and purchasing instructional materials that involved parents and teachers in purchases (Gifford, Phillips, & Ogle, 2000). The largest proportion of these schools employed either a computerized or a self-developed curriculum. The curriculum used by Connecticut charters varied in its origins. Some schools employed a "prepackaged" (The Evaluation Center, 1998, p. 15) version that was adapted to meet the charter's needs. In other schools, individual teachers devised their own curriculum.

Instruction. Common instructional approaches found in charters include small classes, low student-teacher ratios, personalized learning, interdisciplinary projects, an emphasis on connecting the school to the community, and other methods promoted by reforms such as multiage student grouping, cooperative learning, and portfolio assessment (Schwartz, 1996; Wohlstetter & Griffin, 1997b). Additional approaches found in charter schools include "hands-on learning, foreign languages in the early years, unconventional approaches to special and bilingual education, and all manner of assessments" (Manno et al., 1997b, p. 5).

In Texas, the most common pedagogical techniques found in state-sponsored at-risk charters included "multi-age grouping . . . mainstreaming, project-based learning, interdisciplinary teaching, and alternative assessments" (Taebel et al., 1998, p. 30). Pedagogical techniques most commonly employed in non-at-risk schools also included multiage grouping and mainstreaming; but unlike their at-risk counterparts, they tend to use technology more frequently. Instructional approaches found in California's charter schools suggest a broad range of techniques, including "project-based learning, service learning, Waldorf-based strategies, development grouping of students, International Baccalaureate programs, arts-based 'Reggio-Emilia' curricula, and mainstreaming of special education students" (Premack, 1996, p. 62).

Some unique scheduling is present in charter schools. There are "longer days, longer years, before- and after-school programs, and other breaking of the bounds of traditional school days and calendars" (Manno et al., 1997b, p. 7). The 1996–97 Center for Education Reform Charter School Survey found that approximately 60% of respondents had a traditional school schedule. Other common scheduling structures include an extended day (17%), year-round (16%), and extended year (13%). A Michigan study noted the use of block scheduling in several schools (Khouri et al., 1999).

Parent Involvement

Parent involvement in their child's educational experience is a cornerstone of many charter school visions, and it is an area where some charters "have clearly been successful" (Rothstein, 1998b, p. 1). Over one third of charter schools in the U.S. Department of Education fieldwork sample had "extensive and systemic parent involvement" (RPP International & University of Minnesota, 1997, p. 8). While parent involvement is often a central component of a charter's mission, there is a large degree of variation in the types and amount of activities that are characterized as parent involvement in these schools (Good & Braden, 2000; Manno et al., 1998b). Evidence comparing levels of parent involvement with traditional public schools supports multiple conclusions.

Parent Involvement Activities

The term "parent involvement" can constitute a wide range of activities, including involvement in learning at home and participation in decision making (Epstein, 1992). There are numerous ways in which parents have been involved in charter schools, including traditional types of involvement such as serving on governing boards, parent contracts, and teaching classes. Typical parent involvement activities such as parent-teacher meetings and fund-raising also take place in charter schools (Manno et al., 1998b). Charter parents are involved in a wider range of activities at the school and are more likely to serve on the board (Good & Braden, 2000).

Conventional types of parent involvement, such as home-school communication and parent representation on governing boards or committees, occurred in 19% of the schools visited by the U.S. Charter Schools team (RPP International & University of Minnesota, 1997). Divergent types of parent involvement were present in 43% of schools visited and included activities such as workshops, support groups, referrals to other service agencies, and regular parent meetings; volunteer opportunities for parents; learning activities linked to curriculum goals that parents do with their child at home; and parent signatures on homework.

Evidence from Colorado, Connecticut, Massachusetts, and Los Angeles indicate parent involvement at "high levels of responsibility" (Fitzgerald, 2000, p. 41), such as a presence on governing boards. In addition to governance-type activities, parents help with school operations such as maintenance, fundraising, and instruction. For example, New Jersey charter parents are involved in "operation, instruction, and fund-raising" (Kane, 1998, p. 17). Connecticut charter schools reported parent meetings, fund-raising, building maintenance, and classroom and kitchen volunteering (The Evaluation Center, 1998). Some Los Angeles charters offer parent training in helping students study at home and in job-related skills (Izu et al., 1998). In Texas, all state-sponsored charters provide opportunities for parents to volunteer at the school. The majority offer "workshops or support groups for parents and regularly scheduled parent-teacher meetings" (Taebel et al., 1998, p. 32).

Evidence from Texas suggests that the focus of the charter has implications for the types of parent involvement that take place. Differences in parent involvement exist between schools that target at-risk students and those that serve non-at-risk children (Taebel et al., 1998). Charters serving at-risk students tend to offer referrals to social and health agencies and, more frequently, require parents to sign student homework. Parent involvement in non-at-risk charter schools was more likely to involve regularly scheduled parent-teacher meetings and participation on the school's governing board. Parents provided instruction in two thirds of the non-at-risk charter schools but in none of the at-risk schools.

Many charter schools place some sort of requirements on parents in the education of their children at the school. The first-year report of the National Charter School study found that almost half of the surveyed schools reported "some form of parent or family participation requirement" (RPP International & University of Minnesota, 1997, p. 7). In many Texas charter schools, "parents are expected (even required) to serve on campus committees with real decision making authority" (Fusarelli, 1998, p. 12).

A common device used to garner involvement is the parent contract. Parent contracts in California charters spell out the "required behavior of parents and students [and] mandated parent involvement" (Wells et al., 1998, p. 23). Parent contracts were found in over half of charter schools in Minnesota and New Jersey (Kane, 1998; Lange et al., 1998). Of responding Colorado charter schools, 37% required a parent contract (Fitzgerald, 2000). These contracts outlined school "expectations of parents related to their involvement in the school and in their children's education" (p. 43). Parent contracts have received mixed reviews. Until the California law was revised in 1998, charter schools could deny admission to students if the parents were not willing to meet parent involvement requirements (Good & Braden, 2000). Concerns have been raised that requiring parent involvement contracts may discourage or even restrict access for low-income families. Those parents who are able to enroll their child in the charter are "more likely to have the time and resources to be highly involved in their child's education" (p. 162).

Amount of Parent Involvement

There are conflicting reports about the amount of parent involvement. Good and Braden (2000) contend that the overall parent involvement rates in charter schools and traditional schools are very similar. These authors believe that for the most part, important decisions are made by school administrators, particularly in the case of for-profit schools. In Texas charter schools, participation in parent conferences, Parent Teacher Organization meetings, and school activities declined when compared to these parents' participation in their child's former school (Taebel et al., 1998). This was true regardless of whether the child was in an at-risk or non-at-risk school. In contrast, parents in Minnesota charters report being more involved than they were at their child's previous school (Lange et al., 1998). New Jersey and Michigan studies suggest higher levels of parent involvement among charter parents (Kane, 1998; Khouri et al., 1999). Connecticut charter schools provide an illustration of the range in average parent volunteering time among the schools—20 hours to 2,160 hours (The Evaluation Center, 1998).

Self-selection may provide one explanation for increased parent involvement in charter schools. Higher involvement reflects the proactive characteristics possessed by parents who will go through the process of removing their child from a traditional school and enrolling him or her in a charter (Khouri et al., 1999). The absence of transportation provides another rationale. Parents are more likely to be on campus on a regular basis if they must pick up and drop off students. Kane (1998) offers yet another insight based on her work in New Jersey. She contends that parent involvement may be integral to the design of a charter school because "the absence of support staff has made parent involvement a necessity rather than a luxury" (p. 13).

SUMMARY

As we have demonstrated throughout this chapter, there are many differences across charter schools. Much of this variation can be attributed to the legal and fiscal parameters that define the landscape in which these schools operate. The relationships forged with public and private entities further cast the character of charters. As a result, an individual charter school is defined by its autonomy and the associated tension that that level of freedom or constraint brings as the school goes about the process of educating children.

While it is difficult to make definitive statements about any single aspect of charter schools, available national, state, and local data do allow us to note trends within that variation. Collectively, these trends allow us to "define what the charter school movement is, and what it is not" (Nathan, 1996a, p. 1). Our understanding deepens as we turn to the next chapter to explore the sociopolitical and economic context in which the charter school movement has found fertile ground.

CHAPTER 4

The Supporting Climate for Charter Schools

We see charter schools as being caught between the politics of modernity, in which the liberal project promised—often unsuccessfully—to provide more equal distribution of material resources along with universal rights and freedoms, and the politics of postmodernity, which are punctuated by fragmented social movements, identity politics, and the struggle for recognition. (Wells, Lopez, Scott, & Holme, 1999, p. 174)

In this chapter, we continue our quest for understanding of the charter school movement by examining the scaffolding supporting charter activity. In the first part of the chapter, we step back to explore external forces that are fueling the rapid growth of charters. We review shifts underway in the social, economic, and political environments in which schools reside. In the second section, we look internally, exploring how continuing concerns about the effectiveness of schooling support charter activity. We discuss concerns about educational productivity and examine questions about existing governance arrangements.

A SUPPORTIVE ENVIRONMENT FOR REFORM VIA CHARTERS

At the broadest level the emergence of charter schools can be seen as part of a larger political movement to fundamentally alter relationship between government and the governed. (McGree, 1995a, p. 3)

The argument for charter schools is dominated by economic, not educational, ideas. (Molnar, 1996, p. 5)

A fundamental premise of our work in the area of school reform is that the meaning of education is dependent on the political, social, and economic environments in which schools reside. Our basic hypothesis is that there are powerful forces afoot in the economy, the polity, and society that suggest a

recasting of the liberal democratic state that has defined the contours of pub-
lic-private activity in society and which has given focus to our understanding
of schooling for nearly a century. Our second hypothesis is that these shifts
have bolstered the development of the charter school movement. We explore
these issues below, examining first the changing social and political foundations of the liberal democratic state and then the shifting economic infrastructure of our nation.

Sociopolitical Environment

An Unraveling

The political and social environment appears to be undergoing two important
changes. First, there has been a loosening of the bonds of democracy. Thus
according to a number of scholars in this area, "our American democracy is
faltering" (Elshtain, 1995, p. 1), with a concomitant "loss . . . to our ways of
living and working together and to our view of the worth of the individual"
(Tomlinson, 1986, p. 211). Second, the infrastructure of civil society has been
impaired. Analysts discern fairly significant tears in the fabric known as
modern civil society. The composite picture has been labeled "The Disunity
of America" by Dahrendorf (1995, p. 23) and characterized as "the weakening . . . of the world known as democratic civil society" by Elshtain (1995,
p. 2).

   One strand of this sociopolitical mosaic is plummeting support for government. In many ways, Americans "have disengaged psychologically from
politics and governance" (Putnam, 1995, p. 68): "The growth of cynicism about
democratic government shifts America toward, not away from, a more general-
ized norm of disaffection" (Elshtain, 1995, p. 25). Not surprisingly, these indicators of dissatisfaction and discontent provide ample support for the claim
that something is happening to traditional approaches to public governance in
general and school governance in particular.

   Critics maintain that government in the United States is troubled and is
becoming more so—"that conventional ways of doing business in the public
sector [have] failed to deliver acceptable results" (Hassel, 1999a, pp. 35–36).
They discern a sense of hopelessness about civic government (Katz, 1992) and
a crisis of confidence in public institutions and representative government.
They point to surveys and opinion polls showing that citizens are distrustful
of government agencies and regularly opposed to government sector programs
and policies. Other chroniclers of this unrest speak of a mounting sense of
skepticism about the public sector in general (Fitzgerald, 1988) and "skepticism as to the ability of government to implement social goals" (Hula, 1990a,
p. xiii) in particular. They believe that a "philosophy borne of suspicion for

big government may underlie this revolution in America" (Fitzgerald, 1988, p. 20).

Still other reviewers discern a "deeper ... and much more dangerous" (Savas, 1982, p. 1) cynicism toward (Hula, 1990b), distaste for (Donahue, 1989), or distrust of government and government officials among citizens (De Hoog, 1984). They describe a "culture of resistance, bitterness, and adversariness" (Bauman, 1996, p. 626). They paint a picture of "'political bankruptcy,' a vaguely defined state of popular alienation and disaffection from government which stops short of revolution" (Hood, 1994, p. 91). These analysts portray a growing discontent with activist government (Hirsch, 1991) and the rise and spread of an antigovernment philosophy. They describe a "fundamental concern that government simply 'doesn't work.' Planning is seen as inadequate, bureaucracy as inefficient and outcomes highly problematic" (Hula, 1990a, p. xiii). They go on to argue that the consent of the governed is being withdrawn to a significant degree. In its softest incarnation, this cynicism leads citizens to argue that government is no longer a reasonable solution to all problems (Florestano, 1991) and to question the usefulness of much government-initiated activity. At worst, it has nurtured the belief that government is fated to fail at whatever it undertakes (Starr, 1991). In many cases, it has nurtured the development of a variety of antigovernment political and social movements. There is little question that this widespread discontent has spilled over into public education (Katz, 1992) and that it provides part of the foundation on which charters are being constructed.

The changing sociopolitical environment is also anchored in a growing sense of social malaise. Many analysts, for example, have chronicled the growing story of the underclass or "the trend toward private wealth and public squalor" (Bauman, 1996, p. 627). According to Dahrendorf (1995), this economically grounded trend represents a new type of social exclusion—the "systematic divergence of the life chances for large social groups" (p. 24). He and others are quick to point out that this condition seriously undermines the health of society: "Poverty and unemployment threaten the very fabric of civil society. . . . Once these [work and a decent standard of living] are lost by a growing number of people, civil society goes with them" (pp. 25–26).

Consistent with this description of diverging life chances is a body of findings on the declining social welfare of children and their families. These data reveal an emerging society populated increasingly by groups of citizens that historically have not fared well in this nation, especially ethnic minorities and citizens for whom English is a second language. Concomitantly, the percentage of youngsters affected by the ills of the world in which they live—for example, poverty, unemployment, illiteracy, crime, drug addiction, malnutrition, poor physical health—is increasing.

According to Himmelstein (1983), society is best pictured "as a web of shared values and integrating institutions that bind individuals together and restrain their otherwise selfish, destructive drives" (p. 16). Some reviewers have observed a noticeable attenuation of these social bonds (Finn, Manno, & Vanourek, 2000; Rofes, 1995), a failure of social theory (Hood, 1994) or what Elshtain (1995) describes as a "loss of civil society—a kind of evacuation of civic spaces" (p. 5). The splintering of shared values, the rise of "fragmented social movements" (Wells, Lopez et al., 1999, p. 174), and the accompanying diminution in social cohesiveness have been discussed by Dahrendorf (1995) and Mayberry (1991) among others. Few, however, have devoted as much attention to the topic of changing patterns of civic engagement and political participation as Robert Putnam (1995). According to Putnam, the "democratic disarray" (p. 77) that characterizes society and the polity can be "linked to a broad and continuing erosion of civic engagement that began a quarter-century ago" (p. 77). Dahrendorf (1995), in turn, reminds us that citizens "without a sense of belonging or commitment to society . . . [have] no reason to observe the law or the values behind it" (p. 28).

Another piece of the story, one related to the themes of declining social cohesion and political abstinence but one even more difficult to ignore, is the issue of "social breakdown and moral decay" (Himmelstein, 1983, p. 15) or rents in the "sociomoral" (Liebman, 1983, p. 229) tapestry of society (Boyd, Lugg, & Zahorchak, 1996; Wuthnow, 1983). Of particular concern is the perception that state actions have contributed to the evolution of social mores that are undermining the adhesiveness that has traditionally held society together (Heinz, 1983; Liebman & Wuthnow, 1983; Mayberry, 1991)—that "the welfare bureaucracy is irreversibly opposed to the established social morality" (Gottfried, 1993, p. 86).

A Reweaving

New ideas are emerging to fill the sociopolitical spaces left after the unraveling of the liberal democratic welfare state that has dominated education for the past 75 years. One of the key elements involves a recalibration of the locus of control based on what Ross (1988) describes as "a review and reconsideration of the division of existing responsibilities and functions" (p. 2) among levels of government. Originally called "democratic localism" (p. 305) by Katz (1971), it has more recently come to be known simply as localization or, more commonly, decentralization (McGree, 1995a; Wells, Lopez, et al., 1999). However it is labeled, it represents a backlash against and a reversal of nearly exclusive reliance on professional control (Rofes, 1998b).

A second ideological foundation can best be thought of as a recasting of democracy, a replacement of representative governance with more populist conceptions (Rofes, 1998b), especially what Cronin (1989) describes as direct democracy. While we use the term more broadly than does Cronin, our conception shares with his a grounding in: (1) the falling fortunes of representative democracy, (2) a "growing distrust of legislative bodies . . . [and] a growing suspicion that privileged interests exert far greater influence on the typical politician than does the common voter" (p. 4), and (3) recognition of the claims of its advocates that greater direct voice will produce important benefits for society—that it "could enrich citizenship and replace distrust of government with respect and healthy participation" (p. 48).

A third foundation encompasses a rebalancing of the control equation in favor of lay citizens while diminishing the power of the state and (in some ways) educational professionals (Tyack, 1992). This line of ideas emphasizes parental empowerment by recognizing the "historic rights of parents in the education of their children" (Gottfried, 1993, p. 109). It is, at times, buttressed by a strong strand of "profound dissatisfaction with and disappointment in many members of the so-called 'educational establishment'" (Wells, Grutzik, et al., 1999, p. 525) or antiprofessionalism that subordinates "both efficiency and organizational rationality to an emphasis on responsiveness, close public [citizen] control, and local involvement" (Katz, 1971, p. 306).

The ideology of choice is a fourth pillar supporting emerging conceptions of education (Bauman, 1996). Sharing a good deal of space with the concepts of localism, direct democracy, and lay control, choice is designed to "deregulate the demand side of the education market" (Beers & Ellig, 1994, p. 35) and to "enable parents to become more effectively involved in the way the school is run" (Hakim, Seidenstat, & Bowman, 1994, p. 13). It means that "schools would be forced to attend to student needs and parent preferences rather than to the requirements of a centralized bureaucracy" (Hill, 1994, p. 76).

Finally, it seems likely that something that might best be thought of as democratic professionalism will form a central part of the political infrastructure of schooling in the postindustrial or postmodern world. What this means is the gradual decline of control by elite professionals—by professional managers and more recently by teacher unions—that marked the politics of schooling in the industrial era.

Two things become clearer as one steps back and reviews the analyses of the unraveling and reweaving of the social and, especially, the political aspects of the educational environment. First, the dismantling of the dominant foundations of the democratic welfare state has undercut the currency of traditional notions of schooling in general and governance in particular (Fuller, Elmore, & Orfield, 1996; Hassel, 1999a). A good deal of space in the quest for school improvement has been opened. The reform game need no longer be played on the margins. Or stated alternatively, construction does not need to proceed by welding additions onto existing structures.

Second, the new trends in the sociopolitical environment are pushing education into new channels. In the process, they are providing considerable nourishment to the burgeoning charter school movement. In particular, the political ideology defining the postmodern world—localism, direct democracy, enhanced lay control, choice, and democratic professionalism—privileges reform via charters.

Economic Environment

An Unraveling

It is almost a fundamental law that at the turn of the 21st century, the economy is undergoing a significant metamorphosis. There is widespread agreement that we have been and continue to be moving from an industrial to a postindustrial economy. Key aspects of the new economy include the globalization of economic activity, the demise of the mass-production economy, a privileging of information technology, an increase in the skills required to be successful, and an emphasis on the service dimensions of the marketplace (Marshall & Tucker, 1992; Murnane & Levy, 1996). What is also becoming clearer to many analysts is that with the arrival of the postindustrial society, "we are seeing the dissolution of the social structure associated with traditional industrialism" (Hood, 1994, p. 12) and an environment that is less hospitable to government intervention. With the ascent of the global economy, there is an emphasis on new markets (Lewis, 1993), "a loosening of the constraints of the labor market" (Dahrendorf, 1995, p. 21), and a "break[ing] of the state monopoly on the delivery of human services so that private enterprise can expand" (Lewis, 1993, p. 84)—conditions that provide many of the seeds for the debate about appropriate governance structures for tomorrow's society. At the same time that the economic policy habitat is evolving, the current foundations of the economy—especially the public sector—appear to be crumbling. In particular, the economic principles that have provided the foundation for government actions have been called into question.

The important question here is: What accounts for this discontent and skepticism about the public sector of the economy that is helping fuel the quest for new institutional forms? Given the cyclical nature of policy development and other value expressions in American society, it should surprise no one to learn that some of this rising tide of dissatisfaction with public sector initiatives can be characterized as a response to the nearly unbroken growth of government over the last three quarters of the 20th century—a counterreaction to the progressive philosophy that has dominated the policy agenda for so long. According to Hood (1994), for example, the growth of the public sector contained the seeds of its own destruction. The public sector model is, in many ways, simply aging and wearing out. Once a major economic model gains ascendancy, "dissatisfaction builds up over time. Unwanted side-effects of the policy [become] more clearly perceived. . . . At the same time, the shortcomings of the alternative orientation [the market, direct democracy, and voluntary association in this case] [are] forgotten, because they have not been recently experienced. Pressure then starts to build for the policy orientation to go over on the other track" (p. 15).

Another piece of the puzzle focuses on the widespread perception that the state is overinvolved in the life of the citizenry. Critics note that more and more citizens are chafing under the weight and scope of government activity. They characterize a government that has gone too far (Hirsch, 1991)—"public ownership that is more extensive than can be justified in terms of the appropriate role of public enterprises in mixed economies" (Hemming & Mansoor, 1988, p. 3). They argue that the state has become involved in the production of goods and services that do not meet the market failure tests (Pack, 1991) and that government agencies have pushed "themselves into areas well beyond governance. They [have] become involved in the business of business" (President's Commission on Privatization, 1988, p. 3). The results are predictable: The state, it is claimed, occupies an increasingly large space on the economic landscape, welfare loss due to collective consumption increases, and citizens experience an increasing need for more nongovernmental space (Florestano, 1991). Calls for a recalibration of the economic equation are increasingly heard.

Expanding numbers of citizens begin to experience "some public sector institutions as controlling rather than enabling, as limiting options rather than expanding them, as wasting rather than making the best use of resources" (Martin, 1993, p. 8). Of particular concern here is the issue of values. An increasing number of individuals and groups have come to believe that state intrusiveness includes efforts to establish value preferences (Cibulka, 1996)—values that they believe often undermine their ways of life. Others argue that, at least in some cases, through interest group and bureaucratic capture, some public sector institutions have actually destroyed the values that they were established to develop and promote (Hood, 1994).

The wearing out of economic foundations of the liberal democratic state can also be traced to recent critical analyses of the model of public sector activity developed to support expanded state control. The critique here is of three types. First, when examined as they are put into practice, the assumptions anchoring public sector activity over the last 30 years look much less appealing than they do when viewed in the abstract (i.e., conceptually). Indeed, "many of the assumptions and predictions on which the earlier growth of government was based have proved either to be false or at least to be subject to much greater doubt" (President's Commission on Privatization,

1988, pp. 249–250). Thus, the attack on extensive state control rests on the way in which its limitations have become visible. However, much of the critique of the market economy upon which public sector growth has been justified, especially market failure, has been weakened with the advent of sociotechnical changes associated with a shift from industrial to postindustrial society (Hood, 1994).

Second, "structural weaknesses inherent in the nature of public-sector supply itself . . . which undermine the whole basis on which it is established" (Pirie, 1988, p. 20) have become more visible—visible to the point that some advocates claim that state ownership and management are inherently flawed. Concomitantly, both the efficiency and effectiveness of governmental activities have begun to be questioned seriously.

Third, it is suggested that the reforms that created the large public sector are themselves much in need of change. Reform is increasingly seen in terms of alternatives to, rather than the repair of the existing public sector.

The discontent with and expanded skepticism about public sector economic activity are reinforced by a growing suspicion that government intervention is becoming less an instrument to provide services to the general citizenry and more and more a vehicle to establish values and to transfer income and wealth to individuals and groups (Donahue, 1989; Gottfried, 1993). Such transfers are of three types: (1) income and benefit premiums (or "rents," in the economics lexicon) available to government employees—that is, additional income and benefits enjoyed by civil servants over that received by employees in comparable jobs in the private sector; (2) affirmative action employment policies that shift wealth in the direction of targeted groups of citizens; and (3) particular programs that are created primarily to redistribute income.

Central to efforts to overhaul the economic infrastructure are developing beliefs that government is "incompetent and that its inefficiency is a key factor behind the chronic fiscal crisis that plagues the public sector" (Richards, Shore, & Sawicky, 1996, p. 42); that it is the poor performance of the public sector itself that is leading both to the abandonment of the assumptions used to forge a strong public sector and to calls for reshaping economic structures. The sentiment that government is becoming increasingly ineffective and inefficient is expressed along a continuum, from those who read the evidence as a mandate for a reduced public sector to those "advocates [who] want us to think about government as irredeemably incompetent [and prefer] to empty out the portfolio of public responsibilities altogether" (Starr, 1991, p. 35).

The recasting of public sector economic policy can also be attributed to stories of gross government incompetence or scandal and a mounting body of evidence that government enterprises are often inefficient, that it costs more to accomplish tasks in the government than in the private sector. Or, stated alternatively, government is consuming more of the nation's resources than it should: "The government provision and production of many goods and services, including the regulation of market activities, generates substantial deadweight losses" (De Alessi, 1987, p. 24). While widespread concern over the growing costs of government is an important variable in the algorithm of discontent—especially perceived waste and inefficiency—an even more significant factor is the expanding disillusionment about the overall effectiveness of government action (Hula, 1990b), particularly the perceived inability of government to meet its goals. Perhaps nowhere is this perception more vivid than in the arena of the large-scale egalitarian programs initiated in the 1960s and 1970s (Hula, 1990b). A number of critics of government control argue that the conditions that led to the development of these policies have not been ameliorated and that they will "not disappear as a result of having responsibility for them transferred from the private to the public sector" (Savas, 1987, p. 290). In fact, they maintain that such transfers often worsen the situation and create even more problems. They go so far as to suggest that many of our social problems are in reality cratogenic—that is, created by the state.

This widespread dissatisfaction with public sector economic activity has led some to question "whether public production . . . is so inherently inefficient that it results in even greater resource misallocation than do the market failures it aims to correct; whether regulation [government control] is even more costly to society than the initial resource misallocations" (Pack, 1991, p. 282). In tangible terms, it has helped foster a taxpayer revolt and has given birth to an array of citizen initiatives designed to seize control away from existing government structures. At the core of these reactions is the "feeling that there must be a better way of doing all those things that governments do not do too well" (Savas, 1985, p. 17): "If government is failing in its efforts to provide essential services, should we not reconsider the role we have given government in these areas?" (Carroll, Conant, & Easton, 1987, p. x).

A Reweaving

As was the case with the political environment, new ideas are emerging to define the economic domain of society in a postmodern world. Most of these are contained in what can be described as a recalibration of the equation of market-government provision, with considerably more weight being devoted to the market aspects of the algorithm. Stated more directly, the core idea for the reformulation of economic activity is the introduction of significant market forces into the public sector, or, for our industry, the privatization of schooling (Murphy, 1996; 1999). And as we explain below, charter schools are "at the forefront of marketization and privatization of the public school system" (UCLA Charter Schools Study, n.d., p. 62).

Privatization covers a good deal of ground and has several different meanings (Florestano, 1991). Indeed, analysts have been quick to note that privatization is a multilayered construct (Butler, 1991). A particularly helpful definition has been provided by De Alessi (1987):

> The term *privatization* is typically used to describe the transfer of activities from the public sector to the private sector and includes contracting out as well as reducing or discontinuing the provision of some goods and services by government. More accurately, privatization entails a move toward private property and away from not only government and common ownership but also from government regulations that limit individual rights to the use of resources. (p. 24)

At the most basic level, two elements are common to these, and nearly all other, definitions of privatization—a movement away from reliance on government agencies to provide goods and services and a movement toward the private sector and market forces.

An especially helpful way to see how a reweaving of the economic sector supports charter schools is to examine the objectives of the privatization movement. Some authors perceive privatization to be a vehicle to help "restore government to its fundamental purpose to steer, not to man the oars" (Savas, 1987, p. 290). Others who view "privatization as part of a wider neo-liberal policy package" (Martin, 1993, p. 99) maintain that a key objective, for better or worse, is to reconstruct the "liberal democratic state" (Starr, 1991, p. 25), to redefine the operational "set of assumptions about the capacities of democratic government and the appropriate sphere of common obligation" (p. 25). Privatization here is viewed, in particular, as a vehicle to overcome the "dependency culture" (Martin, 1993, p. 48) associated with a social order dominated by government activity. Another aim is to depoliticize service operations (Hanke & Dowdle, 1987). As Pirie (1988) argues, "the actual transfer to the private sector . . . can take the service into the purely economic world and out of the political world . . . freeing it from the political forces which acted upon it in the state sector" (pp. 52–53) and overcoming "structural weaknesses inherent in the nature of public sector supply" (p. 20).

Perhaps the central purpose and most highly touted objective of privatization is "reduction in the size of the public sector" (Pack, 1991, p. 284), "reducing public spending and taxation as proportions of gross domestic product" (Hardin, 1989, p. 20). The goal is to "downsize or rightsize government" (Worsnop, 1992, p. 984). Based on the belief that government is too large and too intrusive and that "government's decisions are political and thus are inherently less trustworthy than free-market decisions" (Savas, 1982, p. 5), the focus is on "rolling back either the rate of growth or the absolute amount of state activity in the social service delivery system" (Ismael, 1988, p. 1).

A further objective is to enhance the overall health of the economy: "If reducing the size of the public sector is the dominant theme in the work of privatization advocates, enhancing the efficiency of the economy as a whole and the public sector in particular is their *leitmotif*" (Pack, 1991, p. 287). The secondary aims are to enhance "efficiency and responsiveness" (Bell & Cloke, 1990, p. 7); to promote "savings, investment, productivity, and growth" (Starr, 1987, p. 126); "to increase the use of scarce resources" (Miller & Tufts, 1991, p. 100); to ensure that customers are "served more effectively" (Hanke & Dowdle, 1987, p. 115); and to promote cost effectiveness by "help[ing] get prices right" (Starr, 1991, p. 32). Related to the issue of cost effectiveness is still another objective of privatization: "to reduce the power of public sector trade unions" (Hardin, 1989, p. 30; see also American Federation of Teachers, 1996) and thereby to exercise "control of wage rates" (Bell & Cloke, 1990, p. 7).

Finally, privatization is often portrayed as a tactic for promoting "choice in public services" (Savas, 1987, p. 5): "The key word is *choice*. Advocates claim that privatization will enlarge the range of choice for individuals while serving the same essential functions as do traditional programs" (Starr, 1987, p. 131). According to Gormley (1991b) and other analysts, "privatization enable[s] individual consumers to pursue their private choices more freely" (p. 309). These same analysts further posit that "greater freedom of choice will generally lead to a more just distribution of benefits" (Starr, 1987, p. 131), serve the interest of equity, and promote democracy (Bell & Cloke, 1990; Thayer, 1987).

Analysts on both sides of the privatization debate acknowledge that "privatization is more a *political* than an *economic* act" (Savas, 1987, p. 233): "It is not possible to discuss privatization as if it consisted of techniques and not of ideas. . . . Privatization comes to us in a political bundle, not logically, but ideologically connected" (Starr, 1991, p. 26). A review of the literature in this area shows that privatization represents a particular "public philosophy" (Van Horn, 1991, p. 262) and that advocates of privatization fall into a distinctive ideological camp.

In particular, privatization draws strength from "a general political movement toward the right" (Brazer, 1981, p. 21) and the fact that "Americans have turned to conservatives for the answers to the most important problems facing the U.S." (Pines, 1985, p. v). The fusion of a political agenda increasingly dominated by "conservative politics" (Martin, 1993, p. 46) and an "economic theology . . . undergoing a return to fundamentalism" (Thayer, 1987, p. 165) has given birth to the doctrine of neoliberalism (Seldon, 1987) and to "the ideological and profit-oriented agenda of the New Right" (Martin, 1993, p. 182), "the conservative view of government as an economic black-hole" (Starr, 1987, p. 126). In the process, "an ideology which has long lurked in the darkest shadows of right-wing thinking [has been] transfer[red] into an apparatus at the very centre of the policy process" (Bell & Cloke, 1990, p. 4).

Undergirding privatization, then, are a particular set of values and political goals (McCabe & Vinzant, 1999) and a specific "concept of the relationship between the individual and the state" (Martin, 1993, p. 48). Economic growth and individual choice are the movement's predominant goals, and the market, which is seen as "consistently and wholly benign" (p. 47), is touted as the best vehicle to secure those objectives. Not surprisingly, the "language of 'choice' and 'empowerment'" (p. 188) is woven throughout the privatization literature: "People should have more choice in public services. They should be empowered to define and address common needs" (Savas, 1987, p. 4). Alternative approaches to government intervention and bureaucratic structures, it is argued, must "buttress individual liberties" (De Alessi, 1987, p. 24); they must minimize interference with individual freedom and the market (Martin, 1993).

When viewed through a pragmatic lens, privatization is about the more efficient delivery of higher quality goods and services. However, "as an ideological principle, privatization equals smaller government, lower taxes, and less government intervention in public affairs" (Van Horn, 1991, p. 261). Fueled by citizen discontent with activist government and fiscal stress, newly formed conservative winds are pushing society away from the agenda of the progressive era and toward a "reconstructing [of] the liberal democratic state" (Starr, 1991, p. 25).

Earlier analysis captured much of the emerging populist view against large government. On the one hand, there has been a weakening of the progressive vision and a lessening of the influence of progressive philosophy—a widespread "reaction against the theories and results of Progressive thought" (President's Commission on Privatization, 1988, p. 230), focusing particularly upon the appropriateness of public provision of goods and services that are highly redistributive in nature. Thus, privatization is seen "as a means to get rid of 'dependency culture'" (Martin, 1993, p. 48). Critics argue that "government is too big, too powerful, too intrusive in people's lives and therefore is a danger to democracy" (Savas, 1987, p. 5). This critique of large government is grounded in an analysis of interest group government and "the excess of current interest group politics" (President's Commission on Privatization, 1988, p. 233); of "distant and unresponsive organs of government" (Savas, 1987, p. 7); "meddling by ministers and civil servants" (Bell & Cloke, 1990, p. 14); groups who are "able to use the political system to secure and maintain benefits at the general expense" (Pirie, 1988, p. 58); and programs that "have too often operated mainly to enlarge the income, status, and power of the industry of bureaucratic and professional service producers, whether governmental or private" (Kolderie, 1991, p. 259).

Finally, consistent with an increasingly popular libertarian philosophy, there is an ongoing reassessment of the appropriate size of government, in general, and particular units of government, in particular (Tullock, 1988), an emerging "belief that small is beautiful when applied to domestic government" (Fitzgerald, 1988, p. 21), and a rekindling of belief in the appropriateness of self-help and local initiative, especially of "traditional local institutions" (Savas, 1987, p. 10). As noted earlier, these winds are blowing us in the direction of decentralization, a "rebuilding America from the bottom up—and the trend away from reliance on political institutions in favor of individual self-help initiatives" (Fitzgerald, 1988, p. 16). New attention is being devoted to "the potential of 'mediating structures'" (Savas, 1987, p. 239)—and the deleterious effects of large government on these structures—that are situated between "the individual and the mechanism of government" (Fitzgerald, 1988, p. 26), such as families, churches, neighborhood groups, and voluntary associations. According to proponents of privatization, based on the belief that "creative local initiatives, informal person-to-person efforts, local role models, and intra-community pressures are more likely to be effective than bureaucrats" (Savas, 1987, p. 239), "we are witnessing the revival of self-help strategies and voluntarism as expressions of independence from government" (Fitzgerald, 1988, p. 26).

Critique of large government represents the negative case for the dismantling of the liberal democratic state. It is balanced on the positive side by the growing belief that "free market economics provide the path to prosperous equilibrium" (Thayer, 1987, p. 168); by "the political pendulum swing toward market-oriented solutions" (Seader, 1991, p. 32). Supported by the intellectual pillars of market theory and theories of the firm and by the public choice literature, there is a "new spirit of enterprise in the air" (Hardin, 1989, p. 16)—a renewed interest in "private market values" (Bailey, 1987, p. 141) and in the "virtues of private property" (Hirsch, 1991, p. 2), and a "pro-market trend" (President's Commission on Privatization, 1988, p. 237) in the larger society.

Although analysts are quick to point out the fallacy of this emerging belief in the infallibility of private business (Baber, 1987) and to remind us that "idealization of the market's invisible hand has served to conceal the grubbier ones directing it" (Martin, 1993, p. 6), there is little doubt that the privatization movement is anchored firmly on "belief in the superiority of free market forms of social organization over the forms of social organization of the Keynesian welfare state society" (Ian Taylor, cited in Martin, 1993, p. 48). This expanding reliance on the market moves individuals in the direction of "exercis[ing] choice as consumers rather than as citizens" (Starr, 1991, p. 27).

As discussed above, the expansion of pro-market sentiment is powered to some extent by the picture painted by some of "a bloated, parasitic public sector blocking the bustle and growth of a more free flowing private economy" (Starr, 1987, p. 124). Two beliefs are central to this line of reasoning: (1) that "the structural organization of the public sector itself" (Pirie, 1988, p. 34) is flawed and (2) that political decisions "are inherently less trustworthy than free-market decisions" (Savas, 1987, p. 5). Starting from here, we find many analysts are adopting an increasingly skeptical stance on the usefulness of government intervention (Tullock, 1988, 1994a, 1994b). Their revisiting the case for public action (Fixler, 1991) "has caused mainstream economists . . . to narrow significantly the circumstances thought to require government intervention to correct market failings" (President's Commission on Privatization, 1988, p. 237). Accompanying this reconsideration of the case for public action has been a reanalysis of the supposed problems of markets and, according to privatization advocates, a recognition that because "market forces can find ways round or through vested interests" (Seldon, 1987, p. 133), "the regulation which the market imposes in economic activity is superior to any regulation which rulers can devise and operate by law" (Pirie, 1988, p. 10). This demonstrates a feeling that because "the level of efficiency of government action is apt to be low, and the possibility of damage through erratic, ill-informed decisions is great, government action should be resorted to only when the social cost emanating from the market is quite great" (Tullock, 1988, p. 103).

Central to this reweaving narrative is a set of key ideas, some more explicit than others, but nearly all of which support the construct of charters as a school reform mechanism. Some of these overlap and reinforce the bundles of ideas we saw emerging in our analysis of the shifting political environment, ideas such as decentralization, choice, and the privileging of citizen control over government action. Others, such as the power of voluntary association, competition, an emphasis on enhancing supply, and the empowerment of the consumer, are additions to the reform engine powering the charter movement.

CONTINUED CONCERNS ABOUT THE EFFECTIVENESS OF SCHOOLING

Charter schools rest on a devastating critique of the present system. (Sarason, 1998, p. 18)

The uniting forces are a general concern with the academic performance of pupils in district public schools and a belief that charter schools can improve the situation. (Garn, 1998, p. 48)

As Hood (1994) reminds us, "policies and institutions can often be their own undoing. . . . They can trip over their own feet and dig their own graves" (p. 13). Focusing specifically on education, we can see that the struggle to recast schooling can be traced to two broad areas: discontent with educational outcomes and critical reviews of the core system of schooling. Discontent with outcomes draws strength from three problems: (1) the perceived inability of public schooling to deliver a quality product, (2) the seeming failure of education to heal itself, and (3) a growing disconnect between the public and public education. Critiques of extant governance systems center on two topics: (1) frustration with the government-professional monopoly and (2) critical analyses of the basic management-governance infrastructure—that is, bureaucracy.

The consequence of the above noted forces is a significant reinforcement of the "common and widely reiterated observation of a declining confidence in public education . . . [and] the mounting criticisms of the established form and content of publicly-funded educational systems" (Mayberry, 1991, p. 1), along with a growing sense "that the existing system [is] unwilling or unable to change from within, and this change from outside the system [is] required" (Bulkley, 1998, p. 78). Whitty (1984) reinforces this latter point, noting that "it is important to recognize that . . . public education fails to serve the majority of its clients and hence makes them potential supporters of reactionary proposals" (p. 54).

Concerns about Educational Productivity

Outcome Concerns

Richards and his colleagues (1996) hit the mark directly when they report that "today the public discourse about American education tends to be preoccupied with failure" (p. 15), with the sense that "the public school establishment is . . . failing America's children" (Powers & Cookson, 1999, p. 105) and that public education is a "troubled institution" (Nathan, 1996a, p. xx). The most recent decade contains a "raft of hopeless narratives on public education" (Fine, 1993, p. 33). What analysts see as frustration over the continuing inadequacies of primary and secondary education in the United States is a multifaceted phenomenon (Public Agenda, 1999). Or, stated in an alternate form, the perception that the level and quality of education in the United States is less than many desire is buttressed by data on a wide variety of outcomes (Finn, Manno, & Vanourek, 2000; Immerwahr, 1999). Specifically, according to many analysts, data assembled in each of the following performance dimensions provide a not-very-reassuring snapshot of the current performance of the American educational system: (1) academic achievement in basic subject areas (compared to student performance in other countries); (2) functional literacy; (3) preparation for employment; (4) the holding power of schools (dropout rates); (5) knowledge of specific subject areas such as geography and economics; (6) mastery of higher-order skills; and (7) initiative, responsibility, and citizenship (Committee for Economic Development, 1994; Marshall & Tucker, 1992; Murnane & Levy, 1996). Perhaps even more important than the data is the fact that "the experience of most Americans tells them that the nation's school system is in trouble and that the problems are getting worse" (Mathews, 1996, p. 1).

Two issues in particular define forward-looking analyses of educational outcomes: (1) the inability of the educational enterprise to enhance levels of productivity to meet the needs of the changing workforce and (2) the failure of schools to successfully educate all of the nation's children, especially the poor (Fusarelli, 1999; Northwest Regional Educational Laboratory, 1998). While analysts acknowledge that student achievement has remained fairly stable over the last quarter century, they fault the education enterprise for its inability to keep pace with the increasing expectations from a changing economy (Committee for Economic Development, 1994; Consortium on Productivity in the Schools, 1995). In other words, "the requirements the world was placing on school graduates were dramatically higher, but performance had stayed the same" (Marshall & Tucker, 1992, p. 79).

One side of the problem these critics discuss is the belief that systems that hold steady in today's world are actually in decline. While others see stability, they see "increasing obsolescence of the education provided by most U.S. schools" (Murnane & Levy, 1996, p. 6), and they question "why schools have remained what they were and are despite the lack of desirable outcomes" (Sarason, 1995, p. 110).

The other side of the productivity issue raised by these reviewers is the claim that because of the changing nature of the economy outlined earlier, the level of outcomes needed by students must be significantly increased (Shanker, 1988):

> Today's schools look much like Ford in 1926. The products they produce—student achievement levels—are not worse than they were 20 years ago; in most respects they are sightly better. But in those 20 years, the job market has changed radically. Just as the Model T that was good enough in 1921 was not good enough in 1926, the education that was adequate for high-wage employers in 1970 is no longer adequate today. (Murnane & Levy, 1996, p. 77)

Critics find that the schools are not meeting this new standard for productivity, that they are not adequate "to the needs of the future in which today's students will live" (Hill, Pierce, & Guthrie, 1997, p. 27). They argue that "the majority of students fail to leave school with the skills they need" (Marshall & Tucker, 1992, p. 67), that "American schools are not providing students with the learning that they will need to function effectively in the 21st century" (Consortium on Productivity, 1995, p. 3); that "American education is in crisis and no longer able to 'raise up' its citizenry to compete in the global market-place" (Rofes, 1998b, p. 52) or "to face international economic competition once it turns up again" (McDonald, 1999, p. 68).

Of special concern to productivity critics is the belief that nearly all the future gains will need to come in the area of educational quality. The Committee on Economic Development (1994) depicts the argument as follows:

> In the past, much of the contribution of elementary education to economic growth has come from increases in the "quantity" of education. Although there is still room for improvement (about 15 percent of twenty-four- to twenty-five-year-olds do not have a high school diploma), much of the future contribution will have to come from increasing the "quality" of students graduating from our high schools. (p. 8)

Another concern is that the outcome standards themselves are being recast:

> The skills that students need are not just more of what the schools have always taught, such as basic skills in mathematics, but also skills that the schools have rarely taught—the ability to work with complex knowledge and to make decisions under conditions of conflicting inadequate evidence. (Consortium on Productivity, 1995, p. 9)

Complicating all of this is the knowledge that high levels of performance must be attained by nearly all of society's children.

> Our task is to shift the whole curve of American educational performance radically upward, and at the same time to close substantially the gap between the bottom and the top of the curve. For the first time in American history, we have to have an education system that really educates everyone, our poor and our minorities as well as our most fortunate. (Marshall & Tucker, 1992, p. 82)

Reviewers, such as those noted above, declare that students who leave school having failed to meet the new performance standards will face increasingly dismal prospects in the 21st-century workplace.

Inability to Successfully Reform

What appears to be especially damaging to public education is the perceived inability of the schooling industry to reform itself (Finn, Manno, & Vanourek, 2000; Sarason, 1998; Wells, Grutzik, et al., 1999). Questions raised by analysts who take the long-term view on this issue are particularly demoralizing. For example, according to Beers and Ellig (1994), over the past 40 years:

Public school leaders have overseen the implementation of many of the most persistently called-for proposals for school reform. The ever-present call for more funding has been met by tripling real per-pupil expenditures from their 1960 levels. The demand for greater teacher professionalism has motivated a 50% increase in average teacher salaries since 1960, adjusted for inflation. Class sizes have fallen by a third since the mid-1960s, and most states have continued to raise graduation requirements. (p. 19)

What has resulted from these efforts, critics argue, has not been an increase in educational quality but rather a proliferation of professional and bureaucratic standards (Hill, Pierce, & Guthrie, 1997), the creation of subsides for bureaucracy (Beers & Ellig, 1994), "a deepening antagonism between professional educators and the public" (Marshall & Tucker, 1992, p. 79), and the strengthening of a centralized educational system (Bulkley, 1998; Tyack, 1992) in which "all risks of failure are shifted onto parents, taxpayers, and children" (Payne, 1995, p. 3). This is a situation in which the existing system transforms the reforms, rather than vice versa (Hill, Pierce, & Guthrie, 1997; Little Hoover Commission, 1996). Beers and Ellig (1994) make this point in dramatic fashion when they claim that "in a very real sense we have tried to run the public schools the same way the Soviets tried to run factories, and now we're paying the price" (p. 20). The effect, critics maintain, is that reform has reinforced the very dynamics that are promoting self-destruction in public education (Buechler, 1996). The natural consequence, they hold, must be the emergence of new forms of educational institutions and new models of school governance (Hakim, Seidenstat, & Bowman, 1994; Lieberman, 1988, 1989). Charter schools are at the top of the list of new forms and new models (Hill, Pierce, & Guthrie, 1997; Sarason, 1998).

Also troubling, if not surprising, given the analysis just presented, is the feeling that the very substantial efforts to strengthen education over the last 15 years in particular have not produced much in terms of improvement across the seven outcome dimensions listed above (Little Hoover Commission, 1996; Sarason, 1998). As Richards and his colleagues (1996) document, public interest in alternative arrangements for schools reflects a profound disappointment that the plethora of school reform initiatives launched over the last 15 years has failed to turn the tide, that "despite considerable energy, initial bursts of optimism, and abundant promises, a good many efforts to reform schools, though not all, are failing in the 1990s" (Mathews, 1996, p. 16). There is an expanding agreement on the need to overhaul school systems as well as an emerging belief that conditions in the area of education are so bleak that any change could hardly make matters worse (Richards, Shore, & Sawicky, 1996) and that charter schools will do much to make them better (U.S. General Accounting Office, 1995b; Loveless & Jasin, 1998): "In response to the public's growing frustration with the pace and scope of school improvement, legislators, educators, and parents are increasingly turning to charter schools as the reform of choice" (McGree, 1995a, p. 1).

Growing Disconnection with the Public

Critics aver that at the same time we are discovering that traditional attacks on our problems not only fail to attack the roots of the nation's educational problems but may be actually crippling public education, we are witnessing a fundamental disconnection between the public and the public schools. Or, as Szabo and Gerber (1996) argue, "Schools have lost their connection to the families and communities they serve" (p. 136). A Public Agenda report, for example, asserts that "in the battle over the future of public education, the public is essentially 'up for grabs'" (cited in Bradley, 1995, p. 1).

The most thoughtful and detailed description of society's deepening loss of confidence in public education has been provided by Mathews (1996). Based on his work, Mathews argues that "the public and the public schools [are] in fact moving apart, that the historical compact between them [is] in danger of dissolving" (p. i). Mathews documents the decline in public confidence in public schools in a number of ways. He cites data from the National Opinion Research Center that reveals a 40% drop (from 37 to 15%) from 1973 to 1993 in those expressing confidence in educational institutions. He also cites data showing an increase of 125% (from 8 to 18%) during this same time frame in citizens expressing low confidence in public institutions (p. 9). Using a more direct measure, he marshals information that reveals that citizens prefer private schools over public ones: "A virtual chorus said that they would take their children out of public schools if they had that option" (Mathews, 1996, p. 22; see also Public Agenda, 1999). Kaufman (1996) adds to this later analysis:

> Parents rank private schools higher in 11 of 13 categories, including preparing students for college, safety and discipline. Public schools rank higher only in serving students with special needs and teaching children how to deal with people of diverse backgrounds. (p. 72)

Questions about Existing Governance Arrangements

Charters are trumpeted as a powerful method of restoring confidence by "re-establish[ing] a social and legal contract between families and their schools" and by providing "meaningful involvement and more direct control over the education of their children" (Szabo & Gerber, 1996, p. 136).

As noted above, critical reviews focusing specifically on governance tend to cluster into two groups: (1) critiques of the governmental-professional model of education—or "concerns about the control of education by a 'monopolistic bureaucracy'" (Bulkley, 1998, p. 126) and (2) attacks on the basic infrastructure of school bureaucracy. Since we have treated the first issue in detail above, we focus here on attacks on educational bureaucracy.

The Larger Narrative

At the heart of the critique of existing governance arrangements is a reassessment of the interests of public employees. Central to this reinterpretation is a dismantling or "undermining of the naive faith in the benevolence of governmental bureaucracy" (Buchanan, 1987, p. 206). According to Niskanen (1971), "The beginning of wisdom is the recognition that bureaucrats are people who are, at least, not entirely motivated by the general welfare or the interests of the state" (p. 36). Rather than accepting the assumption that managers of public agencies are "passive agents [who] merely administer and carry out programs" (Bennett & DiLorenzo, 1987, p. 16) with the sole intent of maximizing public interest, some analysts advance the belief that these "civil servants often [make] decisions in the interest of their own power or income" (Tullock, 1994b, p. 65). Bureaucrats are much like other people, "people who are less interested in the ostensible objectives of the organization than in their own personal well being" (Tullock, 1965, p. 21)—a well-being that is often expressed in terms of "salary, perquisites, rank, prestige, [and] opportunities for promotion" (Bennett & DiLorenzo, 1987, p. 17).

In economic terms, this means "that government employees, like other economic agents, respond to the opportunities for gain provided by the structure of property rights embedded in the institutions used to control their choices" (De Alessi, 1987, p. 24) and that bureaus act as "a type of special interest group" (Hilke, 1992, p. 13). At the most basic level, this results in the notion of the bureaucrat as a public service maximizer giving way to the conception of a manager who attempts to maximize his or her own utility function—a utility function that contains a variety of variables: "salary, perquisites of the office, public reputation, power, patronage, [and] output of the bureau" (Niskanen, 1971, p. 38).

Such an analysis continues to argue that because improving one's utility function is directly dependent on the resources available to the bureau, budget maximization becomes the operant goal of bureau managers (Niskanen, 1971; 1994). Consequently, managers have a strong incentive to engage in "bureaucratic imperialism" (Tullock, 1965, p. 134) or "empire building" (Dudek & Company, 1989, p. 49): "If such a system is applied throughout a whole organization . . . the higher officials will actually encourage their inferiors to build up the size of the whole hierarchy since their own position, as well as that of their inferiors, will depend on the number of subordinates" (Tullock, 1965, p. 135).

Budget maximization and empire building impose real costs on citizens in terms of public control and overall efficiency of the economy (Bennett & Johnson, 1980). The switch from maximizing the public interest to maximizing the discretionary budget means that bureaus have the potential to become "producer-oriented" (Pirie, 1988, p. 26), to capture the agency and to direct its energies toward meeting the needs of government employees (Hardin, 1989; Vickers & Yarrow, 1988). The result is goal displacement (Downs, 1967; Tullock, 1965): "Some public sector activities clearly are serving the interest of their own workforce more than the interests of their customers" (Pirie, 1988, p. 26).

Whatever the causes, because (a) "people are more prodigal with the wealth of others than with their own" (Hanke, 1985, p. 6), (b) "public employees have no direct interest in the commercial outcome" (p. 6) of the enterprise, and (c) "the supply of government services by bureaus generates a net surplus that is shared with members of the government" (Niskanen, 1994, p. 278), it is posited that bureaus are characterized by significant inefficiencies (Hilke, 1992; Niskanen, 1971, 1994; Pack, 1991). A cardinal conclusion of public choice scholarship, for example, is that "the budget of a bureau is too large, the output . . . may be too low, and the production of this output is uniformly inefficient" (Niskanen, 1994, p. 274), or, more succinctly, "inefficiency in production is the normal condition" (p. 274).

Analysts following the line of work noted above see the motivation and behavior of government employees as paralleling the interests and actions of their managers (Solmon, Block, & Gifford, 1999): "The employees' interests in larger budgets are obvious and similar to that of the bureaucrat: greater opportunities for promotion, more job security, etc." (Niskanen, 1971, p. 40). Therefore, because "they benefit from continued operation of the public agencies that employ them . . . [they] thus have a vested interest in maintaining public agencies even when they might not be efficient" (Hirsch, 1991, p. 72). More to the point, it is generally in their interests to have an expanding public sector.

One avenue of this discourse suggests that because public employees are, next to transfer payment recipients, "the most direct beneficiaries of government spending" (Savas, 1987, p. 26), they are likely to use the power of the ballot box to promote the objective of government growth (Tullock, 1994a): "Government employees have a vested interest in the growth of government and, because of this interest, are very active politically. Relative to the general public, they vote in greater proportion and have a correspondingly disproportionate impact on political decisions" (Bennett & Johnson, 1980, p. 372).

A second part of this view holds that public sector unions in particular are key instruments in the growth of bureaus and the concomitant subordination of consumer interests to the objectives of the employees themselves. Ramsey (1987) concludes that when the economic influence of unions is combined with political muscle, public-sector unions have considerable "ability to tax the rest of society" (p. 97).

A final point of this critical analysis asserts that employee self-interest is nurtured in what might, presented in the best light, be thought of as a symbiotic relationship with the bureau's sponsor—the intersection where "the self-interest of the politician [and] a well-organized union cadre" (p. 97) converge to maximize the utility of both groups:

> The political power of public employees and their unions is not restricted to their voting strength. Political campaign contributors and campaign workers are a potent influence on office seekers. The situation lends itself to collusion whereby officeholders can award substantial pay raises to employees with the unspoken understanding that some of the bread cast upon those particular waters will return as contributions. (Savas, 1987, p. 26)

As described above, the well-being of politicians and government employees often comes at the expense of the general citizenry, especially in inefficiencies visible in inappropriate production schedules and unearned rents enjoyed by public servants (Hilke, 1992; Hirsch, 1991; Niskanen, 1971, 1994).

The Education Story Line

Over the past decade, the belief has taken root "that many of the problems plaguing education today originate in the way public schools are organized and governed" (Loveless & Jasin, 1998, p. 10); that "some of public education's troubles, clearly, come not from the problems students bring to school with them but from the educational system that unions, school boards, administrators, and legislators have created" (Nathan, 1996a, p. 76). Or even more directly, "the current governance of public education makes effective action at the school level almost impossible" (Hill, Pierce, & Guthrie, 1997, p. 13). Specifically, too much self-interest and "too much bureaucracy . . . [are] at the heart of educational mediocrity" (Snauwaert, 1993, p. 92): "In recent years, critics have argued that the reforms of the Progressive era produced bureaucratic arteriosclerosis, insulation from parents and patrons, and the low productivity of a declining industry protected as a quasi monopoly" (Tyack, 1993, p. 3). Consistent with the analysis outlined above, there is a sense that producers have "come to dominate most education decisions, and government has become their chosen mechanism for retaining control" (Finn, Manno, & Vanourek, 2000, p. 223)—a feeling that in bureaucracy "the kids can be taken for granted because it's adult interests that matter" (Kolderie, 1994, p. 108). There is growing sentiment that the existing educational governance and management systems are unsustainable (Clark & Meloy, 1989; Little Hoover Commission, 1996; Rungeling & Glover, 1991). Behind this basic critique lie several beliefs: that states are attempting to micromanage schools and that central office staff are too numerous and too far removed from local schools to understand the needs of teachers, children, and families (Garcia & Garcia, 1996; Lieber, 1997); and that bureaucracies may be working well for those who run them but that they are not serving children well (Finn et al., 2000; Fuller, Elmore, & Orfield, 1996; Hill, Pierce, & Guthrie, 1997). It is increasingly being concluded that the existing bureaucratic system of school governance and administration is "incapable of addressing the technical and structural shortcomings of the public educational system" (Lawton, 1991, p. 4).

More finely grained criticism of the bureaucratic infrastructure of schooling comes from a variety of quarters. There are those who contend that schools are so paralyzed by "regulatory excess" (Hill et al., 1997, p. viii) and the "bureaucratic arteriosclerosis" noted above by Tyack (1993, p. 3) that "professional judgment" (Hill & Bonan, 1991, p. 65), "innovation" (Garn, 1998, p. 48; Sarason, 1998, p. 14), "creativity" (Lindelow, 1981, p. 98), "morale" (David, 1989, p. 45), "creative capacity" (Snauwaert, 1993, p. 5), and responsibility have all been stilted (Nathan, 1996a). Other reformers maintain "that school bureaucracies, as currently constituted could [never] manage to provide high-quality education" (Elmore, 1993, p. 37) and, even worse, that bureaucratic governance and management cause serious disruptions in the educational process (Shanker, 1988a, b, c; Wise, 1989), that they are "paralyzing American education . . . [and] getting in the way of children's learning" (Sizer, 1984, p. 206). These scholars view bureaucracy as a governance-management system that deflects attention from the core tasks of learning and teaching (Elmore, 1990). Still other critics suggest that bureaucratic management is inconsistent with the sacred values and purposes of education. They question "fundamental ideological issues pertaining to bureaucracy's meaning in a democratic society" (Campbell, Fleming, Newell, & Bennion, 1987, p. 73) and find that "it is inconsistent to endorse democracy in society but to be skeptical of shared governance in our schools" (Glickman, 1990, p. 74). Other reform proponents hold that the existing organizational-governance structure of schools is neither sufficiently flexible nor sufficiently robust to meet the needs of students in a postindustrial society (Shanker, 1988a, b, c). Finally, some analysts suggest that "the current structure has grown an insulated political culture" (Finn, Manno, & Vanourek, 2000, p. 58). They contend that the rigidities of bureaucracy, by making schools nearly impenetrable by citizens, impede the ability of parents and citizens to govern and reform schooling (Hill, Pierce, & Guthrie, 1997; Sarason, 1995; Tyack, 1992).

Not unexpectedly, given this tremendous attack on the basic organizational and governance infrastructure of schooling, stakeholders at all levels are arguing that "ambitious, if not radical, reforms are required to rectify this situation" (Elmore, 1993, p. 34), that "the excessively centralized, bureaucratic control of . . . schools must end" (Carnegie Forum, cited in Hanson, 1991, pp. 2–3). Some reformers are arguing for redesigning state control of education, to replace it. Other analysts look to replace government control with market mechanisms. Still others see hope in systems that are more professionally controlled. Others appeal to more robust models of democratic governance. And all of these groups see charter schools as an answer to their needs.

CONCLUSION

Chapters 4 and 5 are designed to expose the supporting elements and theories of change in the charter school movement. While some of the embedded logic of charters was noted in this chapter, the bulk of that discussion is scheduled for the next chapter. Here we attended primarily to sets of external and internal dynamics that buttress the charter movement. On the external front, we argued that powerful changes are underway in the sociopolitical and economic environments of the education industry. We saw how these shifts are creating a culture that is conducive to development of charters. Or, coming at the issue from a different direction, charters map well onto the still emerging polity and economy of the postmodern world.

On the internal front, we reviewed the long-playing narrative of schools' inability to reach the goal of providing a high level of education to each youngster in the nation. We reported that their failure to do so has led increasing numbers of reformers to seek more radical solutions to the woes besetting schooling. Charter schools are a particularly well-thought-of stopping point in the search for more aggressive reform efforts.

CHAPTER 5

The Embedded Logic
of Charter Schools

The charter school idea rests on a fairly simple premise. By allowing citizens to start new public schools (or convert existing ones), freeing the schools up from rules and regulations, and holding them accountable for results and "customer" satisfaction, charter school programs will stimulate the formation of promising new educational options for children. And by having money follow children from conventional school districts in charter schools, the programs will place competitive pressure on regular public schools, spurring system-wide improvement. (Hassel, 1997, p. 2)

As with other major reforms, charter schools are powered by theories in action that link the change strategy to desired benefits. Thus at the heart of the concept is a "shared set of assumptions" (Bomotti, Ginsberg, & Cobb, 1999, p. 3), a cluster of "common beliefs" (Izu et al., 1998, p. 3), and "a common set of arguments" (UCLA Charter School Study [UCLA], n.d., p. 9) about how and why charters "will lead to substantial and overlapping educational improvement" (p. 9). And underlying these shared assumptions are "implicit ... theories of organizational and political behavior" (Loveless & Jasin, 1998, p. 10). Bomotti and his colleagues (1999) capture a core part of the theoretical infrastructure undergirding charters as follows:

> In exchange for freedom from burdensome rules and regulations, charter schools will be more accountable for student learning. In addition, charter schools will infuse a healthy competition into a bureaucratic and unresponsive public system by providing more educational choices to parents and students. Because of their enhanced autonomy, they will encourage educational innovation, provide more professional opportunities for teachers, and operate more efficiently than regular public schools. For these reasons, charter schools are also expected to serve as educational research and development laboratories and a spur to reform of the public education system as a whole. (p. 3)

We concur with Lane (n.d.) that "analysis and discussion of the basic assumptions supporting argument for and against charter schools will add considerably to consistent and coherent discussion of the charter school movement, and to education reform in general" (p. 20). We also agree with Hassel (1999a) and others who document that the theories in action in charter schools have been insufficiently investigated to date. In this chapter, we deepen the understanding of the embedded logic of charters in two ways. First, we explore the charter school reform engine itself—the forces that are expected to drive the educational system to more effective performance. We arrange the major assumptions into a framework that includes three key components—autonomy, competition, and accountability. Each has been introduced earlier—autonomy and accountability in Chapter 3 and competition in Chapter 4. Here we weave them into the web of logic that lies at the center of charter schools as a reform strategy. Following the lead of scholars such as Bulkley (1998) and Hassel (1997), we reveal how, in the quest for school improvement, strands of the web of logic receive differential emphasis depending on the political context. Second, we illuminate the dynamics of charter school reform, exploring the path between heightened autonomy, competition, and accountability and the expected benefits of charters, at the individual school level as well as at the educational system level.

THE REFORM ENGINE

> The framework builds from some common beliefs about the purpose and end result of charter schools, namely that *increased parental choice, regulatory flexibility, greater site-based decision-making autonomy,* and *performance-based accountability* will yield improved student outcomes. (Izu et al., 1998, p. 3)

In this section, we provide a picture of the components of the reform dynamic of charter schools—the engine and the benefits. As described, charters are powered by three major concepts—autonomy, competition, and accountability—each of which is comprised of numerous strands of ideas and all of which are deeply intertwined.

Autonomy

Hassel (1997) gets to the heart of the matter when he observes that "perhaps no concept is as central to the charter school idea as 'autonomy'" (p. 117). Without autonomy, analysts conclude, few of the dynamics portrayed in this chapter can materialize. As with much of the ideology in the charter school movement, autonomy is a complex concept. To understand it more clearly, we divide the idea into its three central components: autonomy for suppliers to start charter schools (market), autonomy for families to select charter schools (choice), and autonomy for schools to operate as they see fit (decentralization and deregulation).

Markets for Suppliers

Although underemphasized in the literature, the most unique, and in many ways the most important, contribution of the charter school movement is its focus on opening up the supply side of the choice equation (Kolderie, 1992; Solmon, Block, & Gifford, 1999). That is, "unlike open enrollment policies designed to promote greater choice among existing schools, the charter school movement is intended to increase the number of schools from which parents and students can choose" (McCabe & Vinzant, 1999, p. 363).

By the start of the charter movement, analysts were increasingly concluding that simply cultivating greater growth on the demand section of the choice landscape would be insufficient to reform education, "that choice [does not] mean much if there aren't good, *new* schools to choose from" (Kolderie, 1992, p. 28). They argued that "choice among nearly identical schools was not sufficient" (Educational Excellence Network, 1995, p. 3), that "it was time to open up the supply side, providing different kinds of schools so the right of choice would be meaningful" (Nathan, 1996a, p. 65). Specifically, they held that "the *main* [italics added] purpose of this [charter school] reform strategy rests in its potential to foster marketplace dynamics . . . by increasing and diversifying the 'supply side' of the school reform equation" (Educational Excellence Network, 1995, p. 2).

Nurturing autonomy for providers requires two types of actions, according to charter school reviewers. To begin with, the monopoly over provision enjoyed by local school boards needs to be dismantled (Kolderie, 1992); the state needs to "withdraw from local school boards their exclusive right to create and run schools" (Northeast and Islands Regional Educational Laboratory, 1999, p. 3). Then, provisions must be made to allow alternative suppliers to sponsor schools (Kolderie, 1992; Sautter, 1993), to "allow entities other than traditional school districts to offer something which is considered 'public education'" (Rofes, 1998b, p. 3).

Nourishing supply side autonomy, in turn, is expected to provide "entrepreneurial opportunities" (Nathan, 1996a, p. 1) for an assortment of providers with an array of motives (Arsen, Plank, & Sykes, n.d.). According to the logic of charters, "a variety of suppliers of education will enter the market and offer . . . a varied set of educational services" (Solmon, Block, & Gifford, 1999, p. 2), "increasing the supply of schools" (Wohlstetter, Wenning, & Briggs, 1995, p. 352) and thus "creating a greater variety of schools from which parents can choose" (McCabe & Vinzant, 1999, p. 363). The market dynamic on the supply side of the autonomy landscape is designed to work with the choice dynamic on the demand side of the landscape to create an educational system "where parents are at liberty to select schools they feel are best suited to their children's needs" (Berman, Nelson, Ericson, Perry, & Silverman, 1998, p. 47). In short, the logic of charters asserts that "there will be different types of schools to meet the different tastes and needs of 'consumers' of education" (Solmon et al., 1999, p. 2).[1]

Choice for Consumers

Under charter school legislation, "the school's relationship with its external environment is significantly altered" (Loveless & Jasin, 1998, p. 14), especially relationships with parents. Charter schools are "schools of choice" (Finn, Manno, & Vanourek, 2000, p. 15) for families. A "consumer model of parental involvement in education" (Public Agenda, 1999, p. 25) gains center stage as parents, not government officials, determine where children attend school (Lane, n.d.; Public Agenda, 1999): "Charter schools are intended to be schools of choice where parents are at liberty to select schools they feel are best suited to their children's needs" (Berman et al., 1998, p. 47) and where "they have the ability to remove their children from the school if they are not satisfied with it for any reason" (Bulkley, 1998, p. 42).[2]

While it is important to highlight the structure of choice, "the freedom of parents and students—the education consumers—to choose" (Wohlstetter & Griffin, 1997a, p. 4), and to underscore the dynamics of choice—the fact noted above that such freedom promotes matches between schools and parents (Page & Levine, 1996; Windler, 1996)—perhaps even more critical to the charter school reform movement is the ideology of choice that buttresses demand side logic (Perry, 1998). In charter schools, choice is infused into a market infrastructure that acknowledges parents and students as consumers and clients, a point underscored by Caudell (1997c) when he notes that "perhaps the *biggest shift* in the charter schools concept is the idea that students and their parents are 'consumers' or 'customers'" (p. 1). Charters "regard students and parents, not regulators and bureaucratic overseers, as [their] primary customers" (Hill, Pierce, & Guthrie, 1997, p. 52). As discussed in Chapter 4, in these "consumer-oriented organizations" (Little Hoover Commission, 1996, p. 36), with "the realization that customers are the primary stakeholders" (Manno, Finn, Bierlein, & Vanourek, 1997b, p. 10), there is a new center of gravity in the "education-customer relationship" (Loveless & Jasin, 1998, p. 15) and a shift in authority "from producer to consumer, from experts to the laity" (Manno et al., 1997b, p. 10).

Organizational Autonomy for Schools

For choice to weave its magic, charter school analysts conclude, autonomy must be extended to the school, as well as to suppliers and customers. In short, "school-level autonomy is a necessary . . . condition for improved educational practice" (Bulkley, 1998, p. 29). For many in the charter school movement, "organizational autonomy . . . is what allows charter schools to work" (Educational Excellence Network, 1995, p. 5); "autonomy from the rules and regulations is the key to enabling schools to reflect the wisdom of the educators who work in them and the particular needs of the parents and students who patronize them" (UCLA, n.d., p. 28). The other pieces of the charter school model are likely to lay dormant absent nourishment from this organizational autonomy (Traub, 1999).[3]

Consistent with the shifting political dynamics reviewed in the last chapter, charters set out to strengthen schooling, not by directly attacking the conditions of teaching and learning but by "altering the governance structure within which schools operate" (Bulkley, 1998, p. 3) and the ways in which they are administered (Izu et al., 1998; Traub, 1999) and organized (Loveless & Jasin, 1998; Rofes, 1998a,b). Arsen and his colleagues (n.d.) conclude that charters "represent an experiment in governance in which parents and local communities are granted considerable control over public schools of their own making" (p. 57). They are "publicly funded schools that are more or less self-governing" (Educational Excellence Network, 1995, p. 1). They also "represent a different way of organizing schools into school systems. They support the notion that educational innovations develop best from decentralized, bottom-up sources" (Loveless & Jasin, 1998, p. 14).

Charter school scholars posit that it is organizational autonomy that allows charter schools to distinguish themselves from regular public schools (Garcia & Garcia, 1996; Sarason, 1998). The chain of reasoning for autonomy is nearly identical with the web of logic for the charter concept in general. Autonomy, it is hypothesized, leads to empowered professionals and parents, and such empowerment produces stronger commitment and deeper ownership at the school level (Center for Education Reform, n.d.d; UCLA, n.d.). Committed adults, in turn, respond by creating institutions that are more responsive to the needs and interests of families (Murphy & Beck, 1995; Weiss, 1997). In so doing, they become more innovative (Garn, 1998) and "more efficient in terms of resource allocation and utilization" (Wohlstetter, Wenning, & Briggs, 1995, p. 349). Improved educational practices follow (Bulkley, 1998). In the end, the logic suggests, parents and students will be better served, schools will be improved, and student performance will be enhanced (Izu et al., 1998; UCLA, n.d.).

A central dimension of organizational autonomy in the charter movement is that it attends to "both the internal operations of the organization and its external relations" (Wohlstetter et al., 1995, p. 339), that it addresses both decentralization and deregulation issues (Bulkley, 1998). Manno and colleagues remark: "This means deregulating the schools, freeing them from bureaucratic control and micromanagement. It [also] means allowing individual schools, educators, and parents wide latitude and autonomy in decision-making" (Manno et al., 1997b, p. 11).

As we reported in Chapter 3, deregulation is largely a matter of "regulatory flexibility" (Izu et al., 1998, p. 3), of "freedom from state and district laws, rules, and regulations" (Educational Excellence Network, 1995, p. 5), including union contracts (Weiss, 1997). It includes the extent to which the school has legal and fiscal independence. It also encompasses the extent to which existing laws and regulations are rolled back. Finally, it incorporates a measure of ease by which regulations remaining in place can be circumvented. Decentralization, however, provides autonomy by explicitly placing decision-making power historically housed at higher levels of government in the hands of lay citizens and professionals at the local level (Budde, 1996). Together, deregulation and decentralization ensure that each charter school is a "self-governing community" (Finn, Manno, & Vanourek, 2000, p. 72); "they flip the structure from rule-bound hierarchy to decentralized flexibility by allowing individual schools to shape their own destinies" (p. 70). Equally important, in combination, they have the ability, analysts aver, to reanimate the school—to help change the climate at the school from compliance with rules and regulations to a focus on opportunities for improvement (Bierlein & Mulholland, 1993; Bulkley, 1998).

Unlike earlier reforms, such as school-based management and shared decision making that expected organizational autonomy alone to muscle school improvement, in the charter school movement, decentralization and deregulation are yoked tightly to accountability. (Little Hoover Commission, 1996). In the earlier reforms, the logic held that school improvement would follow "simply by shifting more control and autonomy to the school level" (Bulkley, 1998, p. 27). In the charter movement, however, there is a quite explicit "swapping [of] rules and regulations for freedom *and results* [italics added]" (Manno et al., 1998b, p. 490)—an "autonomy for accountability bargain" (UCLA, n.d., p. 9) or "accountability in exchange for a grant of autonomy" (Hassel, 1999a, p. 159). We examine the topic of accountability in detail below. Our purpose here is simply to introduce the fact that autonomy and accountability in the charter school literature are thoroughly intertwined, that "freedom in return for results is the basic charter bargain" (Finn, Manno, & Vanourek, 2000, p. 242).

Before leaving this examination of organizational autonomy, two points merit attention. First, and hardly surprising given our discussion in Chapter

4, degrees of freedom enjoyed by charter schools vary depending on state and local contexts (Wohlstetter, Wenning, & Briggs, 1995). Differing amounts of autonomy are the result of conditions such as state statutes, "the orientation of those with authority to regulate charter schools" (Hassel, 1999a, p. 98), district policies and regulations, language in charter contracts, and so forth.

Second, autonomy extends to an array of areas at the site level. Key zones of activity in which organizational autonomy unfolds include the following: (a) mission—setting the vision and establishing school goals and objectives; (b) organizational structure—determining the administrative and governance arrangements in schools as well as operational structures (e.g., the length of the school day and year, relationships with employee work groups); (c) finance—establishing budgets, placing amounts in budget lines, and moving funds among accounts; (d) pedagogy—employing instructional approaches (e.g., direct instruction) and setting professional development goals; (e) staffing—determining the preferred mix of professionals and the background needed for employment and then hiring, evaluating, and rewarding or removing administrators and teachers; and (f) curriculum—crafting curricular frameworks, setting standards, choosing materials, and selecting assessment systems (Murphy & Beck, 1995).

Competition

The main reason for increasing autonomy for suppliers and consumers is to introduce the market concept into the educational industry, "to create a more market-driven educational system" (Bierlein & Bateman, 1995, p. 49). And it is this "orthodox economic theory of markets" (Buchanan & Tullock, 1962, p. 17), with its "market-based assumptions" (Loveless & Jasin, 1998, p. 14) about monopolistic behavior and the power of competition, that provides the second building block of the charter school movement (Bulkley, 1998; Little Hoover Commission, 1996). Indeed, it is safe to say that competition is the "nuclear centre" (Hardin, 1989, p. 11) of the entire marketization phenomenon that we laid out in Chapter 4, as well as "the core value of charter schools" (Hill, Pierce, & Guthrie, 1997, p. 116) in particular. In charters, "the primary 'dynamic' is competitive pressure placed on conventional schools" (Hassel, 1997, p. 7).

The Negative Consequences of Monopolies

To begin with, market theory provides a broadside on public sector services that underscores the monopolistic nature of these activities. Specifically, the theory of markets holds that "the underlying structural problem of government monopoly . . . is the dominant factor responsible for malperformance of government services" (Savas, 1987, p. 251); "the monopolistic nature of local-service delivery is the greatest impediment of government effectiveness" (Bailey, 1991, p. 233). Reviewers maintain that public monopolies "induce inefficiencies" (Hilke, 1992, p. 134) and "result in the provision of goods and services substantially lower in quality and higher in cost than those provided in the presence of competition" (Wilson, 1990, p. 65). As a monopoly, it is asserted, "schools continue to exist regardless of educational outcomes" (Garn, 1998, p. 49). As such, they can take students and resources for granted (Manno, Finn, Bierlein, & Vanourek, 1997a; Nathan, 1996a). The conse-quence, critics aver, is that education is "wasteful, overregulated, unresponsive to captive clients, and shockingly inefficient" (Tyack, 1992, p. 14).

According to market theory, these conditions occur because government bureaucracies experience few of the pressures produced by competition, espe-cially those providing incentives (Gifford, Ogle, & Solmon, 1998; Hill, Pierce, & Guthrie, 1997) for organizations to assess and improve the way they conduct business or for individuals to evaluate and revise the way they acquire information with which to make changes (Tullock, 1988; 1994a; 1994b). Most troublesome, according to the theorists who chart this territory, is the fact that "a monopolistic system . . . has no incentive to change because it has no competition" (Bulkley, 1998, p. 25). Because of the absence of competition and incentives—the dual engines of markets—public organizations "tend to absorb resources on internal preference scales" (Bailey, 1987, p. 141). This, so our public choice colleagues tell us, fosters "a redirection of production factors towards political rather than economic ends" (Pirie, 1988, p. 5) as well as the evolution of a producer-oriented system "serving the values and meet-ing the needs of those who direct it and work within it" (p. 7).

> For this reason, no matter how noble the intentions of public employees, no matter how skilled or energetic their efforts, they usually find themselves unable to transcend their bureaucratic restraints to achieve policy goals in a timely, cost-effective manner. (Fitzgerald, 1988, p. 18)

What this means is that "the internal organization is subject to subversion by the bureaucratic process" (Hirsch, 1991, p. 60). The bottom-line effect, ac-cording to Tullock (1988), is that "the government is apt to impose social costs rather than to eliminate them" (p. 93).

The Benefits of Competition

The logical conclusion of this line of reasoning is that markets are to be pre-ferred to government activity, "that competitive markets are more effective than bureaucracies" (UCLA, n.d., p. 10). Competition produces "incentives for improvements in performance" (Hilke, 1992, p. 20) and "tends to motivate organizations to lower prices and sometimes to improve quality" (Brown, 1991, p. 273). Thus, output that can "be described as desirable from the standpoint of almost everyone's preference function" (Tullock, 1994b, p. 66) results, and overall economic efficiency is enhanced. Competition, it is argued, "will force all schools to improve because meeting consumer demand and improving educational quality are synonymous" (Bulkley, 1998, p. 26).

Building from the above analysis, we see that by championing autonomy, the charter school movement breaks the captive market and undermines the monopoly enjoyed by the existing educational system (Nathan, 1996a; Pipho, 1997). Charters introduce competition into the educational industry (Garcia & Garcia, 1996; Goenner, 1996) and "stimulate competition between public charters and traditional schools" (Sautter, 1993, p. 9). Accompanying competition, analysts claim, are rewards and consequences (RPP International, & University of Minnesota, 1997)—"powerful incentives to produce results . . . and grave consequences if they [schools] fail to do so" (Finn, Manno, & Vanourek, 2000, p. 265). Basically, "By creating competitive markets within a public system, contract [charter] schools attempt to change the incentives that drive the participants within public education" (Hill, Pierce, & Guthrie, 1997, p. 62).

Competition and incentives, market theorists assert, provide a powerful "stimulus for reform" (Rosenblum Brigham Associates, 1998, p. 25) that "will trigger responses from unresponsive and bureaucratized school districts" (Rofes, 1998a, p. 111). The calculus of inducement is fairly straightforward. A charter system "creates pressures for performance in the same way that it encourages initiative and responsibility—through competition" (Hill, Pierce, & Guthrie, 1997, p. 74). Schools that fail to meet customer demand will lose students (Little Hoover Commission, 1996). Thus the metric of "improve or perish" (Molnar, 1996, p. 5) is firmly embedded in the charter school philosophy.

> Charter schools are schools of choice; they do not have a captive population. Thus, if district and charter schools must compete for students, market forces will ensure that schools with improved student outcomes will retain students, proponents believe. Conversely, schools that fail to improve outcomes will close when enrollment declines. (Garn, 1998, p. 49)

> Competition will winnow out the weak and reward the successful schools. As a result, test scores will rise, and the United States may once again become competitive economically. (Tyack, 1992, p. 14)

The response of the educational system is also cast in "classically free market" terms (Public Agenda, 1999, p. 19). School staffs will change to attract students (Hill, Pierce, & Guthrie, 1997): "School administrators will respond like business owners who suddenly start losing money to the competition across the street—they will fight to improve their products and services to hold on to their customers and their customers' money" (Public Agenda, 1999, p. 19). As we narrate more fully in the last half of this chapter, a host of "desirable goals" (Bulkley, 1998, p. 228) is then expected to materialize: entrepreneurial spirit (Nathan, 1996a); more responsive (Gifford, Ogle, & Solmon, 1998), more efficient (Powers & Cookson, 1999), and more innovative schools (Collins, 1999); enhanced accountability (Nathan, 1996a); increased productivity (Solmon, Block, & Gifford, 1999), including better quality of services (Educational Excellence Network, 1995); and a significantly improved education system (Rofes, 1998a, b).[4]

Accountability

Accountability is the final piece of the reform engine powering the charter school movement, or stated alternatively, "charters are all about accountability" (Kolderie, n.d., p. 1). According to Finn and his colleagues (2000), "some view accountability as the third rail of the charter school movement, others as the holy grail" (p. 127). For still others, "accountability is the defining element of charter schools" (Lane, n.d., p. 20). For nearly everyone in the movement, "accountability lies at the heart of all charter schools" (Lane, 1998, p. 4); it is "a basic tenet of the charter idea" (Mulholland, 1999, p. 2).

As detailed below, accountability in the charter movement is a three-pronged concept—one that features responsibility to the government through the charter contract, to parents through direct democracy and the market, and to the community through voluntary association (Kolderie, 1992). "Charter accountability can be thought of as a system of checks and balances that maintains public oversight and authority [while] maximiz[ing] the virtues of market forces" (Finn, Manno, & Vanourek, 2000, p. 139).

A Recasting

To begin with, charters infuse considerable new accountability into the educational system (Lane, n.d.). They strive to create "schools that are more accountable than regular public schools" (American Federation of Teachers, 1996, p. 53). In a real sense, they try to make accountability meaningful (Nathan, 1996a). At the same time, they dramatically overhaul the meaning of accountability in education. With regard to content, they shift the center of gravity from adherence to procedures and processes; that is, from "rule-based accountability" (UCLA, n.d., p. 9) to a focus on goal achievement. More specifically, the new focus is on "outcome or performance-based accountability" (p. 10), on "educational results rather than processes or inputs" (McGree,

1995a, p. 2). Manno and colleagues note that "charter schools focus on what children learn and how well they learn it—not on compliance with rules and procedures" (Manno et al., 1997b, p. 10). Regarding method, charters recenter accountability from a nearly exclusive reliance on political activity—from a system in which "accountability is measured through democratic processes" (Garcia & Garcia, 1996, p. 34)—toward heavy emphasis on market or consumer dynamics. And within the political sphere, they recast government from representative democracy to direct citizen control. Thus, with regard to method, charters offer a "kind of direct accountability to public and parents that too often eludes government-run public schools" (Caudell, 1997c, p. 1); "a shift in emphasis from the traditional arbiters of accountability, district and state officials, to a greater focus on accountability to parents" (Bulkley, 1998, p. 146).

Multiple Forms

As noted above, accountability in charters is a shared responsibility (Archer, 2000; Bierlein & Bateman, 1995); it "operates at several levels" (Finn, Manno, & Vanourek, 2000, p. 267). As schools of choice, "they are held to the accountability of consumer demand. And because they are chartered schools, they are legally accountable for their academic results, and their fiscal and legal integrity" (Center for Education Reform, n.d.e, p. 1). Finally, because they are voluntary associations, they are held accountable to the communities that create them: "In exchange for the freedom to be different, they agree to be judged by both the market and by the public agencies monitoring the achievement of their students" (Hassel, 1999a, p. 104).

In the political realm, through contracts, charter schools are responsible to their sponsoring agency for developing goals that are "sound and rigorous" (Center for Educational Reform, n.d.d, p. 5) and that "can be objectively answered" (p. 5), and for meeting the terms of the charter (Nathan, 1996a). As Szabo and Gerber (1996) have concluded, "The promise of accountability is at the heart of the political support for granting a 'charter' as a kind of contract between the proposed school and the state" (p. 139). And generally at the center of the contract is an accountability system that contains "performance standards, assessment strategies, and consequences based on performance" (Wohlstetter & Griffin, 1997a, p. 22). In the political domain, charters trade regulations for results; that is:

> Charter theory prescribes that we be clear, specific, and fairly uniform about ends while allowing wide diversity in the means by which those ends are achieved. Stated differently, the inputs and processes of education can vary greatly from school to school so long as the results are satisfactory. (Manno, Finn, Bierlein, & Vanourek, 1997a, p. 2)

The *quid pro quo* for enhanced freedom is that charters are held accountable for meeting the conditions of their charter (U.S. General Accounting Office, 1998b). In the political realm, securing or renewing a charter depends on documented performance (Manno et al., 1997b).

In the realm of the market, each charter school is "also accountable to its customers via the marketplace: dissatisfied customers can vote with their feet and flee" (Manno et al., 1997a, p. 9). On this piece of the accountability landscape, "parents are the primary accountability mechanism" (Garn, 1998, p. 49), and "the discipline of the market is a primary instrument of accountability" (Arsen et al., n.d., p. 57): "charter schools are totally market-dependent and consumer-driven. This is a very different kind of accountability for public schools" (Windler, 1996, p. 68). Parents and students are empowered to select the school they believe will best serve their needs. As described in the earlier discussion on autonomy, "Charters are schools of choice: families must elect to enroll their children" (Center for Education Reform, n.d.d, p. 5), and "if a school fails to deliver on its promises, parents can move their children to another school along with the money supporting them" (Hill, Pierce, & Guthrie, 1997, p. 66).

Finally, regarding voluntary association, charters are held accountable by community forces—in particular by adherence to the norms of the school community. Economists have long recognized voluntary association as one method, in addition to governments and markets, of providing goods and services (Pirie, 1988; Savas, 1982, 1987). There is a good deal of this community muscle behind the formation and growth of the charter school movement (Finn, Manno, & Vanourek, 2000). It forms the final element in the accountability portfolio, what Bulkley has labeled "community accountability" (1998, p. 186).

THE REFORM DYNAMICS

Change is the major promise of charter schools. (Little Hoover Commission, 1996, pp. 3–4)

The underlying assumption was that the possibility for meaningful reform would be enhanced. (Wohlstetter, Wenning, & Briggs, 1995, p. 343)

The construction of charter schools . . . reflects not one, but two theories of change. One is at the level of charter schools, while the other is at the level of the system of public education, that are separate but simultaneous and mutually reinforcing.

The first theory involves the charter schools themselves, which charter advocates expect to be higher quality than traditional public schools. The second theory involves the entire system of public education, where charter schools [are] expected to spur system-wide reform. (Bulkley, 1998, p. 96)

While the general literature tends to spotlight stories of individual charter schools, it is important to remember that there are two dynamics to this reform, one that engages change efforts at the individual school level and one that fuels improvement at the system level (Sautter, 1993). We explore both dimensions of charters in this section.

Strengthening the Individual School

On one level, charters are about crafting individual centers of excellence. From this vantage point, the charter movement is primarily about creating local schools that work well for students and their parents. The benefits that are expected to follow to families at the school level are mediated by two key variables—community and innovation.

Community

Whether one examines the charter phenomenon with a market lens or with a social-political lens, charter schools succeed by permitting providers to carve out "niche markets" (Arsen, Plank, & Sykes, n.d., p. 74) and by allowing parents to establish or select "clearly defined school communities" (p. 61). As Finn and his colleagues (2000) observe, "Charter schools build . . . communities. They are communities unto themselves" (p. 265).

Analyzing a charter community exposes a handful of key elements that combine to make this reform strategy such a powerful tool for strengthening schools. Underlying nearly all of these elements is the issue of size, specifically the small nature of charters (Collins, 1999; Rofes, 1995). Indeed, small size, in addition to being "a defining element" (Berman et al., 1998, p. 87) of charters, may be, according to the authors of this 1998 national evaluation of charters, "the most important aspect of the charter movement" (p. 45). Small size appears to be so essential because it promotes the creation of powerful dynamics associated with school effectiveness. One of these forces is localism, or local control. Small size, analysts often assert, nurtures local autonomy and "impart[s] a sense of control to people," both parents (Bulkley, 1998; McGree, 1995a) and school-level educators (Wohlstetter & Griffin, 1997a).

Small size also facilitates another core element of community, the development in each school of a "central focus" (Rosenblum Brigham Associates,

1998, p. 6) or a "unifying vision" (Finn, Manno, & Vanourek, 2000, p. 265). It is this "mission driven" (p. 69) aspect of charters that allows these schools "to give themselves a distinctive identity" (Rofes, 1995, p. 31) and to differentiate [their] products from other schools" (Hill, Pierce, & Guthrie, 1997, p. 80). Or as Wells, Lopez, and their colleagues (1999) put it, charters "provide an identity-building space for those who seek it" (p. 194).

This mission-driven infrastructure of charters is often portrayed in terms of shared values or the "bind[ing] of people together in a common spirit" (Rofes, 1995, p. 31). Because they are "privately" organized according to specific educational missions, charter schools broaden the opportunities for transmitting "particularistic values" (Smith, 1998, p. 57). And as Arsen, Plank, and Sykes (n.d.) argue, "The opportunity to focus the attention of students and staff on a common vision, and to call on the shared values of a specific community, is a potentially powerful resource for learning" (p. 71).

Common mission and shared values in turn promote the growth of two other key components of community, one focused on the work of charters and the other dealing with the personal aspects of community. The former includes "distinctive" (Hill, Pierce, & Guthrie, 1997, p. 65) and "more appropriate educational programs" (Rofes, 1995, p. 5), greater "coherence within the school and an integration of many practices toward a single objective" (Rosenblum Brigham Associates, 1998, p. 6), and heightened transparency, including stronger and much more visible linkages between schools and parents (Bulkley, 1998). The human dimension of charters encompasses "a high degree of personal intimacy, social cohesion" (Finn, Manno, & Vanourek, 2000, p. 227), and commitment (McGree, 1995b; Tyack, 1992); "increase[d] parental involvement" (Buechler, 1996, p. 5) in and "oversight of schools" (Rofes, 1995, p. 51); and a heightened expression of "civil society" (Finn, Manno, & Vanourek, 2000, p. 222). It is best to think of these two ingredients of charters as shared work and personalization and democratization, respectively.[5]

Innovation

If community forms the needed culture for charter school success, innovation is the central calculus. That is, "the idea of innovation is the essential intermediate step between passing [a] charter school law and improving student learning" (Bulkley, 1998, p. 185). The starting point in this strategic argument is that "freed from micro-management" (Center for Education Reform, n.d.d, p. 1), autonomy extended to charters "free[s] these schools to be more innovative" (UCLA Charter School Study, n.d., p. 10) and provides "a chance for innovation to flourish" (American Federation of Teachers, n.d., p. 7; see also Garn, 1998). The next step in the argument holds that "due in large part to the need to compete for students" (Bulkley, 1998, p. 101)—by "holding them [charter schools] accountable for results and customer satisfaction" (Hassel, 1999a, p. 1)—charter schools will "encourage more innovative educational practices" (Wohlstetter, Wenning, & Briggs, 1995, p. 332) and "will bring educational innovations" (Collins, 1999, p. 1) to the forefront of the educational enterprise.[6]

Anticipated results from this "conscious fostering of diversity" (Hill, Pierce, & Guthrie, 1997, p. 80) are: the development of "alternative[s] to the bureaucratic and regulated public school system and more variation in the delivery of educational services" (Wells, Lopez, et al., 1999, p. 174); the creation of "alternative and diverse educational programs" (The Evaluation Center, 1998, p. 2) and of "new educational models and options" (Sautter, 1993, p. 6); the expansion of "educational options for students, parents, and teachers" (Bierlein & Mulholland, 1993, p. 7); and the "formation of promising new educational options for children" (Hassel, 1999a, p. 1). In short, charters become "seedbeds of policy and educational innovation" (Finn, Manno, & Vanourek, 2000, p. 70).

The final piece of the logic connects these diverse educational programs, through the objective of "meet[ing] the needs of consumers, namely students and parents" (Wohlstetter, Wenning, & Briggs, 1995, p. 350), to "the ultimate goal of improving student academic achievement" (The Evaluation Center, 1998, p. 21), to "improved school quality" (Bulkley, 1998, p. 101), and to "better, more superior outcomes" (Sarason, 1998, p. 2). We address the proposition linking innovation and school quality in some detail in Chapter 6 when we explore the expected benefits of charters.

Focusing specifically on the innovation activity, the literature suggests that changes associated with charters can be parsed into two related, but somewhat distinct, categories—macrolevel changes and shifts in instructional patterns. At the macro or whole-school level, charters are "expected to allow for a greater variety of public schools" (Bulkley, 1998, p. 96). Public schools with charters "will inevitably come to define different goals and pursue different approaches" (Hill, Pierce, & Guthrie, 1997, p. 81). The focus here is on expanding "the range of public schools" (p. 73), creating "diverse institutions" (Manno, Finn, Bierlein, & Vanourek, 1998b, p. 497), or forging "more options" (Collins, 1999, p. 3) and "new models of schooling" (UCLA Charter School Study, n.d., p. 4), that is, promoting alternatives (Lane, 1998; Nappi, 1999) and creating "a more diverse *system* [italics added] of education" (Bulkley, 1998, p. 145) that provides parents with real options in selecting "schools that more closely match their values and preferences" (Arsen, Plank, & Sykes, n.d., p. 77).

While macrolevel innovation focuses on "increas[ing] the range of options" (McKinney, 1996, p. 23), microlevel innovation deals with translating autonomy and empowerment (Izu et al., 1998; Poland, 1996) into "innovative teaching and learning strategies" (Lane, n.d., p. 12). That is, "charter schools not only serve the function of increasing consumer choice in education, but also aim to implement effective teaching and learning practices in classrooms" (Wohlstetter & Griffin, 1997a, p. 3). Charters, advocates contend, "foster innovation through experimentation with a variety of educational approaches" (McKinney, 1996, p. 23). They can act as "laboratories where new ideas are tested, new methods pioneered" (American Federation of Teachers, n.d., p. 53). In so doing, they are expected to create "innovative learning opportunities" (Weiss, 1994, p. 18); "'break-the-mold' curricular and instructional programs" (Izu et al., 1998, p. 31) and assessment strategies (Buechler, 1996); and "innovative" (Wohlstetter, Wenning, & Briggs, 1995, p. 336), "different" (Sautter, 1993, p. 10), and "better teaching and learning strategies" (Lane, 1998, p. 5).

Not surprisingly, claims by proponents about the innovative nature of charter schools are often challenged. In particular, analysts "suggest that little of what is happening in charter schools cannot also be found in regular schools" (Manno et al., 1998b, p. 493). This conclusion, critics maintain, holds at both the macro level, where they see charters doing little more than copying rather well-known reform models (e.g., Core Knowledge, effective schools); and at the micro level, where they discern fairly conventional patterns of instruction, curriculum, and assessment.

Part of the critique of the innovation proposition centers on the claim by charter advocates that there is a lack of innovation in the regular public school system. Astute reviewers are quick to illuminate the rather "abundant innovation" (Buechler, 1996, p. 5) unfolding in schools and the widespread "cloning [that] has taken place in the public school system" (Anderson, 1997, p. 2). Another pillar of the critical review is built from a close analysis of the legislation and embedded logic supporting charters (Budde, 1996). After conducting just such an analysis, Rofes (1995) concluded that charter schools' form of governance and attenuated regulations do not implicitly require the schools to carry any more responsibility to innovation in curricula, classroom organization, or teaching methods than noncharter schools (p. 38).

Still another strand[7] of the innovation critique focuses on the definition of innovation and the appropriate criteria to assess change (Arsen, Plank, & Sykes, n.d.). As Rofes (1995) has discovered in his extensive work on charters: "The connection between charter schools and innovation . . . is challenging [because] this linkage is accompanied by neither a definition of 'innovation,' nor explicit detailing of the ways in which charter schools will be innovative" (p. 8).

The issue of defining innovation was addressed in the recently completed national examination of charter schools. According to the authors of that study, "a working definition of 'innovation' is a charter school practice that is distinctly different from the practices of other public schools in the charter school's surrounding district(s) or region" (Berman et al., 1998, p. 6). This definition provides considerable comfort to charter advocates. The standard of "charter schools . . . offering students a more innovative and diverse set of curricular options" (McGree, 1995a, p. 8) is dismantled. The criteria for defining innovation are recast. What is critical are not shifts from traditional and extant production practices but changes from what is afoot in the schools in one's own area. Context becomes a key variable in the innovation algorithm (Manno et al., 1997a, 1997b): "School innovation is also situational and relative to the context" (Finn, Manno, & Vanourek, 2000, p. 91).

Employing this definition, schools that replicate well-known, whole-school reform designs (e.g., Success for All) or feature conventional instructional strategies (e.g., direct instruction) can lay claim to the mantle of innovation, for as Manno and his colleagues (1997b) assert, "In their contexts, virtually all charter schools are truly innovative" (p. 5): "The job of charter schools is to satisfy their customers, not to demonstrate to outside analysts that they have devised something never before observed in this galaxy" (Finn, Manno, & Vanourek, 2000, p. 91). Providing this situational ground for innovation takes investigators a fair distance from the textbook definition of innovation as the introduction or creation of something new. And while it allows for considerably more charter activity to be labeled as innovative than would otherwise be the case, schools that adopt practices that are already available in neighboring schools are left outside the community of innovators.

Reforming the Educational System

The Logic of System-Wide Change

Many of the analysts who are closest to the charter movement, especially advocates, assert that charters are primarily about "effecting a systemwide transformation" (Corwin, Carlos, Lagomarsino, & Scott, 1996, p. 6); that is, about "large scale school reform and the possibility for systemwide change" (Lane, n.d., p. 7). Three of the best-known charter proponents make this point as follows:

> The movement for charter schools is not really about the charter schools themselves. It is about systemic change—about the state creating the dynamics that will make the system a self-improving system. (Nathan, 1996a, p. 203)

> The purpose of charter schools is to create dynamics that will cause the mainline district system to change and to improve. The charter

schools, helpful as they may be to the students who enroll in them, are instrumental. (Kolderie, n.d., p. 3)

The charter phenomenon reaches well beyond individual schools and the people they touch directly. It also raises a host of big-picture questions, figures in tough political struggles, alters the practices of entire school districts, bolsters communities, and leaves tracks on American education as a whole. (Finn, Manno, & Vanourek, 2000, p. 151)

According to this line of reasoning, charters act as "agents of change for other schools" (Fulford, Raack, & Sunderman, 1997, p. 1), a "catalyst for improvement throughout the entire public education system" (McGree, 1995b, p. 2), a "spur [for] much needed change throughout the public system" (UCLA Charter School Study, n.d., p. 3), the "doorway to institutional change" (Lieber, 1997, p. 15), "the impetus for . . . a radical restructuring of the public education system" (Lane, n.d., p. 8), a "trigger [for] overall improvement in the district schools" (Rofes, 1998b, p. 70), a "bridge to total reorganizational and cultural change" (Lieber, 1997, p. 16), "a stimulus for enriching and broadening the entire ecosystem" (Finn, Manno, & Vanourek, 2000, p. 73) of education, and as "'shining lights' that will illuminate the future of education" (Teske, Schneider, Buckley, & Clark, 2000, p. 11). In short, in addition to improving the quality of selected institutions, charters are expected to exercise significant leverage on the system of public schooling throughout the nation.

Pathways to Change

System-wide change, it is suggested by most reviewers, is powered in two ways (Buechler, 1996; Little Hoover Commission, 1996; Teske et al., 2000): "by introducing competition into the educational marketplace" (McGree, 1995a, p. 11) and by promoting "imitation of successful practice" (Arsen, Plank, & Sykes, n.d., p. 47) by "creating competition for students that might force existing public schools to become more innovative and flexible [and] by providing examples of innovative instructional practices" (Hill, Pierce, & Guthrie, 1997, p. 118). The competition force is often subdivided into two distinct strategies, replacement and reform. Under the former strategy, competition leads to the replacement of a nonresponsive system of conventional schooling with a new system of charter schools. Under the reform strategy, competition causes the lumbering bureaucratic monopoly known as public education to reinvent itself as a customer-friendly industry (Solmon, Block, & Gifford, 1999).

The Lighthouse Effect. To begin with, some reviewers hold that given some of their defining elements (e.g., freedom from constraints, clarity of mission), it is likely that charters will operate as "'laboratories' for change and experimentation" (Teske et al., 2000, p. 2), serve as sources of "inspiration and energy" (Page & Levine, 1996, p. 29), and act as "laboratories for innovation" (Rosenblum Brigham Associates, 1998, p. 19) to "creat[e] new models of schooling" (UCLA Charter School Study, n.d., p. 3) and to develop best educational practices (Bulkley, 1998), especially to craft "innovations in school management" (Fulford, Raack, & Sunderman, 1997, p. 11) and "new teaching and learning strategies" (Sautter, 1993, p. 16). Ideas that are successful "can be 'exported' to existing schools for broader adoption" (Hassel, 1997, p. 8). Or, stated more proactively, "Other school leaders seeing the success of these charter schools would then copy the best practices, allowing for impact in the public system far beyond individual charter schools" (Bulkley, 1998, p. 181).

Reform. The transformation of the existing system of schooling through competition with charters is part of the same story line we have followed throughout this volume. By way of summary, the argument is that "charter school reform, by creating a competitive market, will force change in the entire public system" (UCLA Charter School Study, n.d., p. 4). Indeed, competition is seen as the "primary dynamic" (Hassel, 1999a, p. 6) or the "primary mechanism" (Bulkley, 1998, p. 151) for strengthening the existing system. Largely by influencing incentives (Caudell, 1997c) to hold onto existing students and resources (Arsen, Plank, & Sykes, n.d.; Budde, 1989)—or more precisely "by creating an economic threat" (Hill, Pierce, & Guthrie, 1997, p. 115)—"charter schools would force traditional public schools to compete by improving their offerings" (Bulkley, 1998, p. 102), including adopting ideas developed in charters themselves. Unpacking this reform design reveals that change occurs "not at the behest of policymakers but in order to compete" (Hassel, 1999a, p. 3).

Replacement. Staying with reform through competition, a "second scenario regarding the entrance of charter schools into the market" (Solmon, Block, & Gifford, 1999, p. 15) opens up "the possibilities of an alternative system of public education" (Berman et al., 1998, p. 9). According to this logic, charter schools are expected to "transform public education not by inducing regular schools to change or by generating good ideas but simply by replacing conventional public schools as the primary providers of public education" (Hassel, 1999, p. 7): "As more and more families choose charter schools, conventional district schools will serve a smaller and smaller fraction of the public school population" (Hassel, 1997, p. 192).

In discussing these pathways to change, Hassel (1997) contends:

> These three mechanisms differ from one another primarily in their assessments
> of conventional school districts' ability to change for the better. The laboratory
> thesis is the most optimistic, positing that the mere demonstration that some idea
> or another "works" will persuade many school districts to adopt the innovation.
> The replacement thesis is the least optimistic, reasoning that conventional dis-
> tricts will muddle along in their familiar fashion until they fade into oblivion.
> The competition [reform] thesis lies in between, hypothesizing that conventional
> districts can change for the better, but only with the introduction of a quasi-
> market for public education. (pp. 192–193)

Response Strategies

Clues about specific strategies that existing school systems might employ in
the face of new ideas and new incentives from charters are scattered throughout the literature. At the least aggressive end of the response continuum districts react with marketing rather than improvement efforts. Moving up the
continuum, the existing systems sometimes employ an incorporation strategy,
borrowing popular elements of neighboring charters (e.g., services for pre-
school children) for their own schools. A still more robust response occurs
when a district clones a charter school. For example, a number of districts
have responded to enrollment threats caused from "back to basic" charters by
establishing more traditional educational programs in neighborhood schools
or by creating back-to-basics magnet schools. The most aggressive reaction of
conventional schools is to reculture the way they do business by embracing
the underlying principles of charters (e.g., providing choice for parents, opening up delivery to a variety of providers).

Concerns about the Viability of Systemic Change via Charters

The ability of charters to power system-wide change, whether as laboratories
of innovation or cauldrons of competition, is not universally acknowledged.
Indeed, there is considerable skepticism about this proposition in the charter
school literature (Rofes, 1998a, b; Teske et al., 2000; UCLA Charter School
Study, n.d.). Reviewers are careful to show that "charter schools face imposing
obstacles that could bar them from the goal many policy-makers hold for
them: to achieve success that has an impact on traditional public school systems" (Medler, 1996, p. 27); basically, "that charter school programs will have
difficulty achieving the system-changing impact their proponents envision"
(Hassel, 1997, p. 209).

    Analysts are especially leery about the lighthouse hypothesis—the belief
that innovations from charters' experiments will be diffused readily to the

traditional system of schooling (Lane, 1998; Hassel, 1999a; Rosenblum Brigham Associates, 1998). Critics are quick to note that given at best the lack of linkages between the two types of schools and at worst open hostility from the conventional system toward charters (Fulford, Raack, & Sunderman, 1997; Weiss, 1997), there is little reason to be optimistic about the innovation proposition. Even under more favorable conditions, they maintain, "introducing innovations into public education which became a widespread and ongoing part of schooling is a tremendous challenge" (Rofes, 1998b, pp. 5–6). The strongest advocates for charters, in particular, are among the most vocal in emphasizing the limits of the "charter-as-test-kitchen" (Finn, Manno, & Vanourek, 2000, p. 214) approach to systemic reform.

Scholars have also demonstrated that existing districts, when confronted by best practices and/or competition, do not necessarily follow the rules of logic laid out by charter proponents (Teske et al., 2000). Solmon, Block, and Gifford (1999) and Hassel (1997) reveal that "districts have a wide variety of other possible responses to competition, none of which hold out hope of enhancing educational quality" (p. 220). For example, it is possible that charters might "function more like a pressure release valve for dissidents than as a fundamental structural change" (Finn, Manno, & Vanourek, 2000, p. 168), that "charters might, at best, be little more than escape valves that relieve pressure for genuine reform of the whole system" (Berman et al., 1998, p. 1) or be a new system of schooling that simply attends to clusters of students who have not been served effectively by the current system (Hassel, 1997). In either case, it might be that "the more involved and educated parents will be siphoned off to other schools and no change will occur for the great majority of students" (McCabe & Vinzant, 1999, p. 371).

Because the "effect of charter schools on the educational system will depend on how potent and how concentrated a threat they pose to traditional public schools" (Solmon, Block, & Gifford, 1999, p. 3), analysts caution that "there will be too few charters to have much of an impact on the public system as a whole" (Rothstein, 1998a, p. 12). Finn and his colleagues (2000) suggest that monopolies can be impacted when 10 to 20% of customers shift to alternative providers. To date, as we recorded in Chapter 2, charters are serving only about 1% of the student population. Medler (1996) also suggests that the small size of the average charter school "might diminish the school's impact on nearby school systems. The reason: Their capacity is too limited to make a dent in the public school enrollment" (p. 27).

In the introductory chapter, we discussed in considerable detail the importance of context in molding charter activity. Studies from a number of charter school scholars also reveal how significant context is in shaping the way regular schools respond to the threats inherent in these new institutions (Teske et al., 2000). For example, at the state level some governments provide funds for districts that are impacted negatively by charters. And districts are likely to "cushion individual schools from the financial impact of declining enrollments and shrinking market share" (Teske et al., 2000, p. 1). Since "the loss of funding is the linchpin needed to spur an aggressive response on the part of the district" (Rofes, 1998b, p. 112), such policies can substantially offset any competitive advantages provided by charters (Solmon, Block, & Gifford, 1999). At the local level, because of the growth of the student population in many areas, the seats left by students departing for charter schools are quickly filled (Teske et al., 2000). In some cases, the loss of students actually helps districts by obviating the need for new construction (Rofes, 1998b). Context—this time at the local level—again unhinges the links in the competitive chain of logic connecting charters with system-wide reform.

SUMMARY

In this chapter, we investigated the embedded logic that powers the charter school movement. We accomplished this task in two ways. First, we examined the assumptions behind the three major variables—autonomy, accountability, and competition—that collectively form the theory in action on which charters rest. Second, we illustrated the dynamics of charter school reform by illuminating the path between heightened autonomy, accountability, and competition and the expected benefits of charters, both at the individual school level and at the educational system level.

NOTES

1. The analysis of autonomy for providers offers insufficient attention to the topic of incentives, consistently overlooking the fact that the profit motive is the real inducement to attract new providers to a service area. The absence of profits considerably detracts from the theory of action supporting charters. In lieu of profits, almost all the incentives in the charter field are negative, the proposition that something will be taken away. While such an incentive structure might cause existing schools to reform, it is difficult to imagine how it will lure new providers into the game.

2. According to Lane (1998), claims that school choice will permit each parent and student to select the most appropriate school "tend to blur the issues and make overgeneralizations about how and why people choose and even their ability to choose. Research has demonstrated that not all parents choose alike. In fact, research on some choice initiatives has demonstrated that even when given the opportunity to choose, many low-income parents fail to make 'rational' choices" (p. 8). There is also "mounting evidence that however sincerely parents want the best for their children, their skills in evaluating schools repeatedly come up short" (Public Agenda, 1999, p. 25).

Finally, it is important to note that "within school" choice has been a central element of public education for most of the latter half of the 20th century (Powell, Farrar, & Cohen, 1985). There is almost no evidence that this choice has been associated with enhanced educational productivity. Indeed, the bulk of the research shows that it has had a deleterious influence on quality.

3. Hassel (1997) reminds us, however, "that independence is a double-edged sword, creating problems for charter schools as it creates opportunities" (p. 191). Autonomy also appears to hinder the spread of reform ideas from charter schools to the regular school system—or to other charter schools for that matter (American Federation of Teachers, n.d.).

Rofes (1995), in turn, observes that "at the heart of many conflicted educators' reluctance to endorse charter schools lies authentic concerns about [the] abrogation of state authority" (p. 25) that provides autonomy for charter schools: "Regulations from which some states' charter schools are freed . . . are not seen as meaningless bureaucratic rigmarole binding the hands of teachers and administrators, but as historically constituted representations of the public will regarding critical educational matters" (p. 25).

4. It is worth noting that the advantages of introducing competition into schools are not universally acknowledged—that "there are reasons to believe that the competition mechanism might not always work as the proponents of charter schools expect" (Hassel, 1999a, p. 135), or, as captured in a recent Public Agenda (1999) report: "There seem to be serious limits to the consumer model of parental involvement in education" (p. 25).

Some analysts, for example, believe that it is cooperation rather than competition that powers real school reform (Traub, 1999). Others argue that the embedded logic is simply not working, that charters are not forcing the changes predicted by market theory (UCLA Charter School Study, n.d.). A subset of this group points out that "districts have a whole array of possible responses to the introduction of competition. Many of these have little to do with improving the quality of public education; some, perversely, are likely to have the opposite effect" (Hassel, 1999a, p. 136). Still others assessing the competitive playing field see negative results, especially for children at risk (Molnar, 1996):

> Our findings suggest that this approach [competition] does not work in education. Instead, greater competition leads privileged schools to become more selective in their admissions and leaves less privileged schools with the students that choice schools did not want. (UCLA Charter School Study, n.d., p. 58)

In conclusion, "Whatever the outcome, it is important to keep in mind that the story will be far more complicated than a rational consumer analysis would suggest" (Public Agenda, 1999, p. 27). It is also important to note that there is a natural tendency for whatever competition is infused into the system to deteriorate. The mutual flow is away from competition and uncertainty toward cooperation and certainty (Murphy, 1996).

Finally, the claim that competition is a necessary element in the struggle to force districts to adopt new practices seems ill-founded. For decades school districts have been slavishly copying the programs of neighboring and/or like districts. Indeed, for much of the 20th century, when change was the calculus of success it was almost imperative that districts match innovations undertaken by similar types of systems.

5. As we discuss in Chapter 6, creating small, homogenous communities based on group identity, common values, and shared agenda is likely to have some negative implications for educational equity. At the micro level, "charters are sometimes faulted for dividing rather than uniting communities" (Finn, Manno, & Vanourek, 2000, p. 235). At a broader level, reviewers express concern that building small, local communities does "little or nothing to overcome larger social inequalities" (Wells, Lopez, et al., 1999, p. 194).

6. Innovation in charter schools can occur in any of the three areas of the organization—the learning and teaching function (the core technology), the management function (organization), and the governance function (the institutional level) (Arsen, Plank, & Sykes, n.d.; Sarason, 1998). While we focus on innovations in the first area in this section, it is important to note that "not all innovations are academic" (Finn, Manno, & Vanourek, 2000, p. 91). Indeed, as we have shown elsewhere in this volume, "change in organizational and institutional arrangements may well prove more significant" (p. 91) than changes in the core technology.

7. The final type of critique is anchored in an empirical analysis of innovation uncovered in charter schools to date. We explore this issue in detail in Chapter 8.

CHAPTER 6

Expected Benefits
and Possible Costs

The promise and appeal of this new educational delivery system is largely based on a popular set of beliefs and assumptions about the efficacy of charter schools. (McGree, 1995a, p. 2)

We contend that in the case of charter schools, questions about the potential gain to individuals in relation to the potential loss of collective values cannot and should not be ignored. (McCabe & Vinzant, 1999, p. 374)

Advocates for charters maintain that the benefits expected from greater reliance on the reform engine and reform dynamics outlined in Chapter 5 are quite extensive, ranging from improved quality to lower costs to enhanced equity. Skeptics, as described in Chapter 2, are quick to question these expected benefits—and even when acknowledging gains that may accrue, they couple such recognition with a thorough analysis of what they see to be the costs of charters. The American Federation of Teachers (n.d.) nicely laid out this contested narrative as follows:

Advocates of charter school reform assume that these schools will:

1. encourage innovation;
2. be more accountable and focus on results;
3. expand public school choices for all;
4. provide new and increased professional opportunities for teachers;
5. require little or no additional money to implement or sustain; and
6. act as a catalyst for improvement of the public system.

Foes of charter schools, not surprisingly, hold a different set of assumptions. They believe that charter schools will:

1. cream off the more affluent students and those with higher academic skills, leaving the public schools bereft of resources and with the responsibility of educating the high-risk, high-cost students;

2. be no more innovative than existing schools, which taken as a whole are not particularly innovative;
3. rely on cheap labor and exploit teachers and other personnel;
4. reduce resources available to public schools; and
5. be no more accountable, or even less accountable, than public schools. (p. 3)

We examine the issue below under the following headings: quality, efficiency, equity, and impact on employees.

QUALITY

The case is often heard that the market forces undergirding charters will enhance educational quality, or increase productivity. Or, as Solmon and his colleagues (1999) put it, "On average, quality in charters should exceed quality in traditional public schools over time" (p. 8). The "competition and entrepreneurship unleashed by 'uncompromised' market-driven choice plans will result in institutional changes in schooling that will ultimately enhance student achievement" (Powers & Cookson, 1999, p. 105), increase parent satisfaction (Fuller, Elmore, & Orfield, 1996), and produce "other positive results" (Wohlstetter & Griffin, 1997a, p. 1): "Innovation, competition, freedom from bureaucracy, accountability, choice—all of these are simply means to an end: improved student achievement" (Buechler, 1996, p. 35). An analysis of the expected benefits and costs of charters in the area of service quality is sketched out below.

Before proceeding, however, it is helpful to highlight the importance of the quality dimension as it applies to charter schools. Although quality of service delivery usually places behind efficiency as a rationale for the marketization of the public sector, as one moves into social services such as education, efforts to improve quality take on much greater significance (Brown, 1991). Thus, in some cases, "distributional and output quality concerns mute the importance of efficiency in production" (Pack, 1991, p. 296). In addition, the saliency of the quality dimension is heightened when attacks on the effectiveness of service delivery are paramount (Butler, 1991), as is the case in the charter school movement.

Possible Benefits

Basing their conclusions on the theoretical propositions we examined in earlier chapters, advocates assert that charters will produce high-quality educational programs (Center for Education, n.d.b, d; Hill, Pierce, & Guthrie, 1997). They claim that because of the dynamics of the marketplace, especially the infusion of incentives, and because many of the dynamics that contribute to substandard performance in the current system will cease to operate, properly implemented, charters offer real potential for enhancing student learning (Finn, Manno, & Vanourek, 2000). At the heart of the logic here is the proposition that because of the sensitivity of markets to their customers, "as opposed to the insensitivity of many publicly held operations to their customers, [markets] can ensure more dependable services" (Butler, 1991, p. 19). Schools are created then to fit the needs of families and kids—not "system planners, state and local regulations, or union contracts" (Finn, Manno, & Vanourek, 2000, p. 10)—"to meet the desires of parents, as opposed to the demands of bureaucrats" (UCLA Charter School Study, n.d., pp. 10–11). Quality is supposedly enhanced by the creation of a "less rigid" (Rofes, 1998b, p. 111), "more responsive system" (Goenner, 1996, p. 32)—responsiveness fostered through innovation (Bulkley, 1998), the development of an array of service options (Cheung, Murphy, & Nathan, 1998), and more direct attention to the varied needs of customers (Arsen, Plank, & Sykes, n.d.; McCabe & Vinzant, 1999).

> Market-driven theorists argue that typical public school systems have a tendency to rely on "one-size-fits all" approaches to meeting the needs of students; whereas, charter schools, in theory, offer parents and students approaches tailored to the needs of particular students. The assumption is that the added value of charter school reform lies not necessarily in developing innovative teaching and learning models but, rather, in the opportunity for educational programs to meet a consumer-driven demand not met elsewhere. (Izu et al., 1998, p. 31)

The effectiveness of service provision is also expected to improve because of the superior flexibility of markets. According to this line of analysis, because "the public sector is notoriously noninnovative and inflexible" (Pirie, 1985, p. 53), government "is slower to adopt new ideas, more hidebound in its accustomed ways, and less adaptable to changing circumstances" (Pirie, 1988, p. 28). As a consequence, quality, as measured in terms of output and customer satisfaction, leaves a good deal to be desired. Charters, conversely, heighten quality by taking advantage of the flexibility associated with markets. Particular aspects of such flexibility that are often cited include the ability to off-load costly in-house functions ("persons with specialized skills can be obtained as needed, and without the constraints imposed by salary limitations or civil service restrictions" [Peters, 1991, p. 58]); to "adjust the size of a program up or down in response to changing demand and changing availability of funds" (Savas, 1987, p. 109); to "purchase new equipment more quickly" (Brown, 1991, p. 273); to undertake new projects more easily (Peters, 1991); and to "hire, promote, reward, and even out workload peaks" (Brown, 1991, p. 273).

A Contested Claim

The belief that marketization and enhanced quality are tightly linked is not universally held, however. Whereas advocates of markets acknowledge "the potential problem of reduced quality of service" (Fixler & Poole, 1987, p. 173), opponents talk in more strident terms. These critics rarely see market forces harnessed to the goal of "improve[d] public service quality" (Martin, 1993, p. 173). Where others perceive vistas of higher productivity and greater effectiveness, analysts in this camp are more likely to discern a much darker horizon—one colored by "the substitution of lower-quality resources and deliberate malfeasance" (Clarkson, 1989, p. 177).

Whether grounded in caution or anchored in critique, a number of specific arguments challenge the proposition that the market forces in charters will result in the delivery of higher quality services. Some analysts assert that, contrary to the claims of charter advocates, "competitive environments . . . and competitive markets bring out the worst, not the best, in human behavior" (Thayer, 1987, p. 148). With for-profit providers, they suggest, profits and quality may be in competition, and quality will be the casualty in the long run. They fear that corners will be cut and service quality will deteriorate (President's Commission on Privatization, 1988). Others propose that charters may lead to reduced services for certain types of consumers, especially poor ones (Molnar, 1996) and ones "who may be particularly difficult and expensive to help, such as disadvantaged clients" (Hatry, 1991, p. 265). Under this dynamic, known as creaming, it is believed that charters "will result in services going only to the easy and profitable customers, while the difficult and unprofitable customers are neglected" (Kolderie, 1991, p. 255). Creaming is a topic to which we return in our discussion of equity, below.

Still others base their apprehensiveness about lower quality upon conditions associated with the dynamics of markets. They are quick to point out the costs connected with monitoring service delivery (Clarkson, 1989). They suggest that rollbacks in civil service regulations will likely diminish the quality of production. The flexibility benefits often attributed to market forces supporting charters have also been called into question. Whereas some see flexibility in the promulgation of multiple providers, these critics worry about fragmented public policy (De Hoog, 1984).

Although the potential for enhanced accountability under charters is acknowledged, the more sophisticated analyses point out both the intended and unintended linkages between quality and accountability (Powers & Cookson, 1999). Indeed, apprehension about the illusive nature of actual accountability in real charter schools is increasingly surfacing in the literature (Archer, 2000; UCLA Charter School Study, n.d.), and with it, concern about the viability of the supposed links between accountability and quality.

EFFICIENCY

Costs

While not as heavily emphasized in the charter school movement as in the larger body of privatization literature, there is a prevalent belief that charters cost less than traditional public schools. The logic here follows one of two strands. One holds that charters are a "no-cost" (Nelson, 1997, p. 1), "revenue neutral" (Buechler, 1996, p. 5), or "cost-free" (McGree, 1995a, p. 3) reform, but one that will lead to the significant improvements that earlier reforms of the last two decades have failed to produce—an idea that Molnar (1996) refers to as "America's enduring faith that major educational reform can be accomplished on the cheap" (p. 4).

The second line of analysis regarding costs suggests that charters may actually reduce costs—that "in most states charters receive less public funding per pupil than do regular public schools" (UCLA Charter School Study, n.d., p. 10). According to the narrative cobbled together here, charters are attractive "because they prove that students can be educated for less and provide one way in which states can save money" (Wells, Grutzik et al., 1999, p. 523) and because they are "leading the way" (p. 524) to a "leaner and less expensive education system" (p. 524).

Efficiency

Advocates maintain that charter schools will also be more efficient than traditional public schools. The principal argument is that charters help attack the three inherent sources of inefficiency in the current system: monopoly power, bureaucratic constraints, and political interference (Bulkley, 1998; Hemming & Mansoor, 1988). Specifically, "Charters endorse the notion that . . . institutions governed by consumer choices are more efficient than institutions governed by democratic processes" (Loveless & Jasin, 1998, p. 14). Charter school reformers assert that it is the subjection of the public sector "to the competitive forces of the marketplace and market incentives" (Bennett & Johnson, 1980, p. 365)—"the introduction of marketlike competition into public service provision" (De Hoog, 1984, p. 18)—that ensures that efficiency gains are realized. Where "competition is absent . . . abuses commonly associated with monopolies are likely to occur" (Hirsch, 1991, p. 83).

Efficiency is also enhanced in three ways, reformers suggest, because charters "focus money and decisions at the school level" (Hill, Pierce, & Guthrie, 1997, p. xi). First, charters reduce the inefficiencies associated with group purchase of services, what economists refer to as welfare loss due to collective consumption. According to this line of reasoning, "Charter schools offer a new kind of local control, instead of forcing all groups in town to accept a single sort of school, they allow a multiplicity of communities to form around shared visions of what a good school can be and what sort of education is best for children" (Nappi, 1999, p. v). In so doing, they promote efficiency by ensuring that customers receive the services they desire, rather than the mix of services that other clients may want. By nurturing the development of multiple providers to match up with varied customer needs, they also reinforce the competitive dynamic of markets (McCabe & Vinzant, 1999).

Second, efficiency is increased because more money flows directly to the school and the classroom (Fusarelli, 1999). This, in turn, reduces resources devoted to bureaucracy, especially administration at the central office level (Solmon, Block, & Gifford, 1999). Finally, within the school, inefficiencies are minimized because schools have the flexibility to allocate and spend funds as needed (Hassel, 1997; Schwartz, 1996). Thus, there is "less waste by charter school operators" (Solmon, Block, & Gifford, 1999, p. 15).

The chain of logic provides that, as a function of the forces generated by competition, public education can be improved. The cardinal principle here is that "the economy of private market values" (Bailey, 1987, p. 144) will produce "a leaner, more efficient delivery system" (Fusarelli, 1998, p. 12): "The discipline imposed by the operation of the market system provides inherent incentives for economic efficiency" (Bennett & Johnson, 1980, p. 369). Specifically, it is held that both allocative and productive inefficiencies common to traditional public schools are reduced.

Allocative efficiency is concerned with "the price efficiency of optional resource allocation" (Hirsch, 1991, p. 76), or ensuring that the educational services desired by consumers are the ones actually provided by schools (McCabe & Vinzant, 1999). Allocative inefficiency can be traced to the monopoly status of public schooling:

> While public ownership per se may lead to productive inefficiency, it can result in allocative inefficiency only when associated with considerable monopoly power—which is often granted by statute—or when some other form of protection from competitive pressures—usually the result of inappropriate financial and trade policies—is implied. (Hemming & Mansoor, 1988, p. 5)

Allocative inefficiency occurs when agencies "fail to allocate . . . assets to their best and highest uses" (Thompson, 1989, p. 205); when "prices are artificially high" (Hilke, 1992, p. 139). The result is that agencies "produce the wrong mix of services, or even do not produce some valued programs at all" (Brown, 1992, p. 288)—"the quantity, quality, and other characteristics of goods and services are not those most valued by consumers" (Hemming & Mansoor, 1988, p. 5). Allocative efficiency is the direct result of the "clarity of the educator-customer relationship" (Loveless & Jasin, 1998, p. 15). In charter schools, the presumption is that "[allocative] efficiency will be achieved because the school's offerings will respond to parental and student needs and desires in a competitive environment" (McCabe & Vinzant, 1999, p. 360).

Productive efficiency focuses on the "input-output production transformation" (Hirsch, 1991, p. 76) or on "the ratio of outputs to inputs" (Scheerens, 1999, pp. 8–9). Here the concern is with ensuring that the same or a higher level of outcomes can be achieved at a lower cost; the idea that charters "will be able to do more with fewer resources" (UCLA Charter School Study, n.d., p. 4). Productive inefficiency "occurs when more inputs (labor, raw materials, energy, etc.) are used than necessary" (Hilke, 1992, p. 139). Unlike allocative inefficiency, it can be traced to all of the three sources of inefficiency listed earlier—monopoly status, bureaucratic failure, and political interference. Productive efficiency, in turn, is often divided into technical and organizational efficiency:

> Technical efficiency involves the availability of choice concerning the appropriate production function and combination of inputs, that is, to what extent cost can be minimized given quality and quantity constraints. . . . Organizational efficiency concerns the question of whether the appropriate production technology is actually known and utilized by decision makers in a manner that maximizes output, given the level of inputs and their prices, and/or minimizes costs for given levels of outputs. Therefore it is mainly concerned with the internal organization of the entity producing the goods. (Hirsch, 1991, pp. 67–68)

Cautionary Notes

Before leaving this section on the expected efficiency benefits of charters, a few notes of caution need to be raised. While we dealt with funding issues in Chapter 3, it is useful to remind ourselves that not everyone agrees that charters are cheaper to operate. Nelson (1997), for example, suggests that "A thoughtful analysis of charter school funding reveals that charter schools impose new costs and that they are not necessarily underfunded when all public revenue sources are matched to the specific kinds of students educated in charter schools. In fact, unless a charter school *primarily* serves at-risk children, the charter school is probably overfunded in comparison to regular public schools" (p. 1). Concomitantly, some analysts suggest that reducing funds to public education—in the name of efficiency or not—is not an especially laudable goal. Those who discern significant underfunding of the current system, especially in our urban and rural areas, are particularly vocal on this point (Molnar, 1996). So too are analysts who believe that "charter schools will siphon badly needed funds from public school systems" (Buechler, 1995b, p. 5).

It is instructive to note that cost and efficiency, while related, are distinct concepts. Specifically, as a number of investigators remind us (De Hoog, 1984; Martin, 1993; Ross, 1988), cost savings are not synonymous with enhanced efficiency: market advocates "appear to equate cost reductions with efficiency increases. The two are not necessarily the same" (Hirsch, 1991, p. 124). Hula argues, "It is clearly inappropriate to identify efficiency as any reduction in cost" (Hula, 1990b, p. 14). Lower costs can result from either "greater efficiency or deteriorating quality" (Starr, 1987, p. 129); from greater productivity or "from reducing the standard of service or by paying lower wages and imposing poorer work conditions on staff" (Bell & Cloke, 1990, p. 12). The goal "is not merely to cut costs but to do so without reducing benefits by a commensurate amount" (Gormley, 1991a, p. 7). "To the extent that cost reductions are achieved by reductions in level and quality of service, claims of increased efficiency are illusionary" (Hula, 1990b, p. 1). Thus, a finding that charter schools have lower unit costs than their counterparts "does not necessarily imply that their contributions to social welfare are greater; questions relating to allocative efficiency and to the quality of goods or services provided also need to be taken into account" (Vickers & Yarrow, 1988, p. 40).

It is also necessary to remind ourselves that not all the stars in the efficiency galaxy line up in support of charters. Especially problematic is the structural efficiency issue of economies of scale:

> The negative impact arises from charter schools' lack of economies of scale. Charter schools tend to be small relative to conventional public schools. More to the point, they are always small relative to public school *districts*. Since they are independent, charter schools are often treated as if they were school districts: required to provide the same level of services to special needs children, to file the same reports, to meet the same requirements for financial and program audits, to manage and maintain their facilities. As small "districts," charter schools have fewer students over which to spread the costs of these activities. And they will have more difficulty participating in bulk, lower-cost purchases that school districts arrange. Their per-pupil costs, then, will tend to be higher than those of conventional school districts. (Hassel, 1997, pp. 163–164)

Charters are also unlikely to realize gains from two other sources of possible efficiencies. First, absent the introduction of the profit motive, the management productivity efficiency rationale is unlikely to come into play. Second, as long as charters remain in the public sector, they are not more likely than traditional public schools to capture efficiencies from more productive use of capital. In both of these cases, the absence of profit incentives found in the private sector is likely to be a more powerful force than marketization energy pumped into the public sector.

Finally, it is not unreasonable to question any system of funding schools that relies as extensively on external support as do charter schools. To date, charters are garnering not insignificant funding from three sources outside the public treasury—cash and materials from private donors, in kind contributions from parents, and "sweat equity" (Wells, Grutzik et al., 1999, p. 524) from school employees (Hassell, 1997). While there is much to be commended in the forging of concerted efforts by the government, private, and voluntary sectors of society, whether current funding schemes undervalue the commitment of the public to the collective good known as public schooling remains an open question. As we discuss more fully below, equity concerns also are tightly woven into the funding tapestry of charter schools.

EQUITY

In earlier sections, we chronicled how charters may contribute to meeting values such as quality and efficiency. As McCabe and Vinzant (1999) remind us, however, "Potential gains in the realization of these values have important implications for how states can and will meet their constitutional mandate for free, equitable, public education" (p. 368). In this section, we examine the equity story line as it is being developed by advocates and opponents of charters, acknowledging up front "that charter schools open up a can of worms with regard to equity" (Harris, cited in Caudell, 1997b, p. 7).

Equity-Enhancing Logic

Reformers who maintain that charters will strengthen the equity fabric of the nation hold that "the charter idea is part of a two-hundred year effort in this country to expand opportunity, especially for those who are not wealthy and powerful" (Nathan, 1996a, p. xiii). They view charters as vehicles to create "opportunity for youngsters, families, and educators" (p. 5). Charter proponents see autonomy, competition, and accountability as powerful forces in the quest for greater equality. They believe that charters will "lead to a more equal allocation of resources among schools than the current system" (Hill, Pierce, & Guthrie, 1997, p. 71) and to the possibility "for groups of parents . . . who have been the least empowered in the state-run system to have a voice in how their children are educated" (Wells, Lopez et al., 1999, p. 193). Most significantly, they yoke equity to outcomes, arguing that "charter schools hold the promise of contributing to the greatest measure of equitable education parity of achievement for all groups of students" (Northwest Regional Educational Laboratory, 1998, p. 8).

The core equity platform for charter advocates is the proposition that these new, autonomous schools will advantage those who historically have been ill-served by public schooling (Vanourek, Manno, Finn, & Bierlein, 1997b): "Proponents of individual equity contend that the purpose of charter schools is to provide all children, especially children at risk, low-income, and minority students, equal opportunity to choose and attend a high quality school" (Lane, n.d., p. 14).

The starting point in this line of analysis is the position that "families whose values are not represented in the mainstream culture and families with low to middle incomes are at a disadvantage in the present structure of public education" (Smith, 1998, p. 57), that "the present-day problems besetting our public school system are disproportionately borne by students who have been traditionally shortchanged in the educational process: lower-income students, racial and ethnic minorities, limited-English-proficient speakers, students with disabilities, and female students" (Northwest Regional Educational Laboratory, 1998, p. 1), and that "the majority of low-income and minority students, especially in our inner cities, are trapped within an educational system that tends to reinforce, or reproduce, existing social class" (Lane, n.d., p. 15).

The next link in this analytic chain holds that minorities and the poor are disadvantaged because they "traditionally [have] had the fewest choices in education" (UCLA Charter School Study, n.d., p. 11), that "they are unable to choose better schools for their children because they cannot afford to purchase homes in the communities where these schools are usually located" (Arsen, Plank, & Sykes, n.d., p. 2). In this scenario, "low-income, minority parents and their children are seen . . . as being trapped by circumstances beyond their control in inferior schools. Providing choice to these parents . . . is seen as providing a way for parents and their children to break free of the constraints of poor schools" (Fuller & Elmore, 1996, p. 189)—or as Arsen and his colleagues (n.d.) put it, "School choice policies reduce the cost of mobility" (p. 79).

The "basic theory of change" (Bulkley, 1998, p. 225) embedded in charter schools—the reform engine outlined earlier—suggests that these new institutions will alter these disenfranchising conditions, that charters will privilege youngsters "who are having difficulty in the traditional public school system" (Fulford, Raack, & Sunderman, 1997, p. 1). While benefits are expected to accrue to all children (Rofes, 1998b), gains, it is argued, will flow disproportionately to "students at risk of academic failure" (McGree, 1995b, p. 2) and to "disadvantaged groups that have had few choices in the past" (UCLA Charter School Study, n.d., p. 42):

> The poor will benefit even more than the prosperous from such a system of choice, for they have lacked the resources to take advantage of existing educa-

tional alternatives such as private schools or public education in affluent suburbs. (Tyack, 1992, p. 14)

Thus charters are seen "as creat[ing] 'homeplaces' for those who have been disconnected and disempowered within the traditional state-run system" (Wells, Lopez, et al., 1999, p. 193).

Potential Deleterious Impact

Critics of charters claim that while "market mechanisms may increase efficiency, and ultimately improve quality for some children . . . they are unlikely to help states address the need for equity" (McCabe & Vinzant, 1999, p. 367). They declare "that market-oriented reforms such as charters . . . [will] increase inequities in public education" (Hill, Pierce, & Guthrie, 1997, p. 71), that "market forces in the educational system will almost certainly have a negative impact on [the] most vulnerable children" (Arsen, Plank, & Sykes, n.d., p. 91). Opponents believe that the charter movement will likely "increase stratification and exacerbate barriers to educational access, undermine democratic education and the public control of schooling, and fail to improve student achievement" (Rofes, 1998b, p. 65).

> Detractors argue that charter schools will "cream off" the best and most motivated students, leaving regular public schools unable to compete; that they will become bastions of race and class segregation; that, exempted from rules, they will engage in actions these rules are designed to prevent, like discrimination, mistreatment of handicapped children, financial misconduct, or simply shoddy educational practice; that they will siphon off energy and resources that could be devoted to improving public schools more generally; or that they will simply serve too few students to make much of a difference. (Hassel, 1997, pp. 8–9)

One line of thinking, underemphasized in the literature, asserts that charters are simply an insufficiently robust tool to produce much gain on the equity agenda. From one end of the political spectrum, Wells, Lopez, and their colleagues (1999) make this point as follows:

> Because charter schools are part and parcel of a larger political push to roll back the welfare state and shrink government size and spending, they have come of age in an era when resources are less likely to be redistributed from wealthy to low-income communities. When we examine charter schools through this wider lens, the emancipatory potential of the reform seems feeble in comparison. (p. 196)

Building on a completely different ideological scaffolding, some critics declare that the charter movement with its weak equalizing potential hinders equity gains that could be realized by employing more powerful market strategies such as contracting and tax credits. These reformers "contend that whatever its merits, the charter movement deflects the needed revolution by stealing the thunder from vouchers and other truly free-market alternatives" (Finn, Manno, & Vanourek, 2000, p. 182). Finally, other analysts raise the possibility that the struggle for enhanced educational opportunity will be insufficiently engaged because charters may siphon off advocates who would be likely to undertake this arduous reform work—or at least would be sufficiently vocal to necessitate others doing something about inequity in the educational system (Arsen, Plank, & Sykes, n.d.). In this scenario, there is a "fear that charter schools might, at best, be little more than escape valves that release pressure for genuine reform of the whole system" (Berman, et al., 1998).

One of the most powerful critiques of the charter school movement is that it weakens the ideals of community, democracy, and the common school, that charters "may undermine the ideas of democratic equality and common citizenship historically embodied in the public school system" (Arsen, Plank, & Sykes, n.d., p. 71). Skeptics are particularly leery of the heavy emphasis on the market ideology that anchors charters (Garcia & Garcia, 1996) and its accompanying stress on "the interests of a narrow unit (the family) over those of society" (Rofes, 1998b, p. 69)—its focus on individuality over commonality (Educational Excellence Network, 1995). The allegation is that "charter schools balkanize American society and weaken the principal institution that knits us together" (Finn, Manno, & Vanourek, 2000, p. 160). According to charter critics, "treating schools simply as the product of market forces subverts an essential democratic institution" (Tyack, 1992, p. 14), undermines the idea of the common school, promulgates a truncated vision of community, and privileges individualism over the collective good:

> Charter schools are built on the illusion that our society can be held together solely by the self-interested pursuit of our individual purposes. Considered in this light, the charter school movement represents a radical rejection not only of the possibility of the common school, but of common purposes outside the school as well. The struggle is not between market-based reforms and the educational status quo. It is about whether the democratic ideal of the common good can survive the onslaught of a market mentality that threatens to turn every human relationship into a commercial transaction. (Molnar, 1996, p. 7)

Some analysts are also openly skeptical of the pronouncements that charters will advantage those who have historically been poorly served by public schools (Fuller & Elmore, 1996). Or, as McGree (1995a) puts it: "There continue to be questions about whether charter schools are designed to substantially increase choice options for at-risk students or, as critics charge, are designed to improve opportunities for students who are already academically and economically advantaged" (p. 7). Critics worry that "school choice movements, such as charter schools, may in fact, increase the disparity between the rich and the poor, the non-minority and the minority" (Lane, 1998, p. 9). They are concerned that equity will be undercut if charter schools "'cream,' or select students who are least at risk of educational failure or . . . skim by covertly choosing those students most at risk" (Mickelsen, 1997, p. 4).

On the creaming issue, reviewers fear that charters will select "academically talented students and highly engaged parents" (Rofes, 1998b, p. 80): "Skeptics say charters will attract all the best students and most involved parents and leave the rest of the public schools with the harder-to-educate and parents who don't care" (Center for Education Reform, n.d.d, p. 1). McCabe and Vinzant (1999) lay out the incentive for charter schools to seek out the best and most committed students and families as follows:

> Like local governments, charter schools must also compete for students by offering a bundle of educational services and programs that will appeal to the parents and students they are trying to attract. In other words, they must position themselves in the market to compete successfully. Like local governments, charter schools have incentives to attract the students of affluent parents. Children of such parents tend to perform better in school than their peers in poorer neighborhoods, and charter schools, if they are to meet the educational standards required for their continued certification, must attract "good" students. Moreover, students with affluent parents, it might be assumed, will benefit because more discretionary resources can be devoted to the children's education. This can be critical as charter schools face the costs of building facilities and/or other start-up costs that traditional public schools receive from their school district. (p. 366)

Given this incentive structure, opponents argue that charters could become "exclusive" (RPP International & University of Minnesota, 1997, p. 32) or "elite facilities" (Collins, 1999, p. 4) or "pseudo-private academies" (Buechler, 1996, p. 5) dedicated to serving "affluent, successful" (Nathan, 1996a, p. 71) and "high achieving" (Little Hoover Commission, 1996, p. 49) students and in the process "unfairly better the quality of education in those communities that have the most access to resources" (Northeast and Islands Regional Educational Laboratory, 1999, p. 14):

> Opponents contend that charter schools, as schools of choice, will appeal to the most successful students and families already highly involved in their children's education. The theory continues that this scholastic and social "cream"—the stereotypical academically-achieving, well-behaved, white, upper-middle-class "normal" children of two-parent PTA-member families—will fill the charter school rosters. Having thus "abandoned" the traditional public school system, their elevating effect on the local schools will no longer be felt, and the local schools, left

to educate the at-risk, minority, poor and poorly-achieving, will sink further into failure. (Center for Education Reform, n.d.d, pp. 1–2)

Creaming, critics contend, could occur because charters might recruit certain types of students and parents and discourage others. In particular, opponents maintain that charters will actively seek out low-cost students (Arsen, Plank, & Sykes, n.d.; Bierwirth, 1997; Zollers & Ramanathan, 1998) and those parents "most committed to their youngsters' education, leaving behind children who receive the least help and encouragement from their families" (Fuller, 1996, p. 39). More important, schools could set in place conditions (e.g., the lack of quality special education services) and require-ments (e.g., parental service mandates) that might reinforce their expectations and help ensure that they received only the types of customers they desired (American Federation of Teachers, 1996; Becker, Nakagawa, & Corwin, 1997; Schwartz, 1996; Zollers & Ramanathan, 1998). In so doing, charters would turn the concept of choice upside down, creating a system in which the schools were choosing families rather than families choosing schools (Arsen, Plank, & Sykes, n.d.).

Finally, creaming might occur, and equity be diminished, because of un-evenness in the market dynamics undergirding the charter movement. The free flow of information is of particular importance to market theory. In the charter movement, this boils down to the issue of "equity in access to informa-tion about charter schools" (Mickelsen, 1997, p. 5). There is concern among charter critics about this issue (Arsen, Plank, & Sykes, n.d.; Mulholland, 1999), with some reviewers claiming that minority and low-income families receive less information than more affluent parents, and are, therefore, less active choosers (Fuller & Elmore, 1996). And as Lane (n.d.) reminds us, "It is not likely that charter schools will be able to promote either individual equity or group equity if steps are not taken to give all parents the ability to choose" (p. 20), for "families that do not take their opportunities for selecting a school seriously [will] end up with less desirable options than those who inform themselves and seek options" (Hill, Pierce, & Guthrie, 1997, p. 85). To the extent that "the subset of people who are influenced by market forces differs significantly from the rest of the customer base" (McCabe & Vinzant, 1999, p. 369), equity may be impeded rather than promoted. Specifically, inequities in the area of educational opportunity might increase because sophisticated families will take advantage of the best opportunities, leaving lower-quality programs for the less informed and less motivated. Or as McGree (1995a) narrates: "There is some concern that charter schools could be established by advantaged parent groups, often at the expense of more disadvantaged parents who have neither the time nor financial resources required to start or maintain a charter school" (p. 8). Under all of these equity inhibiting scenarios, "arguably inferior conventional public schools" (Schwartz, 1996, p. 1) would be left with the "hard to teach children" (Caudell, 1997b, p. 6) and "the neediest students" (Vanourek, Manno, Finn, & Bierlein, 1997b, p. 1)—the "low-income students, at-risk student . . . students with disabilities" (Mickelsen, 1997, p. i), the "least successful students" (McGree, 1995a, p. 8) and high-cost youngsters (Arsen, Plank, & Sykes, n.d.).

An alternative perspective promulgated by some of those who study the equity landscape of charters is that these new, alternative schools will "simply become a dumping ground for kids who don't make it in the traditional public schools" (McCabe & Vinzant, 1999, p. 367), "for the hard to teach children whom the system has given up on" (Caudell, 1997b, p. 6), and for the "academically underprivileged" (Center for Education Reform, n.d.d, p. 5). Whether herded together in alternative institutions such as charter schools or left behind in regular public schools that the more advantaged families have abandoned for charters, the result, critics aver, would be a diminution in society's commitment to equality and a reduction rather than an enhancement of educational equity.

Throughout this volume, we have revealed that charter schools are "fragmented and decentralized localized projects that celebrate difference over uniformity" (Wells, Lopez et al., 1999, p. 174). Consistent with postmodern and postindustrial worldviews, charter schools promote a "distinctive" school as opposed to a "common" school approach to reaching valued ends—a pluralism between schools as opposed to a pluralism within schools approach (Rofes, 1995). Thus "charter schools . . . accelerate the trend toward social separation" (Arsen, Plank, & Sykes, n.d., p. 74) and promote an "increased sorting among schools" (Solmon, Block, & Gifford, 1999, p. 13). The result of "allow[ing] educators and parents to create schools that reflect the culture and values of specific groups . . . is the creation of homogenous school communities, in which children increasingly attend school with children who are like them" (Arsen, Plank, & Sykes, n.d., p. 74).

Earlier, we chronicled the gains that can accrue from this phenomenon. In particular, we reported how charters promote the formation of "community" and the development of "mission," two of the essential building blocks of the school effectiveness edifice (Beck & Murphy, 1996). But, as critics of charters are quick to point out, the creation of homogenous communities is not an unalloyed benefit, especially to the extent that heterogeneity is in and of itself a social goal. Lane (1998) captures the essence of the debate when he notes that "there is a fine line between specialization as a means to enhance education and specialization as a means to exclude the ideas of opposing groups" (p. 15), or members of those groups themselves.

Throughout the charter school literature, there is consternation that advancements in quality from specialization may be more than offset by losses in the area of equity (McCabe & Vinzant, 1999; Powers & Cookson, 1999). We have already explored two dimensions of this phenomenon: gashes in the equity fabric of the democratic welfare state, including the breakdown of traditional ideas such as the collective good and the common school; and the clustering of youngsters at risk, whether by design (into charter schools) or by default (into the remnants of the public school system), in ways that diminish educational opportunity. Related to these issues is a third concern—that even if these fragmented institutions enhance access to quality schools for the disadvantaged and promote fairer distribution of opportunity to learn for poor and minority youngsters, they may still undermine equity by "creating more racial and economic stratification in society" (National Education Association, 1998a, p. 3) and thus "reduce opportunities for interactions across lines of race, class, and religion that are so essential to democratic citizenship" (Arsen, Plank, & Sykes, n.d., p. 7). And, to be sure, while separation is a well-known pattern in the public school mosaic (Murphy, Beck, Crawford, Hodges, & McGaughy, 2001; Northwest Regional Educational Laboratory, 1998), the fear is that "charters will exacerbate the segregation of public education" (Rofes, 1998b, p. 4), or in the words of Collins (1999), they will "advance resegregation" (p. 4).

In our discussion of efficiency, we questioned the viability of funding schemes for charter schools that include considerable support from corporations, foundations, and parents (Izu et al., 1998). We return to the funding issue here to underscore the potential of nontax support to weaken commitment to equity. To begin with, as Wells, Lopez, and their colleagues (1999) reveal, because of this funding arrangement, charters pose some real threats in the area of equal access to resources. Specifically, these authors show how parents in more affluent areas are able to attach the "wealth of their local communities to create the kind of public schools they want" (p. 198). Absent the availability of community resources in the form of (1) monies; (2) donation of services, materials, and labor; (3) social capital; and (4) time, charter parents in poorer communities are disadvantaged. The net result is both a weakening of the equity foundations of schools built up over the last half century from legislative and judicial actions in the area of school finance and reduced resources for poor schools.

Second, because they are able to "circumvent most state and district regulations, charter schools are able to eliminate costs subsidized by more traditional public schools" (McGree, 1995a, p. 8). By converting these traditionally covered costs into "fees and donations" (American Federation of Teachers, 1996, p. 3), such monies may become a "proxy for tuition and therefore make charter schools inaccessible to some students" (p. 3):

> A further concern emerges as inquiries arise as to whether charter schools have costs that are passed on to parents. . . . Parents may be required to provide trans-

portation for their children, volunteer a specified number of hours, and in some cases pitch in as custodians alongside educators. The growing concern emerging from the early charter schools is that economically disadvantaged parents who can't afford the time nor the financial resources will be systemically denied access to charter schools. (Garcia & Garcia, 1996, p. 36)

IMPACT ON EMPLOYEES

As Pirie (1988) succinctly concludes, under marketization initiatives "the issue of jobs is a very sensitive one" (p. 62). It is also, as are many of the topics in the charter realm, long on opinion and short on analyses. However, Dudek and company (1989) provide a useful framework for examining the labor effects of charters. The categories we use in the balance of this section are drawn primarily from their design.

Professionalism

The state of professionalism in the teaching ranks has been a subject of some speculation in the charter school literature. Opponents aver that charters will "undermine teacher professionalism" (McGree, 1995a, p. 10), both collectively and at the individual building level. At the system level, critics predict a diminuation in the professionalism associated with unionism (Buechler, 1996; Rofes, 1998b). They tend to see charters as a naked "vehicle for breaking up teacher unions" (Molnar, 1996, p. 6) and for "destroy[ing] collective bargaining" (American Federation of Teachers, n.d., p. 7). They are concerned that charters "could lead to greater teacher impoverishment" (Sautter, 1993, p. 13), thus further undercutting professionalism. Opponents also view charters as a strategy for undermining traditional pillars of professionalism, such as licensure and certification. They suggest that eliminating certification requirements is "analogous to trying to solve the problems of access to health care by allowing anyone who can attract patients to practice medicine" (Molnar, 1996, p. 5).

   At the individual site level, skeptics also see professionalism breaking down under the onslaught of market forces. Teachers, it is argued, will have a diminished voice and fewer opportunities to influence school policy and operations. Markets, not professionals, will become the fulcrum influencing decisions at the school level. While the current bureaucratic system hardly champions professionalism, critics maintain that market-based systems will create an even less hospitable environment for the elements of professionalism to flourish. They point to the privatization of other public sector domains for support of their assertions.

   Advocates of charters see things quite a bit differently. At the system level, they are leery of the usefulness of traditional pillars of professionalism such as licensure, accreditation, and collective bargaining. In particular, they do not believe that unions are "important to the survival and success of public education" (Buechler, 1996, p. 37). Quite the contrary, they assert that unions have a "stranglehold" (Loveless & Jasin, 1998, p. 15) on the educational enterprise that needs to be broken. In a similar vein, proponents of charters reason that licensure requirements are as likely to exclude qualified teachers from practicing as they are to enhance teacher quality. Not surprisingly, they view market controls, rather than bureaucratic state and professional controls, as more efficacious in ensuring quality in the teaching ranks (Center for Education Reform, n.d.d).

At the school level, supporters proclaim that "charter schools offer increased opportunities for professionalism for teachers" (Garcia & Garcia, 1996, p. 34). They believe that providing teachers "with the increased autonomy, flexibility, and authority necessary to assume responsibility for the development and delivery of new, innovative approaches to teaching and learning at their school sites will empower teachers to be more self-directed professionals" (Bomotti, Ginsberg, & Cobb, 1999, p. 17). In charters, it is suggested, "teachers will gain a stronger voice in the focus and management of their school" (Bierlein & Mulholland, 1993, p. 5). Charters, we are informed, are about "expand[ing] the range of professional options for teachers" (Buechler, 1996, p. 5), "promot[ing] teacher autonomy" (Poland, 1996, p. 2), and "enabling schools to reflect the wisdom of the educators who work in them" (UCLA Charter School Study, n.d., p. 28). They are about "valuing the expertise of teachers and giving them control over instruction" (Garn, 1998, p. 50). Proponents argue that charters afford teachers the opportunity to "use their skills, talents, and energy" more effectively (Nathan, 1996a, p. xvi) and to "reinvent their jobs, take on new challenges, and work 'outside the box'" (Finn, Manno, & Vanourek, 2000, p. 89). These new organizations promote the development of high-quality "professional learning communities" (Wohlstetter & Griffin, 1997a, p. 3):

> Since charter schools confront less red tape, teachers can deploy their professional judgments, set their own instructional priorities, pick their materials, and engage their students in projects and activities that inspire them. They can write their own curriculum or adapt one to fit their pupils' needs. Teachers are included on governing boards of most charter schools. Perhaps even more important is that they *chose* to work there. All this helps forge a professional community in which staff feel a sense of collective responsibility. (Finn, Manno, & Vanourek, 2000, p. 231)

Conditions of Employment

Pulling back the safety net provided by union contracts (e.g., a fixed salary schedule) and state policies (e.g., tenure laws) is either a useful step on the path to reaching the more enlightened state of professionalism envisioned by charter advocates or a calculated effort to undermine the teaching profession and the welfare of individual teachers according to charter opponents. Critics assert that charters are as much about "lowering wages" (Molnar, 1996, p. 6), "decreas[ing] job security" (McGree, 1995a, p. 10), and reducing protective work rules as they are about improving schools. Opponents of charters are concerned about job displacement. They worry that market forces will increase unemployment and produce a cadre of part-time, itinerant workers. Wells, Lopez, and their colleagues (1999) sum up this story line as follows: charters may "lead to lower wages and less job security for educators and other school employees, similar to the unemployment, underemployment, and lower wages experienced by workers in private industry" (p. 181). There is also some wariness about the extent to which charters undercut employment as a social tool, especially the use of public payroll to meet the equity goal of hiring teachers from underrepresented groups.

Review of the literature on the marketization of public services outside of education provides some justification for those who worry about the effects of charters on conditions of employment, especially when private contractors are involved in delivery. While drawing attention to variation among government agencies, Dudek and company (1989) conclude that "private contractors generally pay lower wages than do the government agencies they replace" (p. 2). Reports tracking salaries in industries undergoing privatization via deregulation (e.g., the trucking and airline industries) uncover similar declines in wages (Thayer, 1987). Initial analyses of the effects of marketization on fringe benefits are even more pronounced: Because "the government usually provides much more generous fringe benefits than do contractors . . . the largest difference between the government and the contractor is in the level of the fringe benefits provided" (Dudek & Company, 1989, p. 3). In one of the most thoughtful discussions of this issue, Donahue (1989) demonstrates that, for most services, especially labor-intensive ones such as education, "lower labor costs—both wages and benefits—are a major part of the contractor cost edge" (p. 144). He summarizes our knowledge of the connection between marketization and public employees as follows:

> Two facts are equally evident: Delegating certain functions to private firms usually saves tax dollars, and much of these savings [come] at the expense of public employees. . . . In short, a good deal of what taxpayers stand to gain from privatization comes at the expense of municipal employees. (p. 145)

Thus, in the charter school arena, there is a deep concern that markets will be employed "mainly as a weapon against public sector workers" (Martin, 1993, p. 173) and any gains "come at the expense of compensation" (McGree, 1995a, p. 9).

Proponents of charters examine the available information with different frames of reference and arrive at quite different conclusions. Those who maintain that employees possess an unfair "advantage in the public sector in terms of job security, working conditions and fringe benefits" (Pirie, 1988, p. 59)—who believe that workers "are much better off in the public sector [and] know it" (Worsnop, 1992, p. 982)—discern gains from charters where defenders of the public sector see costs. This group includes a variety of perspectives. Some believe that public schools enjoy "monopoly rents allowed by regulation . . . in the form of higher salaries, reduced hours, and attractive fringe benefits" (Smith, 1987, p. 186). Others focus on restrictive civil service regulations and unchecked and hard-to-control collective bargaining in the public sector that they believe gives unfair advantage to public employees (Loveless & Jasin, 1998). Still others question the income redistribution dimensions of public employment (Donahue, 1989; Worsnop, 1992) that may enhance the position of government workers vis-à-vis their private sector colleagues. Finally, some are troubled by the "political pressure" (Ramsey, 1987, p. 95) that they believe public employees use to distort the budget portfolio in favor of labor and at the expense of capital investments and technological innovations (Hirsch, 1991; Ramsey, 1987). For all these reasons, analysts in this group underscore the benefits of "disarm[ing] public trade unions that are abusing a monopoly position" (Hemming & Mansoor, 1988, p. 6) and "put[ting] personnel practices outside the civil service system and public collective bargaining" (Bailey, 1987, p. 146). They believe the charters provide a powerful vehicle to achieve these goals.

SUMMARY

In this chapter, we built from material developed earlier to explore the benefits of charter schools. We examined four areas in some detail: quality, efficiency, equity, and the impact on employees. In each case, we investigated the claims of charter advocates as well as the logic of critics who have called potential charter benefits into question. In Chapter 7, we review the empirical evidence to date that informs this debate.

CHAPTER 7

Charter School Effects

Yet, despite the hard work and dedication of charter school founders and operators, and the impressive gains that many have made under trying conditions, charter school reform, for the most part, falls short of the broad and comprehensive claims made by many of its proponents. (UCLA Charter School Study, n.d., p. 9)

It is too early to make any definitive statements about the success of charter schools. Some of the available data support initial claims of advocates, while other data give cause for concern of what the ultimate impact of charter schools will be. (American Federation of Teachers, n.d., p. 50)

But the vast majority of today's charters are thriving. Their clients are mostly satisfied. They display promising signs of achievement and productivity gains, as well as positive effects on the larger education system. (Finn, Manno, & Vanourek, 2000, p. 153)

SETTING THE STAGE

Not surprisingly, the policymakers who are encouraging the spread of charter schools are keen to learn whether their continued support is warranted, whether the greater freedom given to charter schools leads to better results than those produced by conventional schools, whether charter schools are more or less efficient, and whether they are properly attentive to such concerns as equal opportunity. The thirst for knowledge about these issues is not limited to the friends of charter schools. Enemies, too, are looking for evidence, if only to buttress their own claims. In short, supporters and doubters—and neutral observers—want to know whether the charter approach is "working" as intended. This is the primary "macro" question. Hence the primary burden of a charter accountability system is to provide policymakers, cognizant authorities, taxpayers, and others with information that answers it. (Manno, Finn, Bierlein, & Vanourek, 1997a, p. 1)

Varying Viewpoints

Depending upon where one looks and to whom one attends, charter schools are either "not support[ing] the advocates' claims" (UCLA Charter School Study, n.d., p. 4) or providing "a statistical portrait [of success] that is compelling" (Vanourek, Manno, Finn, & Bierlein, 1997a, p. 9). Charters are assessed as either an educational strategy doomed from the creation of the conceptual blueprint to "be another well intentioned, very flawed effort at school reform" (Sarason, 1998, p. 71) or a breakthrough design that will dramatically fortify the American educational enterprise (Nathan, 1996a). Critics express feelings ranging from bemusement to outrage over the rapid growth of a movement "with no evidence that it will make a difference" (Garcia & Garcia, 1996, p. 34) while other analysts view the growth itself as evidence of success. For some reviewers, we have a sufficient body of knowledge to support claims of positive effects for charters (Center for Education Reform, 2000b) while others argue that "little information is available on the experiment" (Medler, 1996, p. 26) and hold that it is still "premature to assess the impact of charter schools on their direct consumers or, more generally, their effects on American public schools" (Good, Braden, & Drury, 2000, p. 31; see also McLaughlin & Henderson, 1998). Some scholars cast their gaze over the expanding charter narrative and see "little more than anecdotal puffery and phony statistics . . . and flawed data" (Rothstein, 1998a, p. 52). Others discern more academically supportable claims (Finn, Manno, & Vanourek, 2000). Some who investigate charters view them as a "dynamic force" (p. 99) for large-scale, fundamental change, while others maintain that charters "represent an incremental reform evolving unevenly along a continuum of autonomy" (Wohlstetter, Wenning, & Briggs, 1995, p. 352) and conclude "that charter competition has not induced large changes into district operations" (Teske, Schneider, Buckley, & Clark, 2000, p. 1).

Different Standards

In this concluding chapter, we shed additional light on these and related issues that can be bundled together under the rubric of charter school effectiveness. Unlike in earlier chapters where a variety of perspectives informed the analysis and in which theoretical and conceptual perspectives were privileged, our focus here is exclusively on empirical evidence. Nonetheless, our assignment is still made problematic by a number of issues, many of which we discussed in the introductory chapter. To begin with, there is the relative recency of the charter school movement. At the time of this writing, the charter phenomenon is only 8 years old, and most charters are in the early stages of operation. In short, there is not an overabundance of evidence to examine, or as Finn and his team (2000) have concluded, "definitive data are scarce" (p. 74). While some of this data deficiency problem was hard-wired into the movement via the political dynamics that spawned charters (Sarason, 1998), some is attributable to the fact that reform enthusiasm often outpaces "careful attempts to assess concrete effects" (Fuller, 1996, p. 37), some is due to "the information vacuum that weakens our entire public school system" (Finn, Manno, & Vanourek, 2000, p. 74), and much can be explained by the newness of the charter school movement. Also embedded in this dynamic is the issue of whether findings uncovered in the early stages of this reform movement, when the most committed and most dedicated risk takers hold center stage, are duplicated when a second generation of less zealous reformers moves into the picture (Finn, Manno, & Vanourek, 2000).

At the same time, as we have discussed throughout this volume, charter schools mean quite different things in different states and varied local communities. Forces are arranged to create "a wide diversity in look, method, and circumstances" (Little Hoover Commission, 1996, p. 30) in charters, "differences that make it difficult to perform any meaningful analysis of charter schools based on mere raw numbers or comparative statistics" (p. 30).

In addition, the definition of what counts for "success" is contested territory (U.S. General Accounting Office, 1995a, b; Gifford & Ogle, 1998; Mickelsen, 1997). As Good and his colleagues (2000) assert, "There is no small measure of ambivalence about the standards of evidence and specific criteria to be used in assessing the contributions of charter schools" (p. 1). Or as Vanourek and his colleagues (1997b) aver, "The impact of charter schools can be gauged in many different ways" (p. 11); "Unless we clarify just what it is we're trying to evaluate we are unlikely to have a useful discussion about whether the charter is working" (Kolderie, n.d., p. 1). And because "determining the success of charter schools is very dependent on how one defines their purposes" (American Federation of Teachers, n.d., p. 7) and because politicians, policy entrepreneurs, and "charter school founders engage in this reform to accomplish a wide range of goals" (UCLA Charter School Study, n.d., p. 6), determining what charter schools should be held accountable for is not a straightforward process (Wohlstetter & Griffin, 1997a). For example, a scan of the literature reviewed in Chapters 5 and 6 reveals the following potential anchors by which to judge effectiveness:

political support	academic outcomes/student achievement
number of charter schools opening	
number of potential providers	learning and teaching designs
number of ineffective schools closing	governance and management approaches
charter renewals	
customer demand	curricular focus

employee interest
organizational flexibility
fiscal responsibility
nonacademic outcomes (such
    as safety and orderli-
    ness)
student retention at the school
customer satisfaction
customer involvement
student attitudes

charter objectives and goals
teacher empowerment
competition in the system
equity and equal access
impact on the larger educational
    system
differences from conditions in regu-
    lar public schools
adherence to applicable laws and reg-
    ulations

And within each of these areas the metric applied to determine success can vary significantly. For example, following are differences in the academic outcome criteria by three sets of analysts, all from the same ideological charter school camp:

> Charter schools ultimately can justify their existence *only* by driving improved educational achievement. (Finn, Manno, & Vanourek, 2000, p. 239, emphasis in original)

> I don't think at the beginning of this movement anyone intended for there to be one measure [of success] for these schools. (Jeanne Allen, cited in Bowman, 2000, p. 20)

> Is it the right (and a fair) question to ask charter schools to provide "compelling evidence that they provide superior education"? I don't think so. Did we pledge that they would be better? No. What we asserted is that we would provide meaningful alternative choices for parents and students based on articulated outcomes—a breath of fresh air in a system that too often can't seem to think outside a very confining box. (Gary Hart, quoted in Finn, Manno, & Vanourek, 2000, p. 238)

Variations in the relevant elements to use to determine effectiveness and the appropriate standards to apply to those variables only lengthen as reformers from different points on the reform debate continuum enter the discussions.

The task we have given ourselves is to inform the larger charter school discussion, not to adjudicate disputes over the proper indices of success. In a real sense, the latter objective is beyond the power of empirical data anyway. What we undertake below is an examination of all relevant components that are held in high regard by some segment of the charter school community, assuming that sufficient data exist to make an assessment, however preliminary it may be. We complete that assignment following the conceptual case for effectiveness presented in Chapter 5 under "reform dynamics." We first examine the effects of charters in their own communities and then assess the impact of charters in the larger education system.

INDIVIDUAL SCHOOL EFFECTS

Empirical information examining whether charter schools are improving education is slim and tentative. (Henig, Moser, Holyoke, & Lacireno-Paquet, 1999, p. 5)

In investigating how productive individual charter schools are, we rely on the measures for which sufficient data are available to draw preliminary conclusions: organizational health, customer satisfaction, student achievement, school accountability, and equity.

Organizational Health

While the final arbitrator of charter school success will center on how well these new institutions meet the needs of their customers, enhance student performance, strengthen accountability, and promote equity, as we chronicled in Chapter 6, these outcome measures are mediated through a host of organizational conditions. These bridging variables are what holds our attention here. We concentrate on those factors that are privileged in the theoretical analyses of charters and for which there is sufficient empirical evidence to craft an initial narrative. We commence by examining a cluster of factors that combine into a variable we label organizational and professional culture. We then explore organizational innovation.

Organizational and Professional Culture

Research studies affirm that the culture in charter schools is generally positive (Izu et al., 1998). In particular, "educators in charter schools view their working conditions as high quality and professional" (Wohlstetter & Griffin, 1997a, p. 28) and "deeply satisfying" (UCLA Charter School Study, n.d., p. 52).

Empowerment. To begin with, a large number of studies confirm that teachers in charter schools feel empowered (Little Hoover Commission, 1996; Rosenblum Brigham Associates, 1998). That is, "Charter school status [gives] staff members a sense of empowerment and of being part of a significant reform process" (Anderson and Marsh, cited in Bomotti, Ginsberg, & Cobb, 1999, p. 7), or, as the Hudson Institute national study asserts, "Charters offer teachers entrepreneurial opportunities and more chances to be involved with school policymaking and planning" (Finn, Manno, & Vanourek, 2000, p. 232).

Recent reports from California add weight to these conclusions. For example, in their study, the UCLA research team (n.d.) discovered that "charter school teachers do express a sense of empowerment, derived from their freedom to create smaller, more intimate school communities and their enhanced professional identities" (p. 5). They also uncovered significant decision-making influence for the teachers in the charter schools they visited. Corwin and Flaherty (1995) concluded that compared to their peers in conventional public schools, teachers in charter schools enjoyed more influence and more autonomy. They found major differences in levels of control in all program areas, with charter school staffs enjoying greater influence in almost every area of operation in the sectors of curriculum and instruction, governance, and budget. Finally, Izu and her team (1998) proffer narratives of charter schools that show teachers with "greater opportunities to have a voice in decision making" (p. 59): "Relative to prior experiences, teachers indicated that they [were] 'very much more' (49%) or 'somewhat more' (21%) involved than before" (p. 22).

Data from the national charter school studies completed by Berman and his colleagues (1998, 1999; Nelson et al., 2000) reinforce these early conclusions on empowerment. These investigators ascertained that "the majority of charter schools reported they had primary control over most areas critical to school operations" (Berman et al., 1999, p. 3). In particular, they report:

> In 1998–99, most charter schools had primary control or authority over their administrative operations including: the budget (73%), purchase of supplies and equipment (88%), and hiring of teaching staff (88%). In addition, most charter schools had primary control over the operation of their education program, including: the daily and yearly schedule (95%), curriculum (83%), discipline (87%), calendar (77%), and student assessment policies (72%). A lower percentage of schools reported that they had primary control over their student admissions policies (59%). (Nelson et al., 2000, p. 46)

All of the evidence on empowerment and control does not point in the same direction, however (Izu et al., 1998). In a comparative study in charter and regular public schools in Colorado, Bomotti, Ginsberg, and Cobb (1999) found that "teachers in the traditional schools perceived themselves to be more empowered in the school-wide arena (3.00 and 2.60 respectively) but less so in the classroom with students (3.64 and 4.03 respectively). Effect sizes associated with those mean differences (−0.48 and +0.46 respectively) suggest moderately strong practical significance to those mean differences" (p. 111). They conclude that "for the most part rhetoric and early research findings regarding enhanced teacher 'empowerment' in charter schools outpaces the reality of actual teacher experience when compared to the experiences of teachers in traditional public schools" (p. 17) and that these new institutions "are not delivering on the significantly enhanced level of teacher professionalism hoped for by educational reformers" (p. 18).

Professionalism. As was the case with empowerment, most of the empirical evidence substantiates assertions that charter schools advance the development of a professional culture across an array of elements, that "charter schools foster teacher professionalism" (Finn, Manno, & Vanourek, 2000, p. 266). There is evidence, for example, that charter schools nurture the growth of two flowers at the center of the school improvement garden (Murphy, 1992)—academic press (Bomotti, Ginsberg, & Cobb, 1999; The Evaluation Center, 1998; Vanourek et al., 1997a) and collective responsibility for student success (Wohlstetter & Griffin, 1997a). Careful research also validates theoretical claims that teachers experience substantial collaboration and palpable esprit de corps in charter schools (Izu et al., 1998; UCLA Charter School Study, n.d.). According to Izu and her research team (1998), this professionalism rests on a tripod of "trust, mutual respect and camaraderie" (p. 50) and supports an "orientation toward a continuous improvement" (Wohlstetter & Griffin, 1997a, p. 19), "an openness to sharing and critiquing one another's work" (Izu et al., 1998, p. 59), and a predilection to teamwork (Weiss, 1997).

Community. There is considerable consensus in the empirical literature that "charter schools are characterized by a strong sense of community" (Rosenblum Brigham Associates, 1998, p. 6; see also Goenner, 1996; Sarason, 1998; Vanourek et al., 1997b), communities with the two critical ingredients of small size and clear mission. To begin with, charters generally create "intimate, personal settings" (UCLA Charter School Study, n.d., p. 50), a condition that "may be the most important aspect of the charter movement . . . regardless of the exact nature of the educational program" (Berman et al., 1998, p. 45; see also UCLA Charter School Study, n.d.). Indeed, structural features such as small size "support the development of close-knit communities, where individual students are well known by faculty . . . where parents are welcomed into the school" (Arsen, Plank, & Sykes, n.d., p. 51), and where teachers work together as a learning team.

In analyses of community, the construct of clear mission is often intricately linked with intimate size. It provides the "unity of purpose" (Izu et al., 1998, p. 50) and the sense of consistency and coordination across all aspects of an organization that define high performing schools. As Hassel (1999a) notes, "If charter schools are to serve as a model for conventional public schools, what they appear to be demonstrating is the importance of a coherent focus rather than the value of any particular classroom and management practices" (p. 132).

Flexibility and Sustainability. In our forthcoming discussion of innovation, we explore the possibility that the coherence and durability of alterations in charters may be as important as the nature of the changes themselves. And there are some hints in the research that charters foster this sustainability, particularly by buffering operations from "shifting policy priorities [and] redirection[s] of programmatic resources" (Izu et al., 1998, p. 57) and by freeing schools from bureaucratic encumbrances (Rosenblum Brigham Associates, 1998). There is also a sense in the research that charter schools are more nimble organizations than are regular public schools, that they have enhanced flexibility across a range of areas, including finances, personnel, and curriculum (Manno et al., 1998a):

> PSAs [Public School Academies] also have flexibility to shape staffing patterns to make use of parent volunteers and aides, support services personnel, and leadership positions for teachers, parents, and other community members. They also can experiment with new uses of time, any school's most precious resource. For example, charter schools can alter daily, weekly, and annual schedules to accommodate new curricular and instructional practices. And, they can "bundle" an expanded array of services and programs in the school to better meet community needs and preferences. (Arsen, Plank, & Sykes, n.d., p. 51)

In charters, there is a feeling that "decisions can be made quickly and problems solved more easily than in district schools" (Rosenblum Brigham Associates, 1998, p. 7).

Efficacy and Morale. Documentation to date offers support for assertions that employees find charter schools to be good places to work. We have already reported that teachers in charter schools feel empowered, believing that they have more ability to influence organizational operations than is the case in conventional schools. Charter school teachers also appear to be highly committed, enjoy a sense of efficacy that is often absent in regular public schools, and share an unusually high sense of morale and pride in their work (Izu et al., 1998; UCLA Charter School Study, n.d.). Teachers in these new schools "view their working conditions as high quality and professional, and such conditions clearly offer powerful rewards to the people working in the schools" (Wohlstetter & Griffin, 1997a, p. 28).

Reports almost uniformly uncover "high levels of" (Izu et al., 1998, p. 49), or "great satisfaction" (UCLA Charter School Study, n.d., p. 49) among the teachers in charter schools (Sarason, 1998; Weiss, 1997), with research showing that "nearly all are finding personal fulfillment and professional reward" (Vanourek et al., 1997a, p. 1): "The research suggests that charter school teachers are generally satisfied so far with their experiences despite what appear to be some fairly common concerns, such as heavy workloads, inadequate facilities, relatively low salaries and tenuous job security" (Bomotti, Ginsberg, & Cobb, 1999, p. 5).

It is noteworthy that although charters generally score well on measures that define organizational and professional culture, these new forms of schooling are not without problems. One group of analysts, often those closest to the day-to-day operations of charters, worries about the potential deterioration of positive cultures as the joys of newness fade under the pressures of inadequate funding and the realities that accompany limited resources. Concern is expressed that the honored mantle of autonomy will lead to crippling isolation (Rosenblum Brigham Associates, 1998), especially an absence of much-needed outside support and assistance (Sarason, 1998) and a lack of attention to professional development (Wohlstetter & Griffin, 1997a). Others detect hints that as pressures to perform mount, frustration will develop in the teaching ranks (Weiss, 1997), perhaps undermining the esprit de corps currently enjoyed in many of these schools. The greatest sense of anxiety about a potential deterioration of organizational culture is rooted in analyses of the "long and intense" (Weiss, 1997, p. 13) work schedules often found in charter schools. Indeed, the current reality is that working in charter schools is often more challenging and carries with it more responsibilities than does teaching in traditional public schools (Weiss, 1997). Apprehension is expressed that the work may lead to burnout and high turnover (Little Hoover Commission, 1996; Rosenblum Brigham Associates, 1998; UCLA Charter School Study, n.d.) and that organizational health, in turn, could be compromised.

A second group of reviewers question the robustness of some of the findings on organizational health. For example, Bomotti's research team (1999), in a study more carefully designed than many others, found that while teachers in charters were indeed quite satisfied with their work, they were no more satisfied than were their colleagues in traditional public schools.

Finally, a third group of analysts have uncovered clues that the unique organizational features of charter schools might promote the emergence of unique problems. For example, the barriers between governing boards and teachers in charter schools are much more permeable than they are in regular public schools. Leaders are often nontraditional in substance and style. Parents are more likely to be found "on the playing field" with school staff than is the norm in the public schools. Critics point out that there are potential down sides to these and related organizational realities in charter schools that have received insufficient attention to date.

Innovation

In Chapter 6, we dedicated considerable space to a review of the theoretical literature on charters, establishing hypotheses about the ways these organizations function and about the benefits expected to be found in these new institutions. Central to all of those discussions was the notion that charters would nurture considerable innovation, innovation that would serve as the engine for enhanced practice in charter schools and as the beacon for school improvement in conventional schools and school districts. In short, innovation is at the heart of the charter school reform model (Miron, 1999). The question at hand here is: Do charter schools promote innovation?

Background. The concept of innovation in charters is laced with ambiguity (Reynolds, 2000) and "open to interpretation" (Good, Braden, & Drury, 2000, p. 15). In short, as with most of the patterns in the charter reform tapestry, the answer to our question depends a good deal on the definition of the variable being investigated—innovation, in this case—the criteria used to determine success, and the standards employed to calibrate those criteria. By way of illustration, here are some conclusions of various researchers on this core question. On the pro side of the issue:

> Charter schools typically use unconventional, creative approaches to teaching. (Caudell, 1997b, p. 3)

> Today, many charter schools are fonts of educational and organizational creativity. (Finn, Manno, & Vanourek, 2000, p. 90)

> There is ample evidence that innovation is the norm rather than the exception at charter schools. (Little Hoover Commission, 1996, p. 44)

From the research camp of the skeptics, summary statements have a significantly different hue:

> By and large, we have been disappointed in the area of innovation. (The Evaluation Center, 1998, p. 17)

> Many programs are hardly "innovative" by any common understanding of that word. . . . Virtually all the approaches being employed in charter schools are or have been implemented in regular public schools. (American Federation of Teachers, n.d., pp. 50–51)

Documented educational innovation in charter schools is rare. (Good, Braden, & Drury, 2000, p. 7)

All of this activity in regular public schools raises an important question: With so much innovation already occurring, what are charter schools adding to the mix. The answer may be 'not that much'. . . . Virtually all the approaches mentioned in the list—and in the much larger list of approaches that could be generated— are being tried in regular public schools as well as charter schools. (Buechler, 1996, pp. 28–29)

Innovation As Breakthrough Change. Where is the truth in these observations? If one begins with the theoretical literature in which it often is asserted that charters will produce breakthrough ideas for operating schools and educating youngsters, then it appears that charters fall far short of the mark. While a few researchers have unearthed evidence of "innovative teaching practices" (Weiss, 1997, p. 16) at charters (Little Hoover Commission, 1996) and one study has concluded that "charters are introducing a variety of innovations more frequently than comparison schools" (Corwin & Flaherty, 1995, p. 5), the corpus of empirical work produces much more tempered conclusions. At least nine studies conducted over the past 5 years affirm the finding that "charter schools as a whole cannot be perceived as innovative" (Horn & Miron, 2000, p. 26); Arsen, Plank, and Sykes (n.d.); Bomotti, Ginsberg, and Cobb (1999); Buechler (1996); The Evaluation Center (1998); Hassel (1997); Izu and colleagues (1998); Reynolds (2000); UCLA Charter School Study (n.d.); and Wohlstetter and Griffin (1997a). Most uncover the presence of "educational approaches which build or borrow directly from educational approaches commonly found elsewhere" (Izu et al., 1998, p. 31). While these reports do not gainsay the power of autonomy to open the door to important innovations in teaching and learning, they find that "many charter schools have not taken full advantage of the opportunities that surround them" (Horn & Miron, 2000, p. 26); they do "not capitalize on this power" (Wohlstetter & Griffin, 1997a, p. 34). Indeed, results from these studies indicate that "charter schools [are] not engag[ing] in many 'new' educational practices" (Hassel, 1999a, p. 142):

To be sure, charter schools have done interesting and varied things with their curricula, their instructional practices, their staffing, their budgets, and their governance. But the innovations that charter schools have undertaken are, by and large, innovations that have been proposed elsewhere and, to a limited extent, carried out by existing public schools. (p. 131)

Particularly disheartening are findings that document that charter schools "are not pioneering innovations in teaching and learning" (Arsen, Plank, & Sykes, n.d., p. III). Studies that investigate classroom practices often conclude that "in terms of instructional practices—classroom organization, curriculum, and pedagogy, for example . . . the majority of charter schools employed techniques commonly found in non-charter public schools. The instructional core remained similar to other public settings" (UCLA Charter School Study, n.d., p. 52): "Teaching and learning in most charter school classrooms is indistinguishable from teaching in other public schools" (Arsen, Plank, & Sykes, n.d., p. 50). Thus, it is "unlikely that PSAs will be major sources of innovations related to teaching and learning" (p. 57). And what seems to be the case in the area of instruction appears to hold in the curricular domain as well (Buechler, 1996).

A good summary of the story line here has been tendered by Bomotti and her colleagues (1999): "The fact that the processes surrounding the instructional core remain similar to other public school settings indicates that the charter school movement has not resulted in the degree of educational innovation and experimentation envisioned by its advocates" (pp. 17–18).

Innovation As a Shift from Local Practice. Even strong supporters of the innovation hypothesis are coming to the conclusion that "many charter programs are variations on familiar curricular and pedagogical themes" (Finn, Manno, & Vanourek, 2000, p. 156), that while these new "schools are experimenting with a variety of educational approaches" (Buechler, 1996, p. IX), so too are many regular public schools. At the same time, they have contoured a more nuanced derivation of the initial innovation proposition. The case for innovation here attends much more directly to issues of context in these new schools. The introduction of relatively new ideas as the innovation calculus, or what Finn and his team (2000) label the "inventing [of] brand new educational wheels" (p. 266), is downplayed if not discarded.

In making judgments about the extent of innovation, reviewers in the recalibrated camp assert that "it is important to consider the local context of . . . charter schools" (Weiss, 1997, p. 16). Starting here, the penultimate question is not does the charter school feature a new design, but rather does it, even when "the educational programs . . . offer[ed] may not be substantially different than what could be found in other schools" (Izu et al., 1998, p. 56), represent: (1) a change from the way teachers conducted business in their previous schools, (2) a marked change "from conventional schools in the vicinity" (Finn, Manno, & Vanourek, 2000, p. 266), and/or (3) "something desirable and of added value" (Izu et al., 1998, p. 56). Using this revised scoring system, Manno and his colleagues argue that "in their own contexts . . . virtually all charter schools are truly innovative" (p. 493).

Evidence on this alternative formulation of the innovation hypothesis is less prevalent than are findings on the more robust form of the hypothesis presented above. Nonetheless, even here, investigations of learning and teaching in charters suggest this alternative rendition of the innovation proposition may also be in trouble (Arsen, Plank, & Sykes, n.d.; UCLA Charter School Study, n.d.).

Innovation As Meeting Market Needs. When innovation is contoured from different molds than those noted above, a much more effective landscape of change often is revealed. For example, when innovation is defined not in terms of the characteristics of the activity but as something that attracts clients or in terms of providing for previously unserved or underserved consumer demands, charter schools are much more innovative than they are under the scenarios considered above (Izu et al., 1998; Reynolds, 2000). Horn and Miron (2000) articulate this point as follows: "It can be argued that what has happened with charters is exactly what should have happened, the creation of diverse schools providing parents and students with options from which to choose" (p. 26).

Innovation As Systemic Activity. A number of charter scholars are beginning to posit that innovation might best be thought of in terms of support for systemic or wholistic activity at the school level. The proposition here is that the central ingredient in the success of charters is the development of a "distinct organization with a unique mission aligned with its philosophy and values" (Finn, Manno, & Vanourek, 2000, p. 228). What charter schools accomplish, it is argued by some, is to weave whatever change elements are in play—new or not—into the fabric that comprises this central focus (Finn, Bierlein, & Manno, 1996; Rosenblum Brigham Associates, 1998).

There is some conflicting evidence on this measure of innovation. For example, Wohlstetter and Griffin (1997a) discovered that few of the charter schools in their study "described a well-articulated and integrated instructional program" (p. 21). However, a number of recent investigations (Reynolds, 2000; Rosenblum Brigham Associates, 1998; Solmon, Block, & Gifford, 1999) lend support to the supposition that the key issue in charter school innovation is not the creation of brand-new forms but rather the ability of these institutions to "put in place curriculum and instructional strategies of their own volition to maintain a steady course" (Izu et al., 1998, p. 33; see also Buechler, 1996). Based on their research, Rosenblum and her associates (1998) contend that "most charter schools apparently do not have a collection of individual innovative practices, but demonstrate comprehensive and cohesive *innovative systems* that revolve around a unifying theme or mission" (p. 16). Likewise, Hassel (1999a) asserts that "although the individual practices of most charter schools may not be radically innovative, there is evidence that charter schools link their practices together in comprehensive 'innovation systems' to focus on a coherent mission" (p. 131).

Innovation As Institutional Change. Finally, as we touched upon earlier, and explain in some detail in the last section of this chapter on the system-wide impact of charters, the venue for change—the place to look for innovation, if you will—may be in the institutional forms that shape education rather than in the core technology of schooling (Loveless & Jasin, 1998). To determine if there is innovation in charters, some analysts assert, the spotlight needs to be redirected from the classroom to the management systems, organizational forms, and governance structures that hold the school together: "It may be in these areas, more than curriculum and instruction, where charter schools prove truly innovative" (Buechler, 1996, p. 29). And early research suggests that these reviewers may be, at least partially, correct. Investigators are increasingly documenting innovations in the organization and governance of charter schools (Rofes, 1998a). Arsen and his colleagues (n.d.) concur, concluding that "the most important charter school innovations are not about teaching and learning but rather about control over school operations" (p. 52).

Customer Satisfaction

The Evidence

When we evaluate parent and student satisfaction, at least eight measures merit attention:

1. judgments about the quality of the school in general
2. comparisons of the charter school with institutions previously attended
3. demand as measured by the number of people desiring to attend the charter
4. demand as measured by the expanding number of charters
5. demand as assessed by longevity of student attendance or repeat business
6. customer recommendations
7. parental involvement
8. growth in the number of would-be charter school operators

Data on areas 4 (growth in the number of charters) and 7 (parental involvement) have been presented extensively throughout this volume, most thoroughly in Chapters 2 and 3. Without revisiting the complexities involved in using these measures as proxies for customer satisfaction, the numbers convey the clear impression that charter consumers are quite pleased with the services that these new schools are providing (Becker, Nakagawa, & Corwin, 1997; Bomotti, Ginsberg, & Cobb, 1999; Corwin & Flaherty, 1995; Izu et al., 1998; Little Hoover Commission, 1996). The data for areas 6 (customer recommendations) and 8 (growth in charter operators) are thin but consistent with the overall body of evidence of positive consumer gratification with charters (The Evaluation Center, 1998; Miron, 1999).

In terms of satisfaction measured by voting with one's feet (area 3), "the demand for the option provided by charter schools is high" (Little Hoover Commission, 1996, p. 36). As B. Nelson and his colleagues (2000) discovered in their national study of charters, "The demand for charter schools remains high—7 of 10 charter schools reported that they have a waiting list" (p. 1). Similar results have been affirmed in other studies. The Center for Education Reform (n.d.) reported waiting lists in 65% of the 194 schools they surveyed, with the average waiting list being nearly half the size of the existing enrollment (an average of 295 enrolled students and an average of 135 students on the waiting list) (p. 1). Izu and her colleagues (1998) found that nearly all the charter schools in their study had "waiting lists ranging from 15 to 1000 students" (p. 16). In Michigan, charter schools "receive between three and four student applications for each available seat" (Goenner, 1996, p. 34). In their national study, Vanourek and his team (1997b) also confirmed the presence of "long waiting lists" (p. 8) in charter schools.

Studies addressing longevity or the amount of repeat business (area 5) lend additional credence to claims that customers are quite pleased with the charter schools they attend or to which they send their children. A study in Arizona by Gifford and Keller (1996) revealed that 88% of parents were very likely (68%) or likely (20%) to send their child to the same charter next year while only 6% were very unlikely (2%) or unlikely (2%) to do so (p. 18). In a later study of charter schools in Arizona, Mulholland (1999) found that when the numbers are "adjusted for students who cannot return because the next grade level is not available at the school or because they are moving, 80% plan for their child to return, 6% do not, and 14% are unsure" (p. 13). In a national study based on responses from nearly 3,000 parents in 30 charter schools in nine states, the Hudson Institute established very similar benchmarks (79%, 4%, and 13%) (Vanourek et al., 1997a, p. 8). Investigations by the Little Hoover Commission (1996) and Izu and her colleagues (1998) add support to the finding that longevity is high in charter schools.

Assessments that directly inquire about parent and student satisfaction with charters (areas 1 and 2) are also consistently positive, revealing that "charter schools are very popular with their primary constituents" (Vanourek et al., 1997a, p. 1), although information from parents is more extensive and more positive than are data from students. In assessing general satisfaction, for example, Gifford and Keller (1996) found that 92% of parents in her Arizona study were either very satisfied (57%) or satisfied (35%) with their child's charter school (p. 16). In their examination of charter schools up for renewal in California, Izu and her colleagues (1998) uncovered a similar pattern, with

96% of parents reporting that they were very satisfied (65%) or satisfied (32%) (p. 49). In a second California study, Corwin and his team (1996) reported that 46% of parents were "very satisfied" while another 38% were "satisfied" (p. 16). Studies in Massachusetts and the District of Columbia support the Arizona and California reports (Henig et al., 1999; Weiss, 1997). The data from a large-scale, cross-state study also support assertions of high levels of satisfaction among charter parents and students. The Hudson Institute study, for example, concluded that parents are "satisfied with the education being received and the work being done in charter schools" (Manno, Bierlein, & Vanourek, 1998a, p. 546).

Equally important, research has documented that parents are pleased with nearly all aspects of the charter schools that their children attend (Gifford & Ogle, 1998; Weiss, 1997), especially with the "education-related" (Vanourek et al., 1997a, p. 4) dimensions of the school, such as school and class size, school mission, curriculum, academic standards, and so forth (Corwin, Carlos, Lagomorsino, & Scott, 1996; Izu, et al., 1998; Vanourek et al., 1997a), and with the governance structures and arrangements at the school (Gifford & Ogle, 1998; Weiss, 1997). Finally, these high levels of satisfaction appear to hold for parents from different socioeconomic backgrounds, with students in various classification categories (e.g., special education, bilingual education), and for families from different racial and ethnic groups (Izu et al., 1998; McLaughlin & Henderson, 1998; Vanourek et al., 1997b).

In addition to presenting general measures of the happiness of charter customers, by collecting information on how charter schools stack up to other options available to families, especially schools previously attended, a few researchers have explored comparative indices of parent and student satisfaction. These reports tend to reinforce the story line outlined above. For example, Mulholland (1999) found that "parents of charter school students and the students themselves are much more satisfied with the academic performance of the students at their charter schools than at their former schools" (p. 49). Parents consistently judged the academic program in charters as preferable to the one available in their child's last school in the Gifford and Ogle (1998) study as well:

> Parents were asked to compare their child's charter school with their child's last school in relation to several highly rated factors. More than 90% of parents thought their child's charter school was better than his/her previous school with regard to classroom organization, communication, discipline, school size, teaching methodology, curriculum and technology. A majority of parents thought the charter school was worse with regards to school facility. This was the only area in which charter schools consistently lagged behind, according to parents. (p. 2)

More than 80% of parents also considered their child's charter to be more effective than his or her previous school in the areas of school size, administration, technology, class size, parental involvement, and quality of teaching. Finally, in their analysis, Hudson Institute researchers discovered that:

> Over two-thirds of parents say their charter school is better than their child's previous school with respect to class size, school size, and individual attention from teachers. Over three-fifths say it is better with respect to teaching quality, parental involvement, curriculum, extra help for students, academic standards, accessibility and openness, and discipline. (Vanourek et al., 1997a, p. 1)

As was the case with general measures of satisfaction, these comparative assessments are similar for parents from different economic, racial, and language backgrounds.

Some Cautionary Notes

A number of issues that may temper these conclusions merit attention in this discussion, however. First, while "the number of studies and pattern of results suggest that parents and students are generally satisfied with their charter experience" (Good, Braden, & Drury, 2000, p. 20)—"that satisfaction levels . . . are wide and deep" (Vanourek et al., 1997a, p. 9)—not everything is wonderful in charters, according to parents and students (Corwin et al., 1996). Given the portraits presented in Chapter 3, it is not surprising that customers are often less than thrilled with charter school facilities (Mulholland, 1999; Vanourek et al., 1997a). They often wish for richer offerings outside the core academic program, especially for more extensive sports programs. There are also concerns "about the acceptance of credits earned in a charter school by regular public schools and about the value of a charter school diploma for college admission and scholarship purposes" (Mulholland, 1999, p. 14).

In addition, most studies of customer satisfaction focus on students and parents in charter schools. When a broader definition of the term "customers" is employed (e.g., taxpayers), the results are less impressive. Even when the spotlight is limited to parents and students in charter schools, satisfaction measures decline considerably when parents are queried about their overall level of satisfaction with these alternative forms of schooling. For example, Gifford and Ogle (1998) found that when charter parents were questioned on their thoughts about charters across the state of Arizona, 48% "had a less than favorable opinion" (p. 22) of charters, compared to only 37% who maintained a favorable judgment. That is, "parents overwhelmingly approved of the performance of their child's charter school but most parents (48%) had less than favorable opinions of charter schools in Arizona, generally" (p. 2).

Finally, and perhaps most importantly, the evidence on customer satisfaction:

Must naturally be taken with a pinch of salt, as it is vulnerable to what economists call "revealed preferences" and the biases of self-selection. (Satisfaction with a charter school is influenced by the fact that few people would have chosen the school if they didn't expect to like it.) (Finn, Manno, & Vanourek, 2000, p. 82)

Or, as Windler (1996) states it, we "are becoming more and more aware of the fact that when parents are given the opportunity to choose, they 'will be satisfied with their school of choice because they have exercised their right to choose'" (p. 68). Given this phenomenon, Rothstein (1998a,b) questions whether the size of the satisfaction indices reported in the various studies are really all that impressive. What all this suggests is the need for more refined investigations that separate choice from program, that compare satisfaction quotients in charter schools and with those in other schools of choice.

Student Achievement

Context

Charters are generally seen as being a key force in the quest to reorient how we think about school success and failure, shifting the spotlight from a focus on inputs and processes to a focus on school outcomes (Henig et al., 1999). Thus, for many, student achievement is the sine qua non of the charter movement and the calculus of charter accountability—or as Ciffolillo and Wolf (n.d.) note, "Demonstrating academic achievement is at the core of the charter school accountability system" (p. 17). Can charters pass the "real test" (Caudell, 1997b, p. 1) of school reform? Do they enhance student learning, and are they accountable for their outcomes? We examine the evidence on both of these questions in the next two sections.

While rarely noted, it is important to remind ourselves that achievement discussions that occur under the topic of charter schools in many ways mirror the issues, concerns, and problems extant in the school reform movement writ large (Berman et al., 1998). For example, some charter school operators and analysts have real concerns about the use of standardized tests to measure student learning (Hill, Pierce, & Guthrie, 1997). As in the larger school reform debate in this area, critics assert that standardized tests are a rather clumsy tool for measuring such a complex and nuanced construct as student learning. From an equity perspective, critics raise questions about a movement that insists on portraying results in "universalistic terms without considering the meaning of successful outcomes in different localized communities" (Wells, Lopez et al., 1999, p. 201). From a program perspective, analysts like Sizer (cited in Archer, 2000) aver that standardized assessment measures can undermine the philosophical foundations and distort the unique operational designs of many charters (Wohlstetter & Griffin, 1997a). Critics claim that these assessments promote homogeneity rather than allowing and encouraging the supply side diversity that is so key to the charter movement.

Concomitantly, the lack of a robust testing system in education in general is bedeviling efforts to determine how well charter schools are performing, particularly in comparison to traditional public schools (Berman et al., 1998).

In addition, a number of charter-specific issues confound efforts to gauge student achievement in these alternative schools. There is, of course, the oft-repeated refrain in this volume about the recency of the charter school movement (remember that three quarters of these schools opened in 1997 or later [Henig et al., 1999, p. 56])—a reality that has much to do with the limited body of data available on student learning in charter schools. This is compounded by the fact that in the struggle to give birth to these new entities, many founders have devoted insufficient attention to clarifying levels of desired student achievement and specifying the methods to be employed in judging that performance (Bierlein, 1996; Hill, Pierce, & Guthrie, 1997; Manno et al., 1998a). According to Buechler (1996), "evaluating student achievement in charter schools will continue to be difficult because of the lack of rigor in many of the charters regarding student outcomes and the measurement of those outcomes" (p. 26).

Many charters also are emphasizing the use of more "subjective assessment processes such as portfolios of student work . . . individualized evaluations . . . surveys and self-evaluations [that] are rhetorically rich and statistically vague about what increases in student achievement will constitute success by the schools" (Little Hoover Commission, 1996, p. 32). As Izu and her colleagues (1998) note, "The degree to which these approaches are standardized and used systematically, or analyzed on an aggregate level, is unclear" (p. 39).

Comparing the achievement of students in charters with that of peers in more traditional public schools is made more problematic by two additional conditions. First, because a charter school "is not a learning design, it is not possible as a result to link charter schools and student learning directly. The evaluation has to proceed from an examination of the particular learning programs in use" (Kolderie, n.d., p. 5). Compounding this reality is the knowledge that most charters have a self-selected pool of students and parents: Because of "this self-selection and the lack of baseline data for students in charter schools, accountability systems relying on one-shot test score data may really measure how successful charter schools are at choosing more motivated students rather than how well these schools teach their students" (UCLA Charter School Study, n.d., p. 60).

Data

Given this contextual background, what can we report about student achievement in charter schools? At the end of 2000, the bottom line is that we simply do not have sufficient information to make any definitive claims: "There is then . . . one big gap in our information base: We do not yet know how much and how well the students in charter schools are learning, or whether their academic achievement will surpass that of similar youngsters enrolled in more conventional schools. And in the final analysis, that is how the effectiveness of charter schools must be judged. . . . But not enough charter schools have yet been operating long enough to appraise their academic achievement in any meaningful way" (Manno et al., 1998a, pp. 538–539). Thus, the most powerful conclusion we can draw is that we lack sufficient data to draw any hard and fast conclusions (Teske et al., 2000; Wohlstetter & Griffin, 1997b): the "gap in our knowledge base when it comes to achievement data" (Vanourek et al., 1997a, p. 9) makes "it difficult to evaluate the progress of most charter schools in the very area where they are supposed to make the biggest difference" (Buechler, 1996, p. 26). The fact that "there is as yet no firm evidence of higher performance by students of charter schools" (Teske et al., 2000, p. 17) is, not surprisingly, viewed in different ways. For some, it represents "a lack of compelling evidence" (Fuller, 1996, p. 38) and provides a cautionary tale about how to proceed (Molnar, 1996). For others, it is largely a timing and design issue, suggesting a need for additional charter school programs and for new initiatives to unearth evidence.

Advancing beyond this basic conclusion is a bit problematic. Nonetheless, some evidence is beginning to accumulate on the achievement question. We found two studies that examined student achievement indirectly through parent and/or student perceptions of performance. In the Evaluation Center (1998) study, "students perceived their performance to be much better [statistically significant] at the charter school than at the previous school" (p. 37). Similar conclusions were reported by the investigators in the Hudson Institute study:

> Dramatic improvement occurred in many cases. Among students who report that they did poorly at their previous school, 16.9% are now doing "excellent" work and 43.3% are doing "good" work. Of those failing at their previous school, 19.8% are now doing "excellent" work and 36.5% are doing "good" work. (Vanourek et al., 1997a, p. 3)

> Charter school parents also appraised the academic performance of their children at their previous schools and (as of February 1997) at their charter school. Among parents who report that their children did "below average" work at their previous school, 8.2% indicate that their sons and daughters are now doing "excellent"

work and 23.8% say their child is now doing "above average" work. Of those whose children did "poorly" at their previous school, 18.9% now report "excellent" work and 25.6% report "above average" work by their children. (p. 3)

These results hold for parents and students from different racial, economic, and social groups and for students in bilingual, special education, and other special needs groups and for their parents.

Direct measures of achievement gains in charter schools are not nearly so positive. While information is accumulating on all points of the achievement evidence continuum, the bulk of that still limited data does not support the claims that charters will lead to breakthrough changes in student performance (Good, Braden, & Drury, 2000). While this information has been cast with two very different spins,

> There is little evidence that students are learning more in charter schools than in regular public schools. (Buechler, 1996, p. 26)

> Charter school students are achieving similar academic gains to students attending regular public schools. (Mulholland, 1999, p. 40)

The following summary by Horn and Miron (2000) is a good marker for the knowledge base on student achievement in charter schools to date:

> The data tell us a mixed story about charter schools' impact on student achievement. . . . Based on our analysis of MAEAP results in both our first evaluations and in our current report, one can see that the charter schools as a whole are not performing as well as traditional public schools, nor are they making gains that exceed the traditional public schools. . . . [However,] school-by-school comparisons of individual charter schools and their host district reveals that a good many charters significantly outgained their host districts. (pp. 57, 88, 80)

While there is clear evidence that some charters are promoting improvement in student learning (Farber, 1998; Nathan, 1996a, 1998; Vanourek et al., 1997b; Zollers & Ramanathan, 1998), the data on the upside of the achievement question are often drawn from nonscientific studies. Unfortunately, nonrigorous, ad hoc reports of individual schools that are dramatically boosting student achievement scores lack the power to offer credible evidence of the success of the charter school movement. Even in the few systematic studies that do uncover evidence of enhanced learning in charters, the findings are not especially robust. For example, in the study by Izu and her colleagues (1998), the conclusion is as follows: "For the most part, these three analyses support the same overall theme: students in these five charter schools maintain or slightly improve their performance over time with respect to students in a comparison group of non-charter District schools, with few exceptions" (p. 47). The evidence, in sum, "suggests that overall, improvements in student performance across most of the charter schools is not dramatic" (p. 59). It is comparable.

Accountability

Macrolevel Empirical Backdrop

The first thing we need to remind the reader is that accountability is the fulcrum of the charter school movement.

> Charter school accountability is a serious matter. Not only will it make or break the charter "movement" itself, it will also be the primary source of evidence as to whether that movement is making a valuable contribution to the improved education of American children—and the renewal of U.S. public education—or is another half-tried reform fad that sinks into the sands like so many others. (Manno et al., 1997b, p. 14)

The second reminder is that there are three important domains of accountability associated with charters—market, government, and voluntary association. Which of these domains is most salient and is monitored most heavily depends on the ways in which states approach accountability (Berman et al., 1999) and on the prevailing perspective at the local school level "regarding to whom the charter schools should be most accountable" (UCLA Charter School Study, n.d., p. 60). In short, as Lane (1998) reminds us, "Accountability can mean different things in different contexts" (p. 23).

We also know that the accountability systems that have been forged at state and local levels throughout the country leave a good deal to be desired (Finn, Manno, & Vanourek, 2000). Or stated in a different form, nearly a decade after their inception, "educational policymakers have yet to agree on how the[se] publically financed but largely independent schools should be held accountable for their results" (Archer, 2000, p. 18). The outcome has been that most states have developed accountability language at a fairly high degree of abstraction. They "have passed relatively standard, largely vague provisions stating that charter schools are to be held accountable for results" (Hassel, 1999a, p. 77). The net results are that "state charter school accountability systems remain underdeveloped, often clumsy and ill-fitting, and are themselves beset by dilemmas" (Manno et al., 1997a, p. 1) and that "charter granting agencies are struggling" (Hassel, 1999a, p. 159) with how to deal with accountability issues. Their efforts are regularly hampered by their inability or unwillingness to "specify any clear performance standards or consequences"

(Wohlstetter & Griffin, 1997a, p. 22). Given these dynamics, "promising accountability systems for charter schools are still few and far between" (Finn, Manno, & Vanourek, 2000, p. 155), and a claim of "greater accountability for charters seems unwarranted" (Good, Braden, & Drury, 2000, p. 10).

Not unexpectedly, given this state context, at the school site "the level of specificity of language related to accountability is lower than what would be expected" (Mulholland, 1999, p. 2), and individual charter schools often "do not have sufficient accountability procedures in place" (p. 25). And because chartering documents are often "vague when it comes to their descriptions of student outcomes or benchmarks for achieving them ... local school boards that grant charters generally [have] no clear evidence of academic accountability" (UCLA Charter School Study, n.d., p. 59).

Five recent studies illustrate these conclusions. An investigation in Florida discovered that only 6 of 33 charters "contained measurable goals and objectives" (Archer, 2000, p. 19). In Arizona, Mulholland (1999) found that while 50% of charter applications "contained achievement related goals that were both clearly stated and measurable" (Exhibit B, p. 1), 40% outlined goals that were "either not clearly stated or not measurable, or both" (Exhibit B, p. 1) and "10% of applications did not address goals related to student achievement" (Exhibit B, p. 1). Similar conclusions were formed about the clarity of accountability language in three California studies—by Izu and colleagues (1998), UCLA Charter School Study (n.d.), and Wohlstetter and Griffin (1997a). For example, Izu and her colleagues (1998) report that "in reviewing the charters and visiting these schools, listing and adding up the goals was a complicated, if not impossible, task. This difficulty results from the fact that many of the goals, benchmarks, and measures were vague and not well defined" (p. 41).

Information on Accountability Systems

Different engines power market accountability, accountability through voluntary association, and government accountability. To date there has been no direct assessment of accountability through *voluntary association*. What we do know we must derive from the findings presented earlier on charters as communities. That is, in the aggregate, charters are effective in developing specific missions and in creating unifying connections among stakeholders at the school level. These, indeed, are powerful indices of the viability of accountability through voluntary association. At the same time, much more direct work is required to illustrate and investigate the elements of this model of accountability.

Also, in the area of *market accountability*, little direct evidence has been accumulated. The information that we have comes from cobbling together insights from two strands of market dynamics in charters. To begin with, market accountability works when "schools that attract students and maintain families' trust [are] sustained and those with weaker bases of parental support . . . go out of business" (Hill, Pierce, & Guthrie, 1997, p. 118). Markets will sort the wheat from the chaff. What we know so far in this area is important. First, charter schools are clearly adding new levels of choice for parents in the public school system (Gifford & Ogle, 1998), although concerns remain that in reality it may be the schools that are choosing families. Second, charter school staffs often do feel more accountable to parents and students than do teachers and administrators in more traditional public schools (UCLA Charter School Study, n.d.; Wohlstetter & Griffin, 1997a). Third, the market dynamic itself, as measured by consumers selecting charter schools and continuing to stay with their choices, is fairly robust. At the same time, however, we have been unable to unearth any studies that directly employ a comprehensive economic framework to assess the market component of charter school accountability. We believe that such an appraisal will deepen and expand our understanding of this important piece of the charter school movement.

In addition, market accountability works when the system is transparent and when there is an open flow of good information, especially about product quality. Very little empirical information on these issues has been produced during the first decade of the charter school movement. While, as we discuss below, some data are being generated by chartering boards and other government agencies, it is not especially powerful nor is it clear that it is readily accessible to charter customers. Indeed, given the long-standing tendency of schools to avoid inspecting outcomes, the inadequately conceptualized accountability designs that envelop charters in many states and the active resistance among some educators to spreading the charter school seed, serious questions remain about transparency and information flow in charters.

The most information we have in this area is on *government accountability*, primarily in the form of data required by the agencies that grant charters to schools and information uncovered in the various studies cited throughout this chapter. We know that charter-granting agencies require and that charter schools employ "a variety of assessment and evaluation tools . . . to demonstrate accountability" (Lane, 1998, p. 23). In their comprehensive study of charters throughout the country, Berman and Nelson and their colleagues (Berman et al., 1999; B. Nelson et al., 2000) explored government accountability in some detail. One key question focused on areas of charter schools monitored by the state. The study team concluded:

> Across states, there was greater variance for some areas of monitoring than for others. While a large proportion of schools in most states reported monitoring on student achievement and school finances, there was far greater variance among

the states in other areas, such as student behavior and school governance. (B. Nelson et al., 2000, p. 50)

They also reported:

> More than 9 of 10 charter schools were monitored for accountability in terms of school finances; nearly 9 of 10 for student achievement and for compliance with regulations; more than 8 of 10 for student attendance; and more than 6 of 10 for instructional practices. (p. 3)

In their earlier study, they documented monitoring in the following eight areas: school finances (87% of schools), student achievement (73%), student attendance (70%), compliance and regulation (63%), instructional practices (59%), school governance (34%), student behavior (30%), and school completion (24%) (Berman et al., 1999, p. 55).

Looking at the issue from the charter school out, Berman and his colleagues (1999) found that these new institutions provided information to a variety of different stakeholders, including the chartering agency, private funders, parents, the general community, the school governing board, and the state department of education. Information is generally provided in the form of periodic progress reports and school report cards (Mulholland, 1999; Wohlstetter, Wenning, & Briggs, 1995). Berman and his team (1999) discovered that charter schools used a variety of assessment methods to collect data for these reports, including standardized assessments (86% of the schools), student demonstrations of work (85%), parent satisfaction surveys (81)%, behavioral indicators (75%), state assessment programs (75%), student interviews or surveys (70%), and performance assessments (70%) (p. 60). More than one third of the schools employed at least seven of these measures in making their reports (B. Nelson et al., 2000, p. 3).

When specifically reviewing accountability for student performance, researchers disclose that charter schools employ an assortment of measures of student achievement. Some of them are "well-known traditional standardized tests" (Horn & Miron, 2000, p. 81) and "others are more innovative methods" (Berman et al., 1999, p. 58). The most prevalent of these more innovative "performance-based measures are teacher evaluations, student portfolios, and student presentations" (Cheung, Murphy, & Nathan, 1998, p. 12), although, as Izu and her colleagues (1998) remind us, most of these performance-based assessments are, as they are in traditional public schools, "works in progress" (p. 39).

Information on Consequences

The DNA of charter school accountability is, of course, consequences based on results. Given the recency of the movement, existing norms in education about accountability, and the struggle to get beyond the somewhat vague systems of accountability that have characterized charters during their infancy, our understanding of consequences is rather limited. We do know something about this issue, however. First, consequences in the charter movement are not as visible and, when visible, are not as powerful as one would expect (Manno et al., 1997a). Or as Wohlstetter and Griffin (1997a) put it, "The myth of greater accountability for charter schools far exceed[s] the reality" (p. 22). As is the case with many traditional public schools, results and subsequent actions based on those outcomes often get "lost in the everyday challenges of running a school" (Lutz, 1997, p. 4). In particular, there is less evidence of intermediate consequences and remedial actions for charter schools—short of revoking the school charter (Manno et al., 1997a).

Second, other than the reward of not being put out of business, there is almost no evidence of positive consequences associated with charters. In short, incentives and rewards are conspicuous by their absence. Third, and unanticipated given the heavy focus on using student academic achievement as the touchstone for charter success, the major accountability calculus to date has been fiscal probity (Mulholland, 1999; Wohlstetter & Griffin, 1997a). Many charter boards are "paying more attention to internal matters of school management and finance than to systematic assessments of academic achievement" (Henig, Moser, Holyoke, & Lacireno-Paquet, 1999, p. 60). Many schools are simply not being held accountable for "enhanced academic achievement" (UCLA Charter School Study, n.d., p. 4), and "virtually no schools have been shut down for performance" (P. Herdman, cited in Archer, 2000, p. 18). In short, accountability for academic achievement has been somewhat "illusive" (UCLA Charter School Study, n.d., p. 23). In many places, "The claim of greater school-level accountability for student outcomes via charter school reform has not truly come to pass" (p. 27).

Fourth, there has been little action in the area of high-stakes consequences, or "the system's ability to weed out failure through charter revocations" (Little Hoover Commission, 1996, p. 31). Somewhere in the neighborhood of 4% of charter schools have closed since the first school opened in 1992 (B. Nelson et al., 2000, p. 10), and many of these closed for reasons unrelated to accountability pressures. Most have involved financial hardships in keeping the schools afloat (Manno et al., 1997a).

Equity

As we reported in the last chapter, perhaps no dimension of the charter debate is as contentious and volatile as the effect of these new schools on the equity infrastructure of the American education system. A major conclusion articulated there was that impact has a good deal to do with the equity prism employed for viewing. For example, a homogeneous cluster of students organized around a common vision in a charter school can be seen as:

A wholesome community of common purpose or the unwelcome embodiment of special interests.

An appropriate niche market or a product of entrepreneurial chicanery.

An opportunity to educate more effectively underserved and disadvantaged youngsters or the segregation of poor and minority students.

A vehicle to empower disenfranchised and marginalized families or a scheme to undermine the public good.

Compounding a problem of premature rush to judgment based on deeply held values is the fact that there is still considerable room in the equity empirical warehouse. We have some clues but very few powerful insights and fewer generalizations. In terms of evidence, entire sections of the equity landscape lay fallow.

Nearly all of the data that is available to inform the conversation about the equity impact of charters is concentrated around the question of whether these new schools have a segregating effect on the student population, especially in terms of academic ability, race, and socioeconomic status. We begin reviewing the data on this topic with the knowledge that three factors have the potential to undermine the efforts of charters to enhance, or at least hold steady, the equity fabric of schooling. First, charters are designed to sort students. While this function is fashioned to operate on the basis of "values and beliefs about schooling" (UCLA Charter School Study, n.d., p. 27) and educational mission, the very act of sorting creates potential equity problems. Second, as schools of choice, charters start off in a handicapped position with respect to equity. This is the case because choice, in general, "appears to have a stratifying effect by social class and ethnicity" (Fuller & Elmore, 1996, p. 189). Finally, a variety of factors and pressures inherent to the charter movement have the potential to negate the equity-enhancing dimensions of charters, or, if one prefers, to exacerbate the disequalizing aspects of charters. Among the most salient of these conditions is the ability of charters in some venues to: (1) require preadmission interviews (Horn & Miron, 2000) and/or employ admission criteria (UCLA Charter School Study, n.d.); (2) engage subtle and informed mechanisms to discourage certain students from enrolling (Mulholland, 1999); (3) limit services such as transportation, meals, and sports programs that would discourage less affluent clients from attending (Cobb & Glass, 1999; Dykgraaf & Lewis, 1998; Horn & Miron, 2000); (4) turn the tables and actively select communities and students—rather than allowing students and their families to choose the schools (Horn & Miron, 2000; UCLA Charter School Study, n.d.); and (5) emphasize "parent contracts that require parents to participate in ways specified by the school" (Corwin & Flaherty, 1995, p. 7). In short, in their effort to improve schooling and ensure equity, charters confront some serious obstacles.

Sorting by Ability

Handicapped or not, the question remains: Are charter schools stratifying youngsters on the basis of race, socioeconomic status, and/or achievement? Will they, "as detractors argue . . . cream off the best and most motivated students, leaving the regular public school unable to compete; [will] they become bastions of race and class segregation" (Hassel, 1999b, pp. 7–8)? While the available evidence is mixed and the story line is complicated, in the aggregate, the broadcast is generally, but not uniformly, positive; that is, charters are not stratifying students. We revisit some of the data from Chapter 3 in presenting the case.

To begin with, although considerable concern has been expressed that charters might siphon off the best and the brightest of the student population, there is little evidence that charters are "creaming" off the most academically able students; that is, sorting by academic ability. The following four empirical conclusions are representative of what the research on charters is uncovering on the creaming hypothesis:

> But the weight of evidence pushes toward the opposite conclusion: many charters are conscientiously serving more than their "share" of difficult-to-educate children. Far from "creaming," they are often the recipients of numerous troubled and at-risk youth. (Finn, Manno, & Vanourek, 2000, p. 157)

> "Creaming" involves the selection of only those students who are most able academically, leaving the most difficult students behind. We find little evidence that this is happening in Michigan. In fact, the available evidence (including the relatively low MEAP scores of charter school students) suggests that charter schools are particularly attractive to students who have not done well in regular public schools. (Arsen, Plank, & Sykes, n.d., p. 75)

> Since the passage of the charter school legislation in 1994, charter school organizers/directors have talked about the challenges they face as educators when considering the students they serve while others have surmised that charter schools are "skimming the (academic) cream" off the top. The Goldwater Institute compared standardized test scores of charter school students entering school last fall and the public school population. Charter school students at the fourth and seventh grade levels scored an average of 5 percent lower than the state average and tenth grade charter school students scored an average of 12 percent lower than

the state average, demonstrating that charter schools are not "skimming the cream" off the top. (Gifford & Keller, 1996, p. 2)

While much anxiety about the "creaming" of talented students seemed to appear when charter schools were opened in a particular area, only a small number of the case-study districts seemed to provide evidence that creaming was occurring. (Rofes, 1998b, p. 83)

To the extent that some creaming may be occurring, it involves the parents of charter students. Specifically, even within the same student population (e.g., low-income, average ability white students), there is some evidence that charters are disproportionately populated by parents who are more involved in their children's education and, perhaps, are more educated (Corwin & Flaherty, 1995; Gifford & Keller, 1996). There are hints in some schools that even when focused on low-income students, charter schools tend to serve students "who are better off in terms of having parents who are actively engaged in their education" (Wells, Lopez et al., 1999, p. 175) and families "who are the most advantaged within that group—[those] from smaller and more highly educated families" (Powers & Cookson, 1999, p. 109).

Instead, what we perceive to be occurring to some extent, perhaps unintentionally and unconsciously, is that schools are being organized to exclude students based on a new criterion of undesirability (perhaps "least desirable to teach" or "least desirable to be around"). The criterion being chosen is not the private school's criterion of "ability to pay," nor is it based on academic ability, test-score performance, or record of behavior, nor on racial or ethnic membership. . . . Instead, it is the criterion of having supportive and educationally involved parents. (Becker, Nakagawa, & Corwin, 1997, p. 535)

While the jury is still out on this matter, the evidence accumulated to date argues for more scrutiny of this possible trend in charter schools.

Patterning by Disability

An assortment of "early studies identified special education as one of the key challenges faced by these [charter] schools" (McLaughlin & Henderson, 1998, p. 100). Indeed, it "is one of the most complicated and troublesome areas for charter schools to address. It is also becoming one of the most controversial issues facing charter schools" (Horn & Miron, 2000, p. 27). Some scholars have surfaced the possibility that charter schools may "stimulate us to seek and create school environments that allocate instructional resources and effort more optimally for meeting individual needs" (Szabo & Gerber, 1996, p. 145), and "result in more personalized education for students with disabilities"

(McLaughlin & Henderson, 1998, p. 107). At the same time, these and other investigators have formulated questions about "whether skimming—with the intent of gleaning a pool of the most easy to educate students—is occurring in charter schools" (Dykgraaf & Lewis, 1998, p. 53) and "whether charter schools . . . may be increasing the isolation of students whose needs are greatest or who are the costliest to educate" (Heubert, 1997, pp. 310–311). Still other analysts "express concerns about whether charters [are] resegregating special education students by providing specialized services or niche-focused schools" (Rofes, 1998b, p. 84). In all cases, these chroniclers argue that the special education community must pay attention to the meaning that charters hold for disabled students (Szabo & Gerber, 1996; Horn & Miron, 2000).

Earlier, we revealed some of the general problems that charter schools of choice pose for the equity agenda. Conditions in charters also layer on an additional set of difficulties for efforts to promote equity in the area of special education. At the heart of the problem is the fact that special education has achieved many of its advances through a centralizing strategy, while charter schools privilege site autonomy and localism. McLaughlin and Henderson (1998) expose this issue when they comment that "state legislative provisions can provide specific protections and support for students with disabilities, but individual charters or contracts can differ dramatically with respect to locus of responsibility for meeting the needs of special education students" (p. 107). Szabo and Gerber (1996) reveal another cross section of the problem as they observe:

> Special education, as a national enterprise, depends heavily on the ability of its advocates to inform and influence public school policy. Whether creation of autonomous charter schools will limit the broader community's ability to inform and influence educational planning and programming for students with disabilities is also unknown at this time. (p. 145)

Localism also means that "charter schools will operate, essentially, as one-school districts" (Szabo & Gerber, 1996, p. 144). Szabo and Gerber (1996) and Horn and Miron (2000) worry that economies of scale that are so important in serving high-cost special education students will be a forgone conclusion in charter schools and that, consequently, pressure to underserve disabled youngsters might mount. Szabo and Gerber (1996) also posit that key provisions of charter school legislation "may be challenged by the small scale and variable organizational structure of charter schools" (p. 140).

Localism also creates disjointedness between charters and school districts, and "because the local school district is the usual point of federal program administration, the lack of connection between some charter schools and a local district raises concerns about the flow of federal program funds and locus of accountability" (McLaughlin & Henderson, 1998, p. 100). In addition, because these schools are new and oftentimes out on their own, they confront two additional "problems with respect to special education: unfamiliarity with special education funding processes and lack of preparation to provide assessments and direct services" (p. 100)—a general "unprepared[ness] to accept the challenges of students with disabilities" (p. 100).

Finally, the absence of attention to "the unique problems of cost and scale in providing quality special education" (Szabo & Gerber, 1996, p. 144), coupled with the already documented pattern of general underfunding of charters, may "force charter schools to make programmatic accommodations that may work to the disadvantage of students with disabilities" (p. 144).

The data on patterning of special education students are limited and mixed. No single story line can be discerned at this time. Nonetheless, a hypothesis of underservice merits consideration.

On the equivalence side of the ledger, the UCLA investigators (n.d.) found that "the statewide data show that charter schools enrolled almost equal percentages of special education students as the public school (eight percent in charter schools versus nine percent in public schools)" (p. 14). In their study, the Hudson Institute researchers reported a 12.6% special education population in charters, versus an 11.2% special education population in the rest of the nation's public schools (Finn, Manno, & Vanourek, 2000, p. 81). Becker, Nakagawa, and Corwin (1997) characterized 10.8% of the pupils in the charter schools in their study as special education students versus 12.1% for comparison schools (p. 533). In still another investigation, SRI International reported "little difference between the proportion of children served in charters versus other public schools" (cited in UCLA Charter School Study, n.d., p. 48).

On the nonequivalence side of the ledger, Berman and his colleagues (1999) suggest that charters are serving roughly 27% "fewer students with disabilities than all public schools (8% versus 11%) [with] the percentage of students with disabilities in charter schools and all public schools [being] within 5% in most states" (p. 36). Others have also concluded that special education students are underrepresented in charter schools.

In the Dykgraaf and Lewis (1998) study, "In 10 of the 11 schools ... special education students account[ed] for only 3% of the total enrollment, far below the normal 10 to 13% in traditional public schools" (p. 52). In the McKinney (1996) investigation, special education students comprised only 4% of the student population. Zollers and Ramanathan (1998) also found that charters in their study served a "lower percentage of students with complicated disabilities than [did] local districts" (p. 299).

Finally, Horn and Miron (2000), in their detailed investigation of patterning effects in Michigan, found that "the percentage of enrolled students receiving special education services in charter schools is considerably lower than reported in traditional public schools" (p. 31)—3.74% in charters versus 12.33% in conventional public schools (p. 31). They also discovered important variations "in the nature of the disabling conditions" (p. 32) of the pupils receiving services in charter and in regular public schools. Specifically, "percentages of students identified for services in categorical areas that often require instructional programs outside of the regular education classroom and/or costly related services and equipment . . . are very low or totally unrepresented in charter schools" (p. 32).

While evidence on issues such as the equitable allocation of resources is even scarcer than data on enrollment patterns, the information that is available offers up a cautionary note, especially for for-profit charters (Horn & Miron, 2000). On the funding issue, for example, Garn (1998) revealed that while districts in his study "spent slightly over 10% of their total operating budgets on special needs services" (p. 49), the 46 charter schools devoted only 1.4% of the charter school budget to such services (p. 49). Other researchers have also unearthed configurations of limited resource provision for special education students in charter schools (Dykgraaf & Lewis, 1998), a focus on lower-cost special education students (Horn & Miron, 2000), and sometimes "a pattern of disregard and often blatant hostility toward students with more complicated behavioral and cognitive disabilities" (Zollers & Ramanathan, 1998, p. 298).

Stratification by Race and Class

Given the widespread concern expressed in the literature about the potential stratification of students, considerable attention is being paid to whether charters are sorting youngsters by ethnicity and class. A number of studies have examined this issue by comparing charter school attendance against regular public school enrollments using state and national data (Bierlein, 1996; Gifford, Ogle, & Solmon, 1998; Izu et al., 1998; Little Hoover Commission, 1996; Nathan, 1996a). Consistently, these studies conclude that charter schools "serve a student population comparable to the overall public school population in terms of race and socioeconomic status" (Buechler, 1996, p. IX) and service "disproportionally the families of kids who [are] not succeeding in 'regular' schools or who [are] not well-served by those schools" (Finn, Bierlein, & Manno, 1996, p. 2).

In particular, two national studies of charters lend considerable support to these conclusions. The Hudson Institute, for example, found that 50% of the charter pupils in their study were minorities compared to 34% nationally. Similarly, they reported that 41% of the charter students were eligible for free and reduced-price lunch compared to 37% nationally. The figures for LEP students were 13% charter compared to 7% nationally and for special education were 13% charter to 10% nationally (Vanourek et al., 1997b, p. 2). Their summative conclusions are as follows:

> We do not believe that these numbers sustain the allegation that charter schools are "creaming" or enrolling an "elite" pupil population. (Vanourek et al., 1997b, p. 2)

> In the aggregate, charter schools are serving at least their "share" of disadvantaged youth. (Finn, Manno, & Vanourek, 2000, p. 80)

The 5-year study undertaken by Berman and his colleagues found enrollment patterns similar to those reported by the Hudson Institute team, both at the outset of the investigation (RPP International & University of Minnesota, 1997) and across time as the movement experienced rapid expansion (B. Nelson et al., 2000). In the most recent report, these researchers portrayed enrollment patterns to be minority students (52% charters, 41% nationally), students eligible for free or reduced-price lunch (39% charters, 37% nationally), LEP students (10% charters, 10% nationally), special education youngsters (8% charters, 11% nationally) (B. Nelson et al., 2000, pp. 30, 34, 38, 36). Their penultimate conclusion reads as follows: "Nationwide, students in charter schools have similar demographic characteristics to students in all public schools. However, charter schools in some states have significantly higher percentages of minority or economically disadvantaged students" (p. 2).

Many analysts rightly clamor for caution in employing such aggregate enrollment data to generate conclusions about the equity impact of charters (Cobb & Glass, 1999; Good, Braden, & Drury, 2000; Rofes, 1998b). They assert that local enrollment configurations provide a much more appropriate base from which to draw inferences than do state and national attendance patterns. They maintain that "the aggregated data . . . are powerless to illuminate potential ethnic separation at the level of the school" (Cobb & Glass, 1999, p. 13), "at the level at which it should be measured" (p. 29). Reviewers in this camp indicate that aggregate data can conceal a good deal of the information required to make appropriate assessments of stratification in charter schools (Rofes, 1998b). They hold that "to see . . . ethnic separation . . . one must examine the geography of the situation. The crucial question is not what percents of ethnic groups either are or are not in charter schools; rather, the crucial question is how are ethnic groups distributed between propinquitous charter and traditional public schools" (Cobb & Glass, 1999, p. 8).

When we turn to data from this more nuanced line of work, the conclusions cited above are partially muted. Some reviewers examine the body of research here and determine that "when data are aggregated at the individual school level, or at the level of neighborhood school clusters, the conclusion emerges that charter schools are indeed contributing to increased segregation in American education" (Good, Braden, & Drury, 2000, p. 16). Others are equally resolute in their assessments that "the data clearly demonstrate that the charter schools are providing a variety of choices for parents, not forcing segregation" (Gifford, Ogle, & Solmon, 1998, p. 2). We uncovered a not insignificant number of investigations that help illuminate the question of what disaggregated enrollment patterns reveal about charters' impact on equity. Here is what we learned.

First, some well-designed studies do uncover evidence of the segregating effects of charters—using the more rigorous standard of disproportionate majority enrollment, as opposed to the less rigorous standard of an overconcentration of minority students. In one investigation, SRI International reviewed the demographics of California charters. They discovered that "within-district comparisons showed that in about 40% of charter schools, students were more likely to be white than students in the sponsoring districts, and in about 60% of charter schools, students were less likely to be from low-income families than students in the sponsoring district" (cited in Good, Braden, & Drury, 2000, p. 17).

In a second local unit of analysis study, Becker, Nakagawa, and Corwin (1997) compiled the following demographic portrait: racial and ethnic minorities (45% charters, 46% comparison schools), LEP students (20% charters, 29% comparison schools), pupils eligible for free and reduced-price lunch (35% charters, 48% comparison schools), students qualifying for special education placement (11% charters, 12% comparison schools) (p. 533). Their analysis is as follows:

> Of the seven student characteristics and background variables, three show the charter and comparison schools to be essentially similar—percent from ethnic minority groups, percent qualifying for special education, and percent scoring above grade-level. The other four all show that comparison schools serve a somewhat more difficult-to-teach clientele. Comparison schools have more students who are Limited English Proficient (29% to 20%), more students receiving subsidized school meals (48% vs. 38%), and more students below grade level in achievement (43% vs. 35%). (p. 532)

In a third and especially well-designed study on the issue of segregation at the local level, Cobb and Glass (1999) found that "nearly half of the charter schools exhibited evidence of substantial ethnic separation . . . [and] when comparable nearby traditional public schools were used for comparison, the charters were typically 20 percentage points higher in White enrollment than the other publics" (p. 2). The researchers conclude as follows:

> Clearly, these data show charter schools are more White than the public comparison group. Twenty-six of the public schools were equal to or greater than 70%

White, compared to 38 of the charter schools. That is, two-thirds of the charter schools in metropolitan Phoenix were predominantly White; less than half of the public schools were predominantly White. Described in terms of students, 75% (6493/8676) of the students in metropolitan Phoenix charter schools were in schools that were 70% or more White. In comparison, only 45% (39576/87439) of the students in the public comparison group were in schools 70% or more White. (p. 23)

On the other side of the aisle, a number of studies have examined the stratification issue and have arrived at much less alarming conclusions than did the reports outlined above. In one suggestive study, Arsen and his collaborators (n.d.), employing a methodology that spotlights the geographical location of charters rather than the racial composition of students, uncovered "a systematic negative correlation between PSA [charter] enrollment rates and MAEP [state test] scores" (p. 31). In short, they found that charters were "much more likely to locate in districts with low test scores than in districts with high scores. In districts where less than 40% of the students obtained satisfactory scores, the PSA location quotient is four times higher than in districts where more than 80% of the students obtained satisfactory scores" (p. 31). On the issue of racial patterning, they inform us that in Michigan only about 5% of districts have more than 33% African American enrollment. In their study, they found that charters "are disproportionately located in these 28 districts. Nearly half of the state's PSAs are located in districts where more than a third of the students are African-American. The rate of PSA enrollment in these districts is five times the PSA enrollment rate in districts where less than 1% of the student body is African-American" (p. 30).

There are additional clues from research by Sarason (1998) and Corwin and his colleagues (1996) that charters serve a diverse student population, one "that is fairly representative of the school district student population" (p. 16). In their study in Arizona, Gifford and her research team also uncovered "data that show that charter schools are similar to district schools in most concentrations" (p. 17). While in Minnesota, Nathan's (1998) work reveals that "charter school students are more likely than are students from the districts surrounding the charter to be from low-income groups, to live in communities of color, and to have some form of disability" (p. 502).

In a California study that also employed analysis at the school level, Corwin and Flaherty (1995) found that charters enrolled fewer low-income students than comparison schools, while serving "comparable percentages of minorities" (p. 7). In their summative assessment, they "conclude[d] that while some types of at-risk students tend to be underrepresented, the data do not substantiate sensational claims that charter schools are either creaming the most able privileged students, or skimming out those who traditionally have been underserved" (p. 7).

The comprehensive national study of charters conducted by Berman and his team (1998) supplies additional ammunition to those who conclude that on the equity measuring stick, these new schools compare favorably to schools in the surrounding districts. According to these investigators:

> Sixty-nine percent of charter schools were within 20% of their surrounding district's percentage of nonwhite students, while almost 18% had a distinctly higher percentage of students of color than their surrounding district. Approximately 14% of schools had a lower percentage of students of color than their surrounding district. (B. Nelson et al., 2000, p. 30)

In terms of free and reduced-price lunch eligibility, the Berman team (1998) found that, compared to the average of surrounding districts, about half were not distinct, one quarter served a noticeably higher proportion of low-income students, and one quarter served a distinctly lower proportion of low-income students. They conclude, "Insofar as charter schools are racially distinctive from their surrounding districts, the evidence indicates that they are much more likely to enroll students of color" (p. 56).

What is the summative story line that emerges from our review? First, in the broad sense, it is clear that to date, charters are doing a good job of reaching students from low-income and minority homes. Some of this impact can be attributed to laws that require or encourage a focus on students placed at risk by the current education system. Much can be traced to the visions of those who open charter schools.

More refined studies that use local, as opposed to state and national, comparative data to assess the stratification of youngsters in charter schools provide a more complicated tableau. There are certainly places where charters are undermining the equity infrastructure of education, where equity is defined in terms of racial and class patterns of school enrollments. However, contrary to the claims of some analysts, this is not an inevitable by-product of the charter movement. Rather, as we have reported, much more often than not, charters mirror the socioeconomic demographics of surrounding districts.

We also know that there is a shortage of empirical work on the stratification of students by disability. While conditions appear to be less than might be desired, the situation is far from clear. The reality in terms of sorting appears to rest somewhere between these two assessments:

> The information concerning the education of special needs children in charter schools is mixed. Preliminary data bring both good news and some concerns. As mentioned earlier, some of the schools target children with special needs, but other schools do not. (American Federation of Teachers, n.d., p. 50)

Charter schools are not yet serving the same proportion as traditional public schools of students with disabilities, as determined using federal and state standards and procedures for determining which students have disabilities. (Heubert, 1997, pp. 309–310)

The narrative penned around the stratification issue also leads to the conclusion that vigilance is still the order of the day. The newness of the charter school movement, the absence of compelling data, the presence of conflicting findings, and the likelihood that charters may shift as they mature tells us that continued analysis of the patterning effects of charters must be a priority. The equity landscape does look considerably better than many charter critics suggested. Maintaining these positive contours will require ongoing commitment and work.

In some deep sense, the story line sketched above helps us understand that all equity issues, as are all political topics, are local phenomena. Given this reality and the localizing enhancing, as opposed to centralizing enhancing, dynamics of the charter movement, it is reasonable to expect to continue to see cases that buttress both sides of the equity debate. A reasonable solution to lingering equity concerns, given the totality of information uncovered to date and the patterns those data form, is not to devise improvements that neuter the central features of the charter school movement (e.g., autonomy and local control) by piling back on centralized rules and requirements, but rather to craft safeguards that mesh with the architecture of charter schools.

SYSTEM-WIDE IMPACT

For many educators, the most critical questions in evaluating the charter school movement pertain to how school districts have responded to these schools. In particular: What effects have charter schools had on non-charter schools? (Good, Braden, & Drury, 2000, p. 21)

To achieve the full potential envisioned by charter school advocates, charter schools need to have an influence on other schools and on other students than their own. (Hassel, 1999a, p. 76)

As we discussed in Chapter 5, "One of the most important issues of the many raised by the charter school explosion is the extent to which charter schools affect the behavior of traditional public schools" (Teske et al., 2000, p. 1). The oft stated assumption, carefully delineated earlier, is that these new educational institutions will indeed "act as agents of change for other schools" (Fulford, Raack, & Sunderman, 1997, p. 1) and "as a powerful tool to achieve change within the education system" (Little Hoover Commission, 1996, p. 6). How charters measure up to the theoretical assumptions undergirding systemic change and the system-busting claims of charter advocates will go a long way to determining how "the charter school movement will ultimately be judged" (Weiss, 1997, p. 16).

Background

Although the empirical "evidence is inconclusive on whether or not the growth of charter schools will cause the traditional school districts to improve" (Solmon, Block, & Gifford, 1999, p. 15) and considerable "time and research will be necessary to determine whether charters will have an impact on regular public schools" (Mickelsen, 1997, p. 3), findings to date from the most scientifically credible studies convey the impression that charters are falling far short of expectations in this area, "that charter school competition has not induced large changes in district-wide operations" (Teske et al., 2000, p. 1). In the remainder of the chapter, we unearth knowledge accumulated to date about the system-influencing powers of charters and explore reasons why charters appear to be having considerably less influence as lighthouses of good practice and competitive engines of change than hypothesized.

A few cautionary notes anchor our discussion. To begin with, the movement is relatively new, and "the dynamics of district response to charters are likely to entail a long-term process, the results of which may not yet be apparent" (Hassel, 1999a, p. 130). Thus, even strong charter proponents point out that examples of positive impacts "are still too few really to count" (Finn, Manno, & Vanourek, 2000, p. 46).

In addition, system response can be difficult to assess. In particular, considerable caution is required in drawing parallels between charters and district change. It is important to remember that charters are but one type of school among a complex array of school reforms. Many other powerful reform currents are flowing, and many of them parallel key aspects of the charter movement. Even when we discern temporal connections between the creation of charters and educational and governance changes in neighboring districts, care needs to be taken to test the assumption that the alterations are due to the presence of charters. Change is the norm in public schools. Change, rather than improvement, has historically served as the scorecard to measure organization effectiveness. In a period of massive reform, change is even more prevalent. Therefore, prudence is required in developing attributions about reform activities afoot in districts.

Concomitantly, as we will discover later in this section, forensics in the area of charter school impact need to carefully explore the "structural and attitudinal barriers to replication" (Rosenblum Brigham Associates, 1998, p. 19) that handicap efforts to seed change in surrounding schools and districts.

The definition of impact is contested. For example, here are two views of the findings presented in Rofes's (1998b) comprehensive examination of district response to charters:

> This study finds that 25% of the study districts showed significant signs of response to charters. It is a percentage that is impressive for such a young movement and unprecedented in the history of school reform over the last 30 years. (Center for Education Reform, n.d.e, p. 14)

> A key finding that emerged from this research is that most of the districts did not show signs of strong material impact from the arrival of charter schools in their area. Typically, school districts had not responded with swift, dramatic improvements, as of the time of this study. The majority of districts had gone about business-as-usual and responded to charters slowly and in small ways. (Solmon, Block, & Gifford, 1999, p. 14)

Rofes (1998b) himself argued that the data are consistent with a finding of limited charter school impact on school districts.

Finally, as we have reported throughout this volume, two issues need continual reinforcement. First, "the impact of charters on public schools . . . varie[s] widely across school districts" (Good, Braden, & Drury, 2000, p. 22). Context is critical (Horn & Miron, 2000): "The impact of charters on local school districts was determined in large part by the local context in which public education was being offered and the quantity, quality, and size of local charter schools" (Rofes, 1998b, p. 106). Second, the chain between charter implementation and district response is long and multifaceted and is comprised of links that are often loosely connected. Thus, "Rather than a simple, predictable pattern of response to charters, what has emerged from the data is a complicated portrait involving conflicting tendencies towards resistance, response, refusal to act, and aggressive action" (Rofes, 1998, p. 141).

The Impact Narrative: The Positive Story Line

Reform Pillars and Institutional Arrangements

There is some literature that claims that in addition to benefitting their own students, charters are having an important impact on the larger education system (Goenner, 1996; Hadderman, 1998; Thomas & Borwege, 1996; Vanourek et al., 1997b; Windler, 1996); that "charters are impacting individual schools, changing the attitudes of whole districts, and benefitting public education over all" (Center for Education Reform, n.d.d, p. 1); and that they are "helping stimulate broader system improvements" (Nathan, 1996a, p. 179) and are having a ripple effect on traditional public schools (Center for Education Reform, 2000e). It is useful to consider three overlapping themes that are woven into the impact story line—changes in the basic foundation of schooling, the development of new institutional arrangements, and the promotion of changes in schools and school districts. To begin with, charters can be conceptualized as the engine of larger school reform. Finn and his colleagues (2000) expose this view of charter influence when they posit that these new institutions "are at the epicenter of America's most powerful educational reform earthquake" (p. 219). Another way to cast charter impact as an engine of reform has been provided by Rosenblum Brigham Associates (1998). They hypothesize that it may not be the replication of specific elements of charters that matters most but rather the inculcation of a new mindset about what public education is and what its responsibilities are.

Gathering evidence on the role of charters in reforming American education writ large is a difficult task and an assignment not yet embraced by many in the research community. The question at hand is: To what extent are charters responsible for the growth of choice options in education; the creation of new accountability measures; the spread of autonomy, local control, and decentralized decision making; and other major features on the educational reform landscape? Although charter proponents are often willing to attribute to the charter movement recent changes to the core foundations of our education system, there is very little evidence to this effect regarding this extremely important and complex issue.

A second and related impact theme spotlights the role of charters in promoting the reconfiguration of institutional arrangements in the larger education system. Hassel (1999a) articulates this point when he hypothesizes that charters "might serve as laboratories, not so much for the classroom and management practices they adopt but for the broader set of arrangements under which they work—as examples of institutional form rather than as innovators in curriculum or assessment or some other aspect of practice" (p. 132; see also Loveless & Jasin, 1998). At the institutional level, for example, charters might act to "loosen regulations surrounding teacher certification" (Rofes, 1998b, p. 161), change the balance of power between districts and schools (Hill, Pierce, & Guthrie, 1997), and reshape the relational calculus between districts and employee unions (Nathan, 1996a) and between districts and their constituents (Goenner, 1996).

In many ways, the most significant part of the story regarding impact focuses on the power of charters to reshape the pillars of the current system of education and the related institutional forms of schooling. Yet it is precisely in these areas where we know the least about the influence of charters.

Conditions in Schools and Districts

Most of the discussion regarding system-wide impact centers on changes in school districts and in the schools in communities served by charters. In addition, nearly all the evidence for charter influence is found here. Indeed, advocates for charters have marshalled a body of reports that support the proposition that these new schools are having "a ripple effect well beyond the . . . students being served by them" (Center for Education Reform, n.d.e, pp. 1–2), that some traditional school systems are responding to the competition of charters consistently with the way charter theory suggests they should (Center for Education Reform, n.d.; Finn, Manno, & Vanourek, 2000; Goenner, 1996; Mahtesian, 1998). And a fair reading of the situation supports these assessments: "Indeed, several districts around the country have made changes that are clearly in response to the existence, or the threat of the existence, of a charter school" (Buechler, 1996, p. 35).

An assortment of reviewers have catalogued the ways in which charters have seeded change in surrounding districts and neighboring schools (Buechler, 1996; Center for Education Reform, n.d.e, 2000; Nappi, 1999; Nathan, 1996a; Reynolds, 2000; Rosenblum Brigham Associates, 1998). The most popular positive responses of school districts to charters are of two types: (1) the cloning of school designs, the appeal of which were confirmed by the creation of charters in the district (e.g., a back-to-basics school at the elementary level or an international baccalaureate high school), and (2) the adoption of popular programs or components of neighboring charter schools (e.g., the creation of an after-school program, the use of a longer school day, the development of an elementary foreign language program, the establishment of an all-day kindergarten program) (Arsen, Plank, & Sykes, n.d.; Center for Education Reform, n.d.; Finn, Manno, & Vanourek, 2000; Nappi, 1999; Rofes, 1998a, b). This is what Arsen and his research team (n.d.) characterize as change by adding on rather than by transformation—the addition of "single reforms . . . without changing . . . standard operating procedures" (Teske et al., 2000, p. 14).

The Impact Narrative: The Negative Story Line

While there are numerous places where it can be shown that charter schools have influenced activities in neighboring venues, these reports provide an inadequate foundation from which to build the case for a robust impact of the charter school movement on the larger education system. The problem, as we observed earlier, is that almost all of these reports are anecdotal in nature (Finn, Manno, & Vanourek, 2000). And as Hassel (1999a) reminds us, "While the charter school literature contains . . . many such anecdotes, . . . anecdotes about nonconstructive responses are just as prevalent" (p. 140).

But the charter school movement also faces additional trouble in the court of evidentiary findings. That is, not only is the base on which the case for a positive impact has been built to date academically indefensible, but a growing body of scientifically credible studies arrive at a less-than-sanguine conclusion about the ability of charters to influence the larger education system in a positive manner. Specifically, over the last few years, a handful of well-designed investigations have produced considerable skepticism about the ability of charters to spread change across neighboring schools and districts.

In one study, Buechler (1996) discovered that with a few exceptions, "The effect of charter schools on the public system as a whole has been fairly limited" (ix). Rosenblum Brigham Associates (1998) arrived at a similar conclusion after uncovering "no significant sharing or dissemination of practices from charter schools to district schools at this time" (pp. 1–2). So, too, did the team that conducted the UCLA Charter School Study (n.d.). These investigators uncovered "little evidence to support the claims of charter advocates that charters will infuse productive competition into the educational system or that they will serve as vibrant laboratories where regular public schools can learn about meaningful innovations in education" (p. 56). They found that charters were not serving as "models of positive change and reform throughout the system [and] had not led to any systematic change in the day-to-day functioning of nearby public schools" (p. 54). Based on work in Michigan, Arsen and his colleagues (n.d.) concur with these findings, as does Hassel (1997), based on case studies in four states.

Two additional studies that made the issue of charter school influence the central feature of their investigations arrived at similarly disappointing conclusions. In their examination of charters in Worcester, Massachusetts, Jersey City and Trenton, New Jersey, and the District of Columbia, Teske and his colleagues (2000) "found that charter competition has not induced large changes in district-wide operations" (p. 1). In an earlier investigation of 25 school systems, Rofes (1998b) discovered that 48% of the districts "experienced either high (five or 20%) or moderate (seven or 28%) impact from charter schools and slightly more than half (13 or 52%) experienced either no impact (nine or 36%) or low impact (four or 16%)" (p. 105). His basic observations are that there "was little evidence of laboratory effects" (p. 126) and that the "typical district response to charters [was] business as usual" (p. 114): "Typically, the school districts in this study had not responded with swift, dramatic improvements" (p. 115).

Explaining Disappointing Results

A survey of the information and assessments presented so far on the question of system-wide charter school impact reads as follows: At the macrolevel, on the issue of whether charters are leading a revolution in education and/or reshaping institutional arrangements in schools, little evidence is available. It may turn out that seismic activity here provides the real legacy of the charter school movement. To date, however, while that claim can be formulated, it cannot be supported. At the microlevel, on the issue of whether charters are reshaping neighboring school districts, charters are not having the impact on the regular public school systems for which proponents had hoped. The evidence for positive effects is largely anecdotal and, therefore, suspect. In addition, the more systematic studies almost uniformly fail to support the impact claims that fill the pages of the charter school literature.

One conclusion that might be reached, therefore, is that charter theory is too anemic to power change—that the underlying assumptions of the charter movement do not hold. Or perhaps, using a more refined lens, it may be that the charter power grid is a good deal more complex and considerably less predictable than it is often portrayed to be. The research presented in this chapter certainly lends credence to this initial pathology.

At the same time, our attention is drawn to other explanations as well. For example, we may be confronted not so much with a weak theory as with poor implementation of the design. Some assert that the theoretical infrastructure has been undermined and delinked in so many places that the likelihood for successful impact has been seriously handicapped. As a result, "Several factors have limited the effects of charter schools on traditional public schools" (Teske et al., 2000, p. 4). The consequence, as Sarason (1998), Hassel (1997), and others have ascertained, is that "Charter school programs, as now constituted, do not have much chance of exerting broad systemic impact on public education" (Hassel, 1997, p. 219). They are "currently ill-positioned to have the system-changing effects on public education that charter proponents envision" (p. 224). Others expose the iatrogenic nature of the problem, suggesting that a less-than-stellar performance on the part of charter operators dissuades others from learning from these new institutions. In the remainder of this section, we examine clues that can be culled from the empirical literature to help explain the less-than-hoped-for influence of charters on system-wide operations.

Legislative Compromises

Analysts, like Finn and his colleagues (2000), Hassel (1997), and Teske and his team (2000), reveal that legislative compromises hinder the ability of charters to work their cross-site magic before they even open up shop: "In most states with charter laws, the statutes are too far removed from ideal charter legislation for anyone to say whether charter schools are working or not" (Hassel, 1999a, p. 148). For example, laws that create numerical caps on the number of available charters hinder the formation of the critical mass required to promote change in regular public schools (Finn, Manno, & Vanourek, 2000). In addition, legislation that "cushion[s] the financial blow to existing districts when students choose charter schools . . . [can] lessen the incentives to respond" (Hassel, 1997, p. 198).

Diffusion Problems

Researchers have also observed weaknesses in diffusion theories that hold special relevance for charters. To begin with, as we explained in our discussion of "organizational health" earlier in this chapter, there is not a great deal of evidence that charters are creating new, innovative products and programs that regular public schools might want or need.

In addition, there are almost no mechanisms to facilitate the exchange of ideas and products between charters and more traditional public schools (Good, Braden, & Drury, 2000), "and there has been little incentive to try and create such linkages" (Rosenblum Brigham Associates, 1998, p. 26): "There are virtually no mechanisms in place that would allow traditional public schools and PSAs to learn from each other" (Arsen, Plank, & Sykes, n.d., p. III). Indeed, "Most charter schools lack the time and resources for meaningful collaboration" (UCLA Charter School Study, n.d., p. 55), and given the tendency to frame charters as "responses to inadequate school districts" (Rofes, 1998b, p. 142), it may be difficult to ever "create lines of communication which allow for laboratory effects to be transferred between charter and district schools" (p. 142). As Hassel (1999a) asserts, "It is difficult to imagine charter schools spreading purely on the basis of their success" (p. 133), and with "so little regular communication or interaction between the charter schools and the public schools, it is difficult to imagine how charter schools will serve as laboratories for public schools" (UCLA Charter School Study, n.d., p. 55).

And all of this is made even more problematic by the fact that attention to assessing the quality of innovations that do emerge from charters is conspicuous by its absence (Sarason, 1998). With "as yet no track record of demonstrable success of innovations established in charter schools" (Rosenblum Brigham Associates, 1998, p. 24), public schools find it difficult to determine what is worth replicating (Sarason, 1998) and confront "no compelling reason" (Rosenblum Brigham Associates, 1998, p. 24) to adopt much of anything.

After reviewing the literature on the conditions of knowledge use, Rosenblum and her team (1998) discovered that "virtually none of these conditions apply to the charter school, school district dissemination/knowledge use phenomenon" (p. 26). Neither, they maintain, is there much "convincing evidence that the innovations of charter schools are either free standing or independently replicable" (p. 27). Nor is much attention being devoted to overcoming "long-standing norms of how things are done" (p. 20) in the importing district.

Cushioning Effects

There is considerable evidence that districts and schools are being buffered from the work of charters that is supposed to power reform. Most important, many districts and schools have been made immune to the competition virus that is at the core of the charter school design and thus "feel little to no pressure from the charter schools to change the way they do business" (UCLA Charter School Study, n.d., p. 5).

There are often two layers to this deflecting material. First, in many districts student enrollments are on the rise. As Teske and his colleagues (2000), the UCLA research team (n.d.), and others have documented, this "rising population of school-age children . . . serves to mitigate some of the strongest potential impact of charters" (Rofes, 1998b, p. 109). Indeed, in some places "charters can be viewed as a positive way to deal with space problems" (Teske et al., 2000, p. 8). Second, "Many state policies generally cushion districts from the financial effects of parting students" (p. 1):

> Districts also cushion individual schools from the financial impact of declining enrollments and shrinking market share. They tend to provide constant resources to shrinking schools, in some cases sending extra money to failing schools to "prop them up." (p. 1)

If one accepts the logic of charter theory that "the loss of funding is the linchpin needed to spur an aggressive response on the part of the district" (Rofes, 1998, p. 112), it is easy to envision how such state policies and district practices can decouple the reform engine from the change driveshaft.

District Dynamics

A number of forces afoot in school districts also help deflect the impact of charter schools. There is a feeling in many regular schools that the schools "are being asked to compete on an uneven playing field" (UCLA Charter School Study, n.d., p. 7), that charters are placed in an advantaged position. As the UCLA team hypothesizes, educators who are feeling that they are being treated unfairly are "much less likely to respond to competitive forces in the manner economic theory would suggest" (p. 7). Researches have revealed "substantial skepticism" (Rosenblum Brigham Associates, 1998, p. 24), "an atmosphere of competition, negativism, and animosity" (Horn & Miron, 2000, p. 16), and "hostility between the sectors that limits the spillover from charter schools to traditional public schools" (Teske et al., 2000, p. 11)—hostility that can heighten when charter schools are "created outside the control of school districts" (Powers & Cookson, 1999, p. 116). Rosenblum and her colleagues

(1998) assert that these "attitudinal barriers to communicating and sharing between district and charter schools are greater than the structural barriers" (p. 21).

Even when communication lines may be open and a hostility-free environment prevails, most charter schools are operating on overload and are stretching their resources about as far as possible. There is not an abundance of time and energy—or, for that matter, of incentives or inclinations (Powers & Cookson, 1999) "to share lessons learned with people outside their schools" (Rofes, 1998b, p. 128). Rosenblum and her team (1998) found that "the time and energy required for startup and putting systems in place could not be diverted to disseminating innovations" (p. 24). Finally, charter effects are mediated through an assortment of variables at the district level that can shield impact. One of these is need. It is not unusual for some districts to believe that the need for change is insufficient either to attend to charters or to generate a response. The sense that one is already doing a better job than the competition is hardly a spur to change (Rofes, 1998b). As Arsen and his research team (n.d.) discovered:

> This is especially true in suburban school districts. From the perspective of these administrators, PSAs simply cannot match the teacher quality, facilities, or range of programs available to students in their districts. PSAs do not represent viable competition, and they do not offer useful models for improvement. (p. 60)

A critical component in the need equation is the concept of "critical mass" (Rofes, 1998b, p. 156). Charter competition has to be significant enough to focus the attention of regular public schools. For the many districts that do not have charter competition either at home or close by, this need threshold is rarely reached (Arsen, Plank, & Sykes, n.d.). Even when charter competitors do surface, "As long as charter programs are tiny, most school districts will continue to assume that the costs charters impose do not warrant significant investment in system change" (Hassel, 1997, p. 224). Arsen and his colleagues (n.d.) found this to be the case in Michigan, as did Rofes (1998b) in his study of charter impact in 25 districts. Pipho (1997) wonders at the future regarding this critical mass issue:

> The free-market principle that competition will force the existing system to change will probably remain an elusive goal for some time in the future—that is, unless the education establishment starts sponsoring large numbers of charter schools. (p. 490)

A second variable is incentives, and given the picture we sketched earlier, oftentimes "there is no incentive or stimulus for district schools to learn from charter schools" (Rosenblum Brigham Associates, 1998, p. 27).

Ability to respond is a third condition that mediates the influence of charters. Arsen and his colleagues (n.d.) observed that in some cases district administrators "find themselves unable to respond . . . because the powers that lead students to choose other schools are beyond their power to change" (p. 61). They illustrate this as follows:

> One of the main attractions of charter schools for many parents is their ability to construct a clearly defined school community. Regardless of how widely or intensely such preferences may be held, however, it is generally inappropriate or infeasible for traditional public schools officials to respond to them. PSAs can target niche markets, but traditional public schools must be prepared to serve all of the students living within their attendance boundaries. (p. 61)

Consistent with the larger school reform movement (Beck & Murphy, 1996; Murphy et al., 2001), charter studies have unearthed leadership as the fourth critical mediating variable. Indeed, district leadership may be the key factor in explaining how school systems respond to charters. As Rofes (1998b) discovered in his comprehensive investigation, "The overarching factor [in inspiring district response] appeared to be district leadership. Districts that exhibited a high level of responsiveness to charters usually had reform-minded leaders who seized on charters as a strategic tool to set up reforms in their districts" (p. 151). In districts with less enthusiastic leaders, charter influence is often muted (Teske et al., 2000).

A fifth variable regarding the issue of district reaction is the presence of alternative response moves. Hassel (1999a), for example, has documented the competitive nature of charters. However, he has also observed that "since a constructive response (vast improvement in educational offerings) is so difficult to effect, districts often turn to other ways of dealing with competition, some of which may actually detract from the quality of education" (p. 143). The point, Hassel (1997) contends, is that "even if a charter stimulates a response from its local district, that response may not be aimed at improving education for the district's young people" (p. 205; see also Horn & Miron, 2000; Powers & Cookson, 1999; Rofes, 1998b). In Michigan, for example, Arsen, Plank, and Sykes (n.d.) discovered that "most responses in high-impact districts do not entail basic changes in curriculum or instructional practice. For the most part, these districts do not try to imitate curricula or instructional practices in the PSAs or neighboring districts to which they are losing students" (p. 66). It is not unusual for districts to move scarce resources and energy into their "public relations efforts rather than engage in school reform which target[s] teaching and learning practices" (Rofes, 1998b, p. 141). And some districts spend time and resources attacking the competition and engaging in internecine warfare with charters.

SUMMARY

In this concluding chapter, we brought our analysis of charter schools to a close by reviewing the empirical evidence generated to date on the impact of charters—both on individual charter communities and on the larger educational system. We noted that information about the effects of charters on several important pieces of the conceptual framework of expected benefits detailed in Chapter 6 was too limited to review thoroughly. The two areas where this data void is most visible are efficiency and impact on employees relative to salaries and benefits.

By and large, the picture that emerges from the data we compiled is probably disappointing to charter purists—those who hold that the central goal of charters is to overhaul the extant system of education in the United States. Indeed, at least to date, it is here that the narrative on impact is most bleak. To most other advocates, the evidence will be viewed much more favorably. Certainly, the strident criticisms of many detractors are not supported by the empirical data. With the possible exception of special education, charters are not the sorting and segregating mechanisms that critics envisioned. At the same time, charters are quite effective in building unified communities that are energized by common purpose and mission, two elements on the short list of conditions known to promote school improvement and enhance student learning. Charters are also fairly effective in nurturing the development of professional cultures and in meeting the less rigorous standards for innovation that depend less on "newness" and more on the integration of assorted ideas into a cohesive school program. Still other proponents will be elated with the news that the consumer element of the charter model is working so effectively, as is that sector of the accountability framework that privileges accountability through market forces.

At the same time, while charter proponents can lay claim to a good deal of the battlefield that critics held could not be taken, movements are far from complete. Almost all the results outside the area of customer satisfaction are still tentative. Although explainable, the inability to date of the charter movement to power improvements in the larger educational system is a major problem for this rapidly growing reform model—if not a problem for the average charter school parent or student, then at least for those who created the movement to achieve this goal. The data on student achievement and school accountability, while quite limited, are not nearly as positive as charter advocates had hypothesized. The best that can be said here is that while charters appear to be holding their own on the critical test of whether they can improve student performance (i.e., the question is still open), they are yet to throw off the kind of illumination hoped for by founders of the charter movement. The record on accountability through mechanisms other than markets is even more problematic. And while understandable, the recalibration—downward and employing less stringent criteria—of what counts for success of charters is troubling, especially with regard to the definition of acceptable levels of student achievement.

All in all, charters at this point in time are probably working a good deal better than might be expected given the barren landscape of school reform in the United States and the constraints laid upon charters through the political actions of their opponents and the zealous pronouncements of their advocates. While the long-term health and well-being of the charter movement will be determined by numerous forces more appealing than "empirical evidence of effects," such data will at least have an impact as debates about the future of charters are engaged in and decisions are made. It is our hope that the information provided in this chapter, and throughout this volume, will allow future debates to be well informed.

References

American Association of School Administrators. (2000). *AASA 2000 platform and resolutions*. Arlington, VA: Author. Retrieved November 6, 2000 from: http://www.aasa.org/about/platform2000.htm.

American Federation of Teachers, AFL-CIO. (1988, July 1–6). Resolutions: Education reform. *Convention Report 1988*. San Francisco, CA: Author.

American Federation of Teachers. (1996). *Charter school laws: Do they measure up?* Washington, DC: Author. Retrieved September 10, 1999 from: http://www.aft.org/research/reports/charter/csweb/sum.htm.

American Federation of Teachers. (n.d.). AFT on the issues: Charter schools. Retrieved October 26, 2000 from: http://www.aft.org/issues/charterschools.html.

Anderson, A. B. (1998, March). Charter school finance: Policies, activities and challenges in four states. In *ECS State Notes*. Denver, CO: Education Commission of the States.

Anderson, R. (1997, Spring). Boomers want choice. *Northwest Education Magazine*. Retrieved September 23, 1999 from NWREL database: http://www.nwrel.org/nwedu/spring_97/article 3.html.

Archer, J. (2000, May 17). Accountability measures vary widely. *Education Week, 19*(36), 1, 18–20.

Arsen, D., Plank, D., & Sykes, G. (n.d.). *School choice policies in Michigan: The rules matter*. East Lansing: Michigan State University.

Baber, W. F. (1987). Privatizing public management: The Grace Commission and its critics. In S. H. Hanke (Ed.), *Prospects for privatization. Proceedings of the Academy of Political Science* (Vol. 36, No. 3; pp. 153–163). Montpelier, VT: Capital City Press.

Bailey, R. W. (1987). Uses and misuses of privatization. In S. H. Hanke (Ed.), *Prospects for privatization. Proceedings of the Academy of Political Science* (Vol. 36, No. 3; pp. 138–152). Montpelier, VT: Capital City Press.

Bailey, R. W. (1991). Uses and misuses. In R. L. Kemp (Ed.), *Privatization: The provision of public services by the private sector* (pp. 233–249). Jefferson, NC: McFarland.

Bauman, P. C. (1996, November). Governing education in an antigovernment environment. *Journal of School Leadership, 6*(6), 625–643.

Beales, J. R. (1998, October). *Industry analysis: The private sector in special education*. East Brunswick, NJ: KIDS I.

Beck, L. G., & Murphy, J. (1996). *The four imperatives of a successful school*. Thousand Oaks, CA: Corwin.

Becker, H. J., Nakagawa, K., & Corwin, R. G. (1997, Spring). Parent involvement contracts in California's charter schools: Strategy for educational improvement or method of exclusion? *Teachers College Record, 98*(3), 511–536.

Beers, D., & Ellig, J. (1994). An economic view of the effectiveness of public and private schools. In S. Hakim, P. Seidenstat, & G. W. Bowman (Eds.), *Privatizing education and educational choice: Concepts, plans, and experiences* (pp. 19–38). Westport, CT: Praeger.

Bell, P., & Cloke, P. (1990). Concepts of privatisation and deregulation. In P. Bell & P. Cloke (Eds.), *Deregulation and transport: Market forces in the modern world* (pp. 3–27). London: David Fulton.

Bennett, J. T., & DiLorenzo, T. J. (1987). In S. H. Hanke (Ed.), *Prospects for privatization. Proceedings of the Academy of Political Science* (Vol. 36, No. 3; pp. 14–23). Montpelier, VT: Capital City Press.

Bennett, J. T., & Johnson, M. H. (1980, October). Tax reduction without sacrifice: Private-public production of public services. *Public Finance Quarterly, 8*(4), 363–396.

Berman, P., Nelson, B., Ericson, J., Perry, R., & Silverman, D. (1998). *A national study of charter schools: Second-year report.* Washington, DC: U.S. Department of Education, Office of Educational Research and Improvement.

Berman, P., Nelson, B., Perry, R., Silverman, D., Solomon, D., & Kamprath, N. (1999, May). *The state of charter schools: Third-year report.* Washington, DC: U.S. Department of Education, Office of Educational Research and Improvement.

Bierlein, L. A. (1995–1996, December–January). Catching on but the jury's still out. *Educational Leadership, 53*(4), 90–91.

Bierlein, L. A. (1996). *Charter schools: Initial findings.* Denver, CO: Education Commission of the States.

Bierlein, L. A., & Bateman, M. (1995, November). Opposition forces and educational reform: Will charter schools succeed? *Network News & Views, 14*(11), 48–58.

Bierlein, L. A., & Bateman, M. (1997). Opposition forces and education reform: Will charter schools succeed? In T. A. DeMitchell & R. Fossey (Eds.), *The limits of law-based school reform: Vain hopes and false promises.* Lancaster, PA: Technomic.

Bierlein, L. A., & Fulton, M. F. (n.d.). *Emerging issues in charter school financing.* Denver, CO: Educational Commission of the States (ECS). Retrieved November 4, 1999 from: http:/www.ecs.org/ecs/ecsweb.nsf/23e9e2e827e5df7054b87256667 9005eed71.

Bierlein, L., & Mulholland, L. (1993). *Charter school update: Expansion of a viable reform initiative.* Tempe: Arizona State University, Morrison Institute for Public Policy.

Bierwirth, J. (1997, Spring). Redefine school boundaries. *Northwest Education Magazine.* Retrieved September 23, 1999 from NWREL database: http://www.nwrel. org/nwedu.

Bomotti, S., Ginsberg, R., & Cobb, B. (1999). Teachers in charter schools and traditional schools: A comparative study. *Educational Policy Analysis Archives, 7*(22), 1–23.

Bowman, D. H. (2000, May). Charters, vouchers earning mixed report card. *Education Week, 19*(34), 1, 19–21.

Boyd, W. L., Lugg, C. A., & Zahorchak, G. L. (1996, May). Social traditionalists, religious conservatives, and the politics of outcome-based education. *Education and Urban Society, 28*(3), 347–365.

Bradley, A. (1995). Public backing for schools is called tenuous. *Education Week, 15*(7), 1, 13.

Brazer, H. E. (1981). On tax limitation. In N. Walzer & D. L. Chicoine (Eds.), *Financing state and local governments in the 1980s* (pp. 9–34). Cambridge, MA: Oelgeschlager, Gunn & Hain.

Brown, B. W. (1992). Why governments run schools. *Economics of Education Review, 11*, 287–300.

Brown, S. (1991). A cautionary note. In R. L. Kemp (Ed.), *Privatization: The provision of public services by the private sector* (pp. 272–275). Jefferson, NC: McFarland.

Buchanan, J. M. (1987). *Economics: Between predictive science and moral philosophy.* College Station, TX: Texas A&M University Press.

Buchanan, J. M., & Tullock, G. (1962). *The calculus of consent: Logical foundations of constitutional democracy.* Ann Arbor: University of Michigan Press.

Budde, R. (1988). *Education by charter: Restructuring school districts: Keys to long-term continuing improvement in American education.* Andover, MA: Regional Laboratory for Educational Improvement of the Northeast and Islands.

Budde, R. (1989, March). Education by charter. *Phi Delta Kappan, 70*(7), 518–520.

Budde, R. (1996, September). The evolution of the charter school concept. *Phi Delta Kappan, 78*(1), 72–73.

Buechler, M. (1996). *Charter schools: Legislation and results after four years.* Bloomington, IN: Indiana University, Indiana Education Policy Center.

Bulkley, K. E. (1998, December). *Telling stories: The political construction of charter schools.* Unpublished doctoral dissertation, School of Education, Stanford University, Palo Alto, CA.

Butler, S. (1991). Privatization for public purposes. In W. T. Gormley (Ed.), *Privatization and its alternatives* (pp. 17–24). Madison: The University of Wisconsin Press.

Campbell, R. F., Fleming, T., Newell, L., & Bennion, J. W. (1987). *A history of thought and practice in educational administration.* New York: Teachers College Press.

Carnegie Forum on Education and the Economy. (1986, May). *A nation prepared: Teachers for the 21st century.* Washington, DC: Author.

Carroll, B. J., Conant, R. W., & Easton, T. A. (1987). Introduction. In B. J. Carroll, R. W. Conant, & T. A. Easton (Eds.), *Private means, public ends: Private business in social service delivery* (pp. ix–xiii). New York: Praeger.

Caudell, L. S. (Ed.). (1997a). Basic training department: A determined group of parents fight for a traditional school. *Northwest Education Magazine.* Retrieved September 23, 1999 from Northwest Regional Educational Laboratory (NWREL) database: http://www.nwrel.org/nwedu.

Caudell, L. S. (Ed.). (1997b). Charter for change. *Charters at a Crossroads. Northwest Education Magazine.* Retrieved September 23, 1999 from NWREL database: http://www.nwrel.org/nwedu.

Caudell, L. S. (Issue Ed.). (1997c, Spring). Introduction. *Charters at a Crossroads. Northwest Education Magazine.* Retrieved September 23, 1999 from NWREL database: http://www.nwrel.org/nwedu.

Center for Education Reform. (1998, October). *Charter school legislation: State rankings.* Washington, DC: Author. Retrieved April 14, 1999 from: http://edreform. com/laws/lawrank.htm.

Center for Education Reform. (2000a, May 16). Charters. *CER Newswire, 2*(19).

Center for Education Reform. (2000b, November). *What the research reveals about charter schools.* Washington, DC: The Center for Education Reform. [Also available at: http://edreform.com/pubs/charters.htm.

Center for Education Reform. (2000c, November 28). *Charter school highlights and statistics.* Washington, DC: Author. Retrieved December 19, 2000 from: http:// edreform.com/pubs/chglance.htm.

Center for Education Reform. (2000d). *Charter schools in Indiana.* Washington, DC: Author. Retrieved September 28, 2000 from: http://edreform.com/charter_ schools/states/indiana.htm.

Center for Education Reform. (2000e). *Charter school legislation: Profile of [state] law.* Retrieved March 1, 2001 from: http://edreform.com/charter_schools/laws/.

Center for Education Reform. (n.d.a). *Charter school highlights and statistics.* Washington, DC: Author. Retrieved April 14, 1999 from: http://edreform.com/pubs/ chglance.htm.

Center for Education Reform. (n.d.b). *Charter school legislation: A heartening show of bipartisan support.* Washington, DC: Author. Retrieved July 26, 1999 from: http://edreform.com/laws/bipartisan.htm.

Center for Education Reform. (n.d.c). *Charter school legislation: State rankings.* Washington, DC: Author. Retrieved September 12, 1999 from: http://edreform. com/laws/ranking.htm.

Center for Education Reform. (n.d.d). *Charter school myths and realities: Answering the critics.* Washington, DC: Author. Retrieved September 18, 1999 from: http:// edreform.com.

Center for Education Reform. (n.d.e). *Charter schools: A progress report—Part III: The ripple effect.* Washington, DC: Author. Retrieved September 18, 1999 from: http://edreform.com/pubs/ripple.htm.

Center for Education Reform. (n.d.f). *Charter school survey 1996–1997: Analysis of results.* Washington, DC: Author. Retrieved September 18, 1999 from: http:// edreform.com/pubs.

Center for Market-Based Education. (1998, Fall). *Charter school wage and incentive survey.* Phoenix, AZ: Goldwater Institute, Center for Market-Based Education. Retrieved September 22, 1999 from: http://www.cmbe.org/publications/04_ survey.htm.

Center for Market-Based Education. (1999, May). *Survey of Arizona charter school administrators.* Phoenix, AZ: Goldwater Institute, Center for Market-Based Education. Retrieved September 22, 1999 from: http://cmbe.org/publications/05_ contents.htm.

Cheung, S., Murphy, M., & Nathan, J. (1998, March). *Making a difference: Charter schools, evaluation and student performance.* Minneapolis: University of Minnesota, Hubert H. Humphrey Institute of Public Affairs, Center for School Change.

Cibulka, J. G. (1996, May). Afterword: Interpreting the religious impulse in American schooling. *Education and Urban Society, 28*(3), 378–387.

Ciffolillo, K., & Wolf, R. (n.d.). *Renewal findings: A review of the first fourteen Massachusetts charter school renewal inspection reports.* Boston: Pioneer Institute, Massachusetts Charter School Resource Center.

Citizens League. (1988, November 17). *Citizens League Report: Charter schools = choices for educators + quality for all students.* Minneapolis, MN: Citizens League, School Structure Committee.

Clark, D. L., & Meloy, J. M. (1989). Renouncing bureaucracy: A democratic structure for leadership in schools. In T. J. Sergiovanni & J. A. Moore (Eds.), *Schooling for tomorrow: Directing reform to issues that count* (pp. 272–294). Boston: Allyn & Bacon.

Clarkson, K. W. (1989). Privatization at the state and local level. In P. W. MacAvoy, W. T. Stanbury, G. Yorrow, & R. J. Zeckhauser (Eds.), *Privatization and state-owned enterprises* (pp. 143–194). Boston: Kluwer.

The Clayton Foundation. (1998, January). *1997 Colorado charter schools evaluation study: The characteristics, status and student achievement data of Colorado charter schools.* Denver, CO: Colorado Department of Education.

Cobb, C. D., & Glass, G. V. (1999, January). Ethnic segregation in Arizona charter schools. *Education Policy Analysis Archives, 7*(1), 1–36.

Collins, T. (1999, January). *Charter schools: An approach for rural education.* ERIC Clearinghouse on Rural Education and Small Schools (EDO-RC-98–3). Retrieved September 28, 1999 from: http://www.ael.org/eric/digests/edore983.htm.

Committee for Economic Development. (1994). *Putting learning first: Governing and managing the schools for high achievement.* New York: Author.

Consortium on Productivity in the Schools. (1995). *Using what we have to get the schools we need.* New York: The Institute on Education and the Economy, Teachers College, Columbia University.

Contreras, A. R. (1995, February). The charter school movement in California and elsewhere. *Education and Urban Society, 27*(2), 213–228.

Corwin, R., Carlos, L., Lagomarsino, B., & Scott, R. (1996, May). *From paper to practice: Challenges facing a California charter school.* (Report presented to the San Diego Unified School Board). San Francisco: West Ed.

Corwin, R. G., & Flaherty, J. F. (Eds.). (1995, November). *Freedom and innovation in California's charter schools: Executive summary.* Southwest Regional Laboratory. Retrieved September 15, 1999 from: http://www.wested.org/policy/pubs/full_text/pb_ft_freedom.htm.

Cronin, T. E. (1989). *Direct democracy: The politics of initiative, referendum, and recall.* Cambridge, MA: Harvard University Press.

Cutter, M. (1996, September). City academy. *Phi Delta Kappan, 78*(1), 26–27.

Dahrendorf, R. (1995, Summer). A precarious balance: Economic opportunity, civil society, and political liberty. *The Responsive Community,* 13–39.

David, J. L. (1989, May). Synthesis of research on school-based management. *Educational Leadership, 46*(8), 45–53.

De Alessi, L. (1987). Property rights and privatization. In S. H. Hanke (Ed.), *Prospects for privatization. Proceedings of the Academy of Political Science* (Vol. 36, No. 3; pp. 24–35). Montpelier, VT: Capital City Press.

DeHoog, R. H. (1984). *Contracting out for human services: Economic, political, and organizational perspectives.* Albany: State University of New York Press.

Donahue, J. D. (1989). *The privatization decision: Public ends, private means.* New York: Basic Books.

Downs, A. (1967). *Inside bureaucracy.* Boston: Little, Brown.

Dudek & Company. (1989). *Privatization and public employees: The impact of city and county contracting out on government works.* (Report No. NCEP-RR-88–07). Washington, DC: U.S. National Commission for Employment Policy.

Dunkle, M., Dunn, C., & Rentner, D. (1997). *Flexibility in federal education programs: A guide book for community innovation.* Washington, DC: Center on Education Policy and Institute for Educational Leadership.

Dykgraaf, C. L., & Lewis, S. K. (1998, October). For-profit charter schools: What the public needs to know. *Educational Leadership, 56*(2), 51–53.

Education Commission of the States, & Center for School Change. (1995, August). *Charter schools—what are they up to? A 1995 survey.* Denver, CO: Education Commission of the States and Humphrey Institute of Public Affairs, Center for School Change, University of Minnesota.

Education Commission of the States. (2000, December 12). *ECS State notes: Charter schools: Charter school legislation, 2000.* Denver, CO: Author. Retrieved December 16, 2000 from ECS database: http://www.ecs.org/ecs/ecsweb.nsf/e2addb6ef7 5864c9c94872568b10005d7d8a.

Educational Excellence Network. (1995). *An educational excellence network backgrounder: Charter schools.* Indianapolis, IN: Hudson Institute.

Elmore, R. F. (1990). Introduction: On changing the structure of public schools. In R. Elmore & Associates (Eds.), *Restructuring schools: The next generation of educational reforms* (pp. 1–29). San Francisco: Jossey-Bass.

Elmore, R. F. (1993). School decentralization: Who gains? Who loses? In J. Hannaway & M. Carnoy (Eds.), *Decentralization and school improvement* (pp. 33–54). San Francisco: Jossey-Bass.

Elshtain, J. B. (1995). *Democracy on trial.* New York: Basic Books.

Epstein, J. L. (1992). School and family partnerships. In M. Alkin (Ed.), *Encyclopedia of Educational Research* (6th ed., pp. 1139–1151). New York: Macmillan.

The Evaluation Center. (1998, December). *First annual report of the evaluation of charter schools and the charter school initiative in the state of Connecticut.* Kalamazoo, MI: Western Michigan University.

Farber, P. (1998, March). The Edison Project scores—and stumbles—in Boston. *Phi Delta Kappan, 79*(7), 506–511.

Final fiscal 1997 education appropriations. (1996, October 16). *Education Week, 16*(7), 20.

Final fiscal 1999 education appropriations. (1998, November 4). *Education Week, 18*(10) 30–31.

Fine, M. (1993, Winter). A diary on privatization and on public possibilities. *Educational Theory, 43*(1), 33–39.

Fine, M. (Ed.). (1994). *Chartering urban school reform: Reflections on public high schools in the midst of change.* New York: Teachers College Press.

Finn, C. E., Bierlein, L. A., & Manno, B. V. (1996, January). *Charter schools in action: A first look.* Washington, DC: Hudson Institute, Educational Excellence Network.

Finn, C. E., Manno, B. V., Bierlein, L. A., & Vanourek, G. (1997a, July). *The birthpains and life-cycles of charter schools.* Washington, DC: Hudson Institute.

Finn, C. E., Manno, B. V., Bierlein, L. A., & Vanourek, G. (1997b, July). *The policy perils of charter schools.* Washington, DC: Hudson Institute.

Finn, C. E., Manno, B. V., & Vanourek, G. (2000). *Charter schools in action: Renewing public education.* Princeton, NJ: Princeton University Press.

Fiore, T. A., & Cashman, E. R. (1998, September). *Review of charter school legislation provisions related to students with disabilities* (Report prepared for the Office of Educational Research and Improvement, United States Department of Education). Research Triangle Park, NC: Research Triangle Institute.

Fitzgerald, J. (2000, January). *1998–99 Colorado charter schools evaluation study: The characteristics, status and performance record of Colorado charter schools.* Denver, CO: Colorado Department of Education.

Fitzgerald, R. (1988). *When government goes private: Successful alternatives to public services.* New York: Universe Books.

Fixler, F. L., & Poole, R. W. (1987). Status of state and local privatization. In S. H. Hanke (Ed.), *Prospectives for privatization. Proceedings of the Academy of Political Science* (Vol. 36, No. 3; pp. 164–178). Montpelier, VT: Capital City Press.

Fixler, P. E. (1991). Service shedding—a new option. In R. L. Kemp (Ed.), *Privatization: The provision of public services by the private sector* (pp. 39–52). Jefferson, NC: McFarland.

Florestano, P. S. (1991). Considerations for the future. In R. L. Kemp (Ed.), *Privatization: The provision of public services by the private sector* (pp. 291–296). Jefferson, NC: McFarland.

Fulford, N. (1997). *Charters in our midst: An overview.* Chicago: North Central Regional Educational Laboratory. Retrieved September 23, 1999 from: http://www.ncrel.org/sdrs/pbriefs/97/97–1.over.htm.

Fulford, N., Raack, L., & Sunderman, G. (1997). *Charter schools in our midst: Charter schools as change agents: Will they deliver?* Chicago: North Central Regional Educational Laboratory. Retrieved September 23, 1999 from: http://www.ncrel.org/sdrs/pbriefs/97/97–1.chg.htm.

Fuller, B. (1996, October). Is school choice working? *Educational Leadership, 54*(2), 37–40.

Fuller, B., & Elmore, R. F. (1996). Conclusion: Empirical research on educational choice: What are the implications for policy-makers. In B. Fuller, R. F. Elmore, & G. Orfield (Eds.), *Who chooses? Who loses?: Culture, institutions, and the unequal effects of school choice* (pp. 187–201). New York: Teachers College Press.

Fuller, B., Elmore, R. F., & Orfield, G. (1996). Policy-making in the dark: Illuminating the school choice debate. In B. Fuller, R. F. Elmore, & G. Orfield (Eds.), *Who chooses? Who loses? Culture, institutions, and the unequal effects of school choice* (pp. 1–21). New York: Teachers College Press.

Fusarelli, L. D. (1998, October 30). *Reinventing urban education: Charter schools, small schools and the new institutionalism.* Paper presented at the annual meeting of the University Council for Educational Administration, St. Louis, MO.

Fusarelli, L. D. (1999, February). Reinventing urban education in Texas: Charter schools, smaller schools, and the new institutionalism. *Education and Urban Society, 31*(2), 214–224.

Garcia, G. F., & Garcia, M. (1996, November). Charter schools—another top-down innovation. *Educational Researcher, 25*(8), 34–36.

Gardner, H. (2000, October 19). Paroxysms of Choice. *New York Review of Books, 47*(16), 44–49.

Garn, G. A. (1998, October). The thinking behind Arizona's charter movement. *Educational Leadership, 56*(2), 48–50.

Garn, G. A. (1999, August). Solving the policy implementation problem: The case of Arizona charter schools. *Educational Policy Analysis Archives, 7*(26), 1–17.

Gifford, M., & Keller, T. (1996, April). *Arizona's charter schools: A survey of parents.* (Arizona Issue Analyses No. 140). Phoenix, AZ: Goldwater Institute, Center for Market-Based Education. Retrieved December 12, 1998 from: http://goldwater institute.org/azia/140.htm.

Gifford, M., & Ogle, M. L. (1998, December). *Focus on the parents: Parents talk about charter schools.* Phoenix, AZ: Goldwater Institute, Center for Market-Based Education. Retrieved December 12, 1998 from: http://www.cmbe.org/publications/03_executive.htm.

Gifford, M., Ogle, M., & Solmon, L. (1998, May). *Who is choosing charter schools? A snapshot of geography and ethnicity of charter school students.* Phoenix, AZ: Goldwater Institute, Center for Market-Based Education. Retrieved December 12, 1998 from: http://www.cmbe.org/publications/02_who.htm.

Gifford, M., Phillips, K., & Ogle, M. (2000, November). *Five year charter school study: An overview* [Arizona education analysis]. Tempe, AZ: Goldwater Institute, Center for Market-Based Education.

Glickman, C. D. (1990, September). Pushing school reform to a new edge: The seven ironies of school empowerment. *Phi Delta Kappan, 71*(1), 68–75.

Goenner, J. N. (1996, September). Charter schools: The revitalization of public education. *Phi Delta Kappan, 78*(1), 32–36.

Good, T. L., & Braden, J. S. (2000). *The great school debate: Choice, vouchers and charters.* Mahwah, NJ: Lawrence Erlbaum.

Good, T. L., Braden, J. S., & Drury, D. W. (2000). *Charting a new course. Fact and fiction about charter schools.* Alexandria, VA: National School Boards Association.

Gormley, W. T. (1991). Two cheers for privatization. In W. T. Gormley (Ed.), *Privatization and its alternatives* (pp. 307–318). Madison: The University of Wisconsin Press.

Gottfried, P. (1993). *The conservative movement* (Rev. ed.). New York: Twayne.

Gottstein, R. (1997, Spring). Spark a revolution. *Northwest Education Magazine.* Retrieved September 23, 1999 from NWREL database: http://www.nwrel.org/nwedu/spring_97/article5.html.

Hadderman, M. (1998, February). *Charter schools.* ERIC Clearinghouse on Educational Management (Digest #118). Retrieved November 6, 1999 from: http://eric.voregon.edu/publications/digests/digest118.html.

Hakim, S., Seidenstat, P., & Bowman, G. W. (1994). Introduction. In S. Hakim, P. Seidenstat, & G. W. Bowman (Eds.), *Privatizing education and educational choice: Concepts, plans, and experiences* (pp. 1–15). Westport, CT: Praeger.

Handel, L., Jehl, J., & Rentner, D. (2000). *Understanding flexibility in education programs 2000*. Washington, DC: Institute for Educational Leadership and Center on Education Policy.

Hanke, S. H. (1985). The theory of privatization. In S. M. Butler (Ed.), *The privatization option: A strategy to shrink the size of government* (pp. 1–14). Washington, DC: The Heritage Foundation.

Hanke, S. H., & Dowdle, B. (1987). Privatizing the public domain. In S. H. Hanke (Ed.), *Prospects for privatization. Proceedings of the Academy of Political Science* (Vol. 36, No. 3; pp. 114–123). Montpelier, VT: Capital City Press.

Hanson, E. M. (1991). *School-based management and educational reform: Cases in the USA and Spain*. East Lansing, MI: National Center for Research on Teacher Learning. (ERIC Document Reproduction Service No. ED 336 832)

Hardin, H. (1989). *The privatization putsch*. Halifax, Canada: The Institute for Research on Public Policy.

Harrington-Lueker, D. (1997, August). Reform by charter: Superintendents discover how charter schools fit (or don't) their districts' agendas. *The School Administrator, 54*(7), 6–13.

Hart, G. K., & Burr, S. (1996, September). The story of California's charter school legislation. *Phi Delta Kappan, 78*(1), 37–40.

Hassel, B. C. (1997, June). *Designed to fail? Charter school programs and the politics of structural choice*. Unpublished doctoral dissertation, Harvard University, Cambridge, MA.

Hassel, B. C. (1999a). *The charter school challenge: Avoiding the pitfalls, fulfilling the promise*. Washington, DC: Brookings Institute.

Hassel, B. C. (1999b, January). *Paying for the charter schoolhouse: A policy agenda for charter school facilities financing*. (Charter Friends National Network). Retrieved December 14, 2000 from: http://www.charterfriends.org/facilities.html.

Hatry, H. P. (1991). Problems. In R. L. Kemp (Ed.), *Privatization: The provision of public services by the private sector* (pp. 262–266). Jefferson, NC: McFarland.

Heinz, D. (1983). The struggle to define America. In R. C. Liebman & R. Wuthrow (Eds.), *The New Christian Right: Mobilization and legitimation* (pp. 133–148). New York: Aldine.

Hemming, R., & Mansoor, A. M. (1988). *Privatization and public enterprises* (Occasional Paper No. 56). Washington, DC: International Monetary Fund.

Henig, J. R., Moser, M., Holyoke, T. T., & Lacireno-Paquet, N. (1999, November). *Making a choice, making a difference? An evaluation of charter schools in the District of Columbia*. Washington, DC: The Center for Area Studies, George Washington University.

Heubert, J. P. (1997, Summer). Schools without rules? Charter schools, federal disability law, and the paradoxes of deregulation. *Harvard Civil Rights-Civil Liberties Law Review, 32*(2), 301–353.

Hilke, J. C. (1992). *Competition in government-financed services*. New York: Quorum Books.

Hill, P. T. (1994). Public schools by contract: An alternative to privatization. In S. Hakim, P. Seidenstat, & G. W. Bowman (Eds.), *Privatizing education and educational choice: Concepts, plans, and experiences*. Westport, CT: Praeger.

Hill, P. T., & Bonan, J. (1991). *Decentralization and accountability in public education*. Santa Monica, CA: Rand Corporation.

Hill, P. T., Pierce, L. C., & Guthrie, J. W. (1997). *Reinventing public education: How contracting can transform America's schools*. Chicago: University of Chicago Press.

Himmelstein, J. L. (1983). The New Right. In R. C. Liebman & R. Wuthrow (Eds.), *The New Christian Right: Mobilization and legitimation* (pp. 13–30). New York: Aldine.

Hirsch, W. Z. (1991). *Privatizing government services: An economic analysis of contracting out by local governments*. Los Angeles: University of California, Institute of Industrial Relations.

Hoff, D. J. (1996, October 30). Under new budget charters cash in. *Education Week, 16*(9), 22.

Hood, C. (1994). *Explaining economic policy reversals*. Buckingham, England: Open University Press.

Horn, J., & Miron, G. (2000, July). *An evaluation of the Michigan charter school initiative: Performance, accountability, and impact*. Kalamazoo: Western Michigan University, The Evaluation Center.

Hula, R. C. (1990a). Preface. In R. C. Hula (Ed.), *Market-based public policy* (pp. xiii–xiv). New York: St. Martin's Press.

Hula, R. C. (1990b). Using markets to implement public policy. In R. C. Hula (Ed.), *Market-based public policy* (pp. 3–18). New York: St. Martin's Press.

Immerwahr, J. (1999). *Doing comparatively well: Why the public loves higher education and criticizes K–12*. Washington, DC: The Institute for Educational Leadership, The National Center for Public Policy and Higher Education and the Public Agenda.

Ismael, J. S. (1988). Privatization of social services: A heuristic approach. In J. S. Ismael & Y. Vaillancourt (Eds.), *Privatization and provincial social services in Canada* (pp. 1–11). Edmonton, Canada: The University of Alberta Press.

Izu, J. A., Carlos, L., Yamashiro, K., Picus, L., Tushnet, N., & Wohlstetter, P. (1998). *The findings and implications of increased flexibility and accountability: An evaluation of charter schools in Los Angeles Unified School District*. Los Angeles: West Ed.

Jennings, W., Premack, E., Adelmann, A., & Solomon, D. (n.d.). *A comparison of charter school legislation: Thirty-three states and the District of Columbia incorporating legislative changes through October, 1998*. Washington, DC: U.S. Department of Education.

Kane, P. R. (1998, June 9). *New Jersey charter schools: The first year 1997–1998* (Report prepared for the New Jersey Institute for School Innovation). New York: Teachers College.

Katz, M. B. (1971, Summer). From voluntarism to bureaucracy in American education. *Sociology of Education, 44*(3), 297–332.

Katz, M. B. (1992). Chicago school reform as history. *Teachers College Record, 94*(1), 56–72.

Kaufman, J. (1996). Suburban parents shun many public schools, even the good ones. *Network News & Views, 14*(5), pp. 72–73.

Khouri, N., Cleine, R., White, R., & Cummings, L. (1999, February). *Michigan's charter school initiative: From theory to practice.* Final report prepared for the Michigan Department of Education. Lansing: Michigan Department of Education.

King, K. (1998, January). A charter story. *The American School Board Journal, 185*(1), 20–22.

Kolderie, T. (1990, November). Beyond choice to new public schools: Withdrawing the exclusive franchise in public education. (Policy Report No. 8). Minneapolis, MN: Center for Policy Studies.

Kolderie, T. (1991). Two different concepts. In R. L. Kemp (Ed.), *Privatization: The provision of public services by the private sector* (pp. 250–261). Jefferson, NC: McFarland.

Kolderie, T. (1992, Fall). Chartering diversity. *Equity and Choice, 9*(1), 28–31.

Kolderie, T. (1994, February). Charter schools: States begin to withdraw the "exclusive." *Network News & Views,* 103–108.

Kolderie, T. (n.d.). What does it mean to ask: "Is 'charter schools' working?" *Charter Friends National Network.* Retrieved September 15, 1999 from: http://www.charterfriends.org/working.html.

Lane, B. (1998, September). *A profile of the leadership needs of charter school founders.* Portland, OR: Northwest Regional Educational Laboratory. Retrieved December 12, 1998 from: http://www.nwrel.org/charter/deliverable/index.html.

Lane, B. (n.d.). *Choice matters: Policy alternatives and implications for charter schools.* Portland, OR: Northwest Regional Educational Laboratory. Retrieved July 24, 1999 from: http://www.nwrel.org/charter/policy.html.

Lange, C., Lehr, C., Seppanen, P., & Sinclair, M. (1998, May). Minnesota charter schools evaluation: Final report. Minneapolis: The College of Education and Human Development, Center for Applied Research and Educational Improvement, University of Minnesota.

Lawton, M. (1991). Teenage males said more apt to die from gunshots than natural causes. *Education Week, 10*(26), 4.

Learning Matters, Inc. (1999). Charter schools: Hope or hype? In Alexis Kessler (Producer), *The Merrow Report.* National Public Radio, Learning Matters Inc. in association with WBUR-Boston and Education Week.

Lewis, D. A. (1993). Deinstitutionalization and school decentralization: Making the same mistake twice. In J. Hannaway & M. Carnoy (Eds.), *Decentralization and school improvement* (pp. 84–101). San Francisco: Jossey-Bass.

Lieber, R. (1997, August). What's to fear about charters? *The School Administrator, 7*(54), 14–16.

Lieberman, M. (1988, Winter). Efficiency issues in educational contracting. *Government Union Review, 9,* 1–24.

Lieberman, M. (1989). *Privatization and educational choice.* New York: St. Martin's Press.

Liebman, R. C. (1983). The making of the New Christian Right. In R. C. Liebman & R. Wuthnow (Eds.), *The New Christian Right: Mobilization and legitimation* (pp. 227–238). New York: Aldine.

Liebman, R. C., & Wuthnow, R. (Eds.). (1983). *The New Christian Right: Mobilization and legitimation.* New York: Aldine.

Lindelow, J. (1981). School-based management. In S. C. Smith, J. A. Mazzarella, & P. K. Piele (Eds.), *School leadership: Handbook for survival* (pp. 94–129). Eugene: University of Oregon.

Little Hoover Commission. (1996, March). *The charter movement: Education reform school by school.* Report 138, State of California. Retrieved September 15, 1999 from: http://www.lhc.ca.gov/lhcdir/138rp.html.

Loveless, T., & Jasin, C. (1998, February). Starting from scratch: Political and organizational challenges facing charter schools. *Educational Administration Quarterly, 34*(1), 9–30.

Lutz, S. W. M. (1997). *Charters in our midst: Are charter schools productive schools?* North Central Regional Educational Laboratory. Retrieved September 23, 1999 from: http://www.ncrel.org/sdrs/pbriefs/97/97-lpro.htm.

Mahtesian, C. (1998, January). Charter schools: Learn a few lessons. *Governing, 11*(4), 24–27.

Manno, B. V., Finn, C. E., Bierlein, L. A., & Vanourek, G. (1997a). *Charter school accountability: Problems and prospects.* Washington, DC: Hudson Institute.

Manno, B. V., Finn, C. E., Bierlein, L. A., & Vanourek, G. (1997b). *How charter schools are different: Lessons and implications.* Washington, DC: Hudson Institute.

Manno, B. V., Finn, C. E., Bierlein, L. A., & Vanourek, G. (1998a, Spring). Charter schools: Accomplishments and dilemmas. *Teachers College Record, 99*(3), 537–558.

Manno, B. V., Finn, C. E., Bierlein, L., & Vanourek, G. (1998b, March). How charter schools are different: Lessons and implications from a national study. *Phi Delta Kappan, 79*(7), 489–498.

Marshall, R., & Tucker, M. (1992). *Thinking for a living: Work, skills, and the future of the American economy.* New York: Basic Books.

Martin, B. (1993). *In the public interest? Privatization and public sector reform.* London: Zed Books.

Massachusetts Department of Education. (1998). *Massachusetts charter school initiative: Expanding the possibilities of public education: 1998 report.* Boston: Author.

Massachusetts Department of Education. (n.d.). 603 C.M.R. 1.00. (Massachusetts Regulation). M.G.L. Chapter 71 § 89.

Mathews, D. (1996). *Is there a public for public schools?* Dayton, OH: Kettering Foundation Press.

Mayberry, M. (1991, April). *Conflict and social determinism: The reprivatization of education.* Paper presented at the annual meeting of the American Educational Research Association, Chicago, IL.

Mazzoni, T., & Sullivan, B. (1990). Legislating educational choice in Minnesota: Politics and prospects. In W. L. Boyd & H. J. Walberg (Eds.), *Choice in education: Potential and problems* (pp. 146–176). Berkeley, CA: McCutchan.

McCabe, B. C., & Vinzant, J. C. (1999, July). Governance lessons: The case of charter schools. *Administration & Society, 31*(3), 361–377.

McDonald, J. P. (1999, September 8). The trouble with policy-minded school reform. *Education Week, 19*(1), 68, 46.

McGree, K. (1995a, July). Charter schools: Early learnings. In *Insights on Education Policy and Practice* (No. 5). Austin, TX: Southwest Educational Development Laboratory.

McGree, K. (1995b). *Redefining education governance: The charter school concept.* Austin, TX: Southwest Educational Development Laboratory.

McKinney, J. R. (1996, October). Charter schools: A new barrier for children with disabilities. *Educational Leadership, 54*(21), 22–25.

McLaughlin, M. J., & Henderson, K. (1998, Summer). Charter schools in Colorado and their response to the education of students with disabilities. *The Journal of Special Education, 32*(2), 99–107.

McQueen, A. (1998, November 25). News in brief: A Washington Roundup: Clinton signs school measures into law. *Education Week, 18*(13), 17.

Medler, A. (1996, March). Promise and progress. *The American School Board Journal, 183*(3), 26–28.

Mickelsen, H. H. (1997). *Charters in our midst: Accountability and equity in charter schools.* Chicago: North Central Regional Educational Laboratory. Retrieved September 23, 1999 from: http://www.ncrel.org/sdrs/pbriefs/97/97-lacct.htm.

Miller, J. R., & Tufts, C. R. (1991). A means to achieve "more with less." In R. L. Kemp (Ed.), *Privatization: The provision of public services by the private sector* (pp. 97–109). Jefferson, NC: McFarland.

Mintrom, M., & Vergari, S. (1997, March 24). *Political factors shaping charter school laws.* Paper presented at the annual meeting of the American Educational Research Association, Chicago, IL.

Miron, G. (1999, October). *The initial study of Pennsylvania charter schools: First annual report.* Kalamazoo: The Evaluation Center, Western Michigan University.

Molnar, A. (1996, October). Charter schools: The smiling face of disinvestment. *Educational Leadership, 54*(2), 9–15.

Mulholland, L. A. (1996, March). *Charter schools: The research.* Tempe: Arizona State University, Morrison Institute for Public Policy. Retrieved March 8, 1999 from: http://edreform.com/pubs/morrison.htm.

Mulholland, L. A. (1999, March). *Arizona charter school progress evaluation.* Tempe: Arizona State University, Morrison Institute for Public Policy.

Murnane, R. J., & Levy, F. (1996). *Teaching the new basic skills: Principles for educating children to thrive in a changing economy.* New York: The Free Press.

Murphy, J. (1990). The educational reform movement of the 1980s: A comprehensive analysis. In J. Murphy (Ed.), *The reform of American public education in the 1980s: Perspectives and cases.* Berkeley: McCutchan.

Murphy, J. (1991). *Restructuring schools: Capturing and assessing the phenomena.* New York: Teachers College Press.

Murphy, J. (1992). School effectiveness and school restructuring: Contributions to educational improvement. *School Effectiveness and School Improvement, 3*(2), 90–109.

Murphy, J. (1996). *The privatization of schooling: Problems and possibilities.* Newbury Park, CA: Corwin Press.

Murphy, J. (1999). New consumerism: The emergence of market-oriented governing structures for schools. In J. Murphy & K. S. Louis (Eds.), *The handbook of research on school administration.* San Francisco: Jossey-Bass.

Murphy, J. (2000, February). Governing America's schools: The shifting playing field. *Teachers College Record, 102*(1), 57–84.

Murphy, J., & Adams, J. E. (1998). Educational reform in the United States: 1980–2000. *Journal of Educational Administration, 36*(5), 426–444.

Murphy, J., & Beck, L. G. (1995). *School-based management as school reform: Taking stock.* Newbury Park, CA: Corwin/Sage.

Murphy, J., Beck, L. G., Crawford, M., Hodges, A., & McGaughy, C. L. (2001). *The productive high school: Creating personalized academic communities.* Newbury Park, CA: Corwin Press.

Murphy, J., Gilmer, S., Weise, R., & Page, A. (1998). *Pathways to privatization in education.* Norwood, NJ: Ablex.

Myatt, L., & Nathan, L. (1996, September). One school's journey in the age of reform. *Phi Delta Kappan, 78*(1), 24.

Nappi, C. R. (1999). *Why charter schools? The Princeton story.* Washington, DC: The Thomas B. Fordham Foundation.

Nathan, J. (1996a). *Charter schools: Creating hope and opportunity for American education.* San Francisco: Jossey-Bass.

Nathan, J. (1996b). Early lessons of the charter school movement. *Educational Leadership, 54*(2), 16–20.

Nathan, J. (1998, March). Heat and light in the charter school movement. *Phi Delta Kappan, 79*(7), 499–505.

National Association of Elementary School Principals. (2000). *2000–01 NAESP Platform.* Alexandria, VA: Author. Retrieved October 26, 2000 from: http://www.naesp.org/misc/platform2000.htm.

National Association of Secondary School Principals. (2000, May 6). *Statement of the National Association of Secondary School Principals on charter schools.* Reston, VA: Author. Retrieved October 26, 2000 from: http://www.nassp.org/news/ps_chtr_schols.htm.

National Commission on Excellence in Education. (1983, April). *A nation at risk: The imperative of educational reform.* Washington, DC: U.S. Government Printing Office.

National Conference of State Legislatures. (n.d.). *Education program: Charter schools.* Denver, CO: Author. Retrieved October 26, 2000 from: http://www.ncsl.org/programs/educ/c1schols.htm.

National Education Association. (1998a, January). *Charter schools run by for-profit companies.* Retrieved March 11, 2001 from: http://www.nea.org/issues/charter/corpchar.html.

National Education Association. (1998b, April). *Charter schools: A look at accountabil-*

ity. Retrieved September 30, 1999 from: http://www.nea.org/issues/charter/accnt 98.html.

National Education Association. (1998c, April). *Employee rights and benefits in charter schools.* Retrieved October 1, 1999 from: http://www.nea.org/issues/charter/ employ98.html.

National Education Association. (n.d.a). *In brief: The NEA Charter Schools Initiative.* Washington, DC: Author. Retrieved December 9, 1998 from: http://www.nea.org/ issues/charter/csinit.html.

National Education Association. (n.d.b). *Evaluating state charter school legislation: Questions and answers.* Retrieved April 8, 2001 from: http://www.nea.org/issues/ charter/eval.html.

National Education Association. (n.d.c). *NEA statement on charter schools.* Retrieved October 1, 1999 from: http://www.nea.org/issues/charter/statement.html.

National Education Association. (n.d.d). NEA charter schools resource center. Retrieved September 30, 1999 from: http://www.nea.org/issues/charter/resources. html.

National School Boards Association. (2000, March 31). *2000–2001 resolutions of the National School Boards Association.* Alexandria, VA: Author. Retrieved October 19, 2000 from: http://www.nsba.org/about/resolutions.htm.

National School Boards Association. (n.d.) *Education and the presidential candidates: School choice.* Retrieved October 19, 2000 from: http://www.nsba.org/candidates/ school-choice.htm.

Nelson, B., Berman, P., Ericson, J., Kamprath, N., Perry, R., Silverman, D., & Solomon, O. (2000, January). *The state of charter schools: Fourth-year report.* Washington, DC: U.S. Department of Education, Office of Educational Research and Improvement.

Nelson, H. F. (1997, March). *How much thirty thousand charter schools cost.* Paper presented at the annual meeting of the American Education Finance Association, Jacksonville, FL.

Nelson, H., Muir, E., Drown, R., & To, D. (2000, December). *Venturesome capital: State charter school finance systems* [National charter school finance study]. Washington, DC: U.S. Department of Education.

Niskanen, W. A. (1971). *Bureaucracy and representative government.* Chicago: Aldine-Atherton.

Niskanen, W. A. (1994). *Bureaucracy and public economics.* Brookfield, VT: Edward Elgar Publishing.

Northeast and Islands Regional Educational Laboratory. (1999). *Charter schools: The other public schools.* Providence, RI: LAB at Brown University.

Northwest Regional Educational Laboratory. (1998). *Meeting the equity challenge in public charter schools: Revised edition.* Portland, OR: Author. Retrieved September 23, 1999 from NWREL database: http://www.nwrel.org/cnorse/booklets/ charter/index.html.

Pack, J. R. (1991). The opportunities and constraints of privatization. In W. T. Gormley (Ed.), *Privatization and its alternatives* (pp. 281–306). Madison: The University of Wisconsin Press.

Page, L., & Levine, M. (1996, October). The pitfalls and triumphs of launching a charter school. *Educational Leadership, 54*(2), 26–29.

Payne, J. L. (1995, November). *Profiting from education: Incentive issues in contracting out.* Washington, DC: Education Policy Institute.

Perry, E. (1998, Fall). Charter parents: Involved or not? *Educational Horizons, 77*(1), 37–40.

Peters, T. (1991). Public services and the private sector. In R. L. Kemp (Ed.), *Privatization: The provision of public services by the private sector* (pp. 53–59). Jefferson, NC: McFarland.

Pines, B. Y. (1985). The conservative agenda. In S. M. Butler (Ed.), *The privatization option: A strategy to shrink the size of government* (p. v). Washington, DC: The Heritage Foundation.

Pipho, C. (1997, March). The evolving charter school movement. *Phi Delta Kappan, 78*(7), 489–490.

Pirie, M. (1985). The British experience. In S. M. Butler (Ed.), *The privatization option: A strategy to shrink the size of government* (pp. 51–68). Washington, DC: The Heritage Foundation.

Pirie, M. (1988). *Privatization.* Hants, England: Wildwood House.

Pitsch, M. (1995, October 4). Riley announces first charter-school grants, new study. *Education Week, 15*(5), 18.

Poland, S. V. (1996, April). *Charter schools.* Retrieved September 26, 1999 from: http://www.rdc.udel.edu/pb9602.html.

Powell, A. G., Farrar, E., & Cohen, D. K. (1985). *The shopping mall high school: Winners and losers in the educational marketplace.* Boston: Houghton Mifflin.

Powell, J., Blackorby, J., Marsh, J., Finnegan, K., & Anderson, L. (1997, December). *Evaluation of charter school effectiveness: Part I.* SRI International. (Prepared for Joel Schwartz, Evaluation of Charter School Effectiveness, Office of the Legislative Analyst, State of California.)

Powers, J. M., & Cookson, P. W. (1999, January & March). The politics of school choice research: Fact, fiction, and statistics. *Educational Policy, 13*(1), 104–122.

Premack, E. (1996, September). Charter schools: California's education reform 'power tool.' *Phi Delta Kappan, 78*(1), 60–64.

President Clinton visits nation's first public charter school, announces new steps to support charter schools. (2000, May 4). Washington, DC: Office of the Press Secretary, White House.

President's Commission on Privatization. (1988). *Privatization: Toward more effective government.* Washington, DC: U.S. Government Printing Office.

Prielipp, L. A. (1997, Spring). *We must safeguard equity.* Retrieved September 23, 1999 from: http://www.nwrel.org/nwedu/spring_97/article4.html.

Public Agenda. (1999). *On thin ice: How advocates and opponents could misread the public's views on vouchers and charter schools.* New York: Author.

Putnam, R. D. (1995). Bowling alone: America's declining social capital. *Journal of Democracy, 6*(1), 65–77.

Ramsey, J. B. (1987). Selling the New York City subway: Wild-eyed radicalism or the only feasible solution. In S. H. Hanke (Ed.), *Prospects for privatization. Proceed-*

ings of the Academy of Political Science (Vol. 36, No. 3; pp. 93–103). Montpelier, VT: Capital City Press.

Reynolds, K. (2000). *Innovations in charter schools: A summary of innovative or unique aspects of Michigan charter schools*. Kalamazoo: The Evaluation Center, Western Michigan University.

Richards, C. E., Shore, R., & Sawicky, M. B. (1996). *Risky business: Private management of public schools*. Washington, DC: Economic Policy Institute.

Rofes, E. E. (1995). *Charter schools and the promise of innovation*. Unpublished manuscript.

Rofes, E. E. (1998a, April). *How are school districts responding to charter laws and charter schools?* Berkeley, CA: Policy Analysis for California Education.

Rofes, E. E. (1998b, Fall). *What are the effects of charter laws and charter schools on school districts? A study of eight states and the District of Columbia*. Unpublished doctoral dissertation, University of California, Berkeley.

Rosenblum Brigham Associates. (1998, July). *Innovation & Massachusetts charter schools*. Retrieved September 15, 1999 from: http://www.doe.mass.edu/cs.www/imcs98/798report.html.

Ross, R. L. (1988). *Government and the private sector: Who should do what?* New York: Crane Russak.

Rothstein, R. (1998a, July–August). Charter conundrum. *The American Prospect, 39*, 46–60.

Rothstein, R. (1998b, July–August). Parental involvement. *The American Prospect, 39*, 58. Available: http://epn.org/prospect/39/39rrsbnf.html.

RPP International, & University of Minnesota. (1997, May). *A study of charter schools: First-year report*. Washington, DC: U.S. Department of Education, Office of Educational Research and Improvement.

Rungeling, B., & Glover, R. W. (1991, January). Educational restructuring—The process for change? *Urban Education, 25*(4), 415–427.

Sarason, S. B. (1995). *Parental involvement and the political principle: Why the existing governance structure of schools should be abolished*. San Francisco: Jossey-Bass.

Sarason, S. B. (1998). *Charter schools: Another flawed educational reform*. New York: Teachers College Press.

Sautter, R. C. (1993). *Charter schools: A new breed of public schools*. Oak Brook, IL: North Central Regional Educational Laboratory.

Savas, E. S. (1982). *Privatizing the public sector: How to shrink government*. Chatham, NJ: Chatham House.

Savas, E. S. (1985). The efficiency of the private sector. In S. M. Butler (Ed.), *The privatization option: A strategy to shrink the size of government* (pp. 15–31). Washington, DC: The Heritage Foundation.

Savas, E. S. (1987). *Privatization: The key to better government*. Chatham, NJ: Chatham House.

Scheerens, J. (1999, July). *School self-evaluation: Origins, definition, approaches, methods and implementation issues*. Paper prepared for presentation to the World Bank Effective School and Teachers Group, Washington, DC.

Schnaiberg, L. (1999a, February 10). Building in hand, church leaders float charter ideas. *Education Week, 18*(22), 1, 11.

Schnaiberg, L. (1999b, June 23). Okla., Ore. bump up charter law states to 36. *Education Week, 18*(41), 20, 23.

Schwartz, W. (1996, November). *How well are charter schools serving urban and minority students?* New York: Teachers College. ERIC Clearinghouse on Urban Education (Digest #119). Retrieved October 16, 1999 from: http://eric-web.tc.columbia.edu/digests/dig119.html.

Seader, D. (1991). Privatization and America's cities. In R. L. Kemp (Ed.), *Privatization: The provision of public services by the private sector* (pp. 29–38). Jefferson, NC: McFarland.

Seldon, A. (1987). Public choice and the choices of the public. In C. K. Rowley (Ed.), *Democracy and public choice* (pp. 122–134). New York: Columbia University Press.

Shanker, A. (1988a, Spring). Restructuring our schools. *Peabody Journal of Education, 65*(3), 88–100.

Shanker, A. (1988b, March 31). National Press Club Speech. Washington, DC.

Shanker, A. (1988c, July 10). Where we stand: Convention plots new course—A charter for change. *The New York Times,* E4.

Shanker, A. (1988d, July 17). Where we stand: A charter for change, cont'd.: Less TRUTH—Fewer consequences. *The New York Times,* E9.

Shanker, A. (1988e, November). Charter schools: Option for other 80 percent. *The School Administrator, 45*(10), 72.

Sizer, T. R. (1984). *Horace's compromise: The dilemma of the American high school.* Boston: Houghton Mifflin.

Smith, F. L. (1987). Privatization at the federal level. In S. H. Hanke (Ed.), *Prospects for privatization. Proceedings of the Academy of Political Science* (Vol. 36, No. 3; pp. 179–189). Montpelier, VT: Capital City Press.

Smith, S. (1998, October). The democratizing potential of charter schools. *Educational Leadership, 56*(2), 55–58.

Smrekar, C., & Goldring, E. (1999). *School choice in urban America: Magnet schools and the pursuit of equity.* New York: Teachers College Press.

Snauwaert, D. T. (1993). *Democracy, education, and governance: A developmental conception.* Albany: State University of New York Press.

Solmon, L. C., Block, M. K., & Gifford, M. (1999, August). *A market-based education system in the making: Charter school.* Phoenix, AZ: Goldwater Institute, Market-Based Center for Education. Retrieved September 23, 1999 from: http://cmbe.org/publications/06.htm.

Starr, P. (1987). The limits of privatization. In S. H. Hanke (Ed.), *Prospects for privatization. Proceedings of the Academy of Political Science* (Vol. 36, No. 3; pp. 124–137). Montpelier, VT: Capital City Press.

Starr, P. (1991). The case for skepticism. In W. T. Gormley (Ed.), *Privatization and its alternatives* (pp. 25–36). Madison: University of Wisconsin Press.

Stein, B. (1996, September). O'Farrell community school. *Phi Delta Kappan, 78*(1), 28–29.

Sund, C. (2000, March 3). *Charter schools overview.* Washington, DC: National Education Association. Retrieved October 26, 2000 from: http://www.nea.org/issues/charter/.

Szabo, J. M., & Gerber, M. M. (1996). Special education and the charter school movement. *Special Education Leadership Review, 3*(1), 135–148.

Taebel, D., Barrett, E. J., Chaisson, S., Kemerer, F., Ausbrooks, C., Thomas, K., Clark, C., Briggs, K. L., Parker, A., Weiher, G., Branham, D., Nielson, L., & Tedin, K. (1998, December). *Texas open enrollment charter schools: Second year evaluation.* Arlington, TX: University of Texas, School of Urban and Public Affairs; University of North Texas, Center for the Study of Education Reform; Texas Center for Educational Research; Texas Justice Foundation; University of Houston, Center for Public Policy.

Teske, P., Schneider, M., Buckley, J., & Clark, S. (2000, June). *Does charter school competition improve traditional public schools?* New York: Manhattan Institute for Policy Research.

Thayer, F. C. (1987). Privatization: Carnage, chaos, and corruption. In B. J. Carroll, R. W. Conant, & T. A. Easton (Eds.), *Private means, public ends: Private business in social service delivery* (pp. 146–170). New York: Praeger.

Thomas, D., & Borwege, K. (1996, September). A choice to charter. *Phi Delta Kappan, 78*(1), 29–31.

Thompson, F. (1989). Privatization at the state and local level: Comment. In P. W. MacAvoy, W. T. Stanbury, G. Yorrow, & R. J. Zeckhauser (Ed.), *Privatization and state-owned enterprises* (pp. 202–207). Boston: Kluwer.

Timar, T. B., & Kirp, D. L. (1988, Summer). State efforts to reform schools: Treading between a regulatory swamp and an English garden. *Educational Evaluation and Policy Analysis, 10*(2), 75–88.

Tomlinson, J. (1986). Public education, public good. *Oxford Review of Education, 12*(3), 211–222.

Traub, J. (1999, April 4). A school of your own: It's an idea everybody loves to love. But will charter schools be here tomorrow, or are they just another indispensable innovation of the moment. *The New York Times (Education Life)*, 4A, 30, 42–43.

Tullock, G. (1965). *The politics of bureaucracy.* Washington, DC: Public Affairs Press.

Tullock, G. (1988). *Wealth, poverty, and politics.* New York: Basil Blackwell.

Tullock, G. (1994a). Public choice: The new science of politics. In G. L. Brady & R. D. Tollison (Eds.), *On the trail of homo economicus* (pp. 87–100). Fairfax, VA: George Mason Press.

Tullock, G. (1994b). Social cost and government policy. In G. L. Brady & R. D. Tollison (Eds.), *On the trail of homo economicus* (pp. 65–85). Fairfax, VA: George Mason Press.

Tyack, D. (1992, Fall). Can we build a system of choice that is not just a "sorting machine" or a market-based "free-for-all"? *Equity and Choice, 9*(1), 13–17.

Tyack, D. (1993). School governance in the United States: Historical puzzles and anomalies. In J. Hannaway & M. Carnoy (Eds.), *Decentralization and school improvement* (pp. 1–32). San Francisco: Jossey-Bass.

UCLA Charter School Study. (n.d.). *Beyond the rhetoric of charter school reform: A study of ten California school districts.* Los Angeles: University of California, Los Angeles.

U.S. Department of Education. (1998a, September). *The charter school roadmap.* Washington, DC: Author.

U.S. Department of Education. (1998b, December). Charter schools: A state legislative update. *Research Today.* Washington, DC: U.S. Department of Education, Office of Educational Research and Improvement, National Institute on Student Achievement, Curriculum, and Assessment.

U.S. Department of Education. (2000). *Evaluation of the public charter schools program: Year one evaluation report.* Washington, DC: U.S. Department of Education, Elementary and Secondary Education Division, Planning and Evaluation Service.

U.S. General Accounting Office. (1995a, January). *Charter schools: A growing and diverse national reform movement.* Statement of Linda G. Morra, testimony before the Subcommittee on Labor, Health and Human Services Education, and Related Agencies; Committee on Appropriations; U.S. Senate. Washington, DC: Author.

U.S. General Accounting Office. (1995b, January). *Charter schools: New model for public schools provides opportunities and challenges. Report to congressional requesters.* Washington, DC: Author.

U.S. General Accounting Office. (1998a, March). *Charter schools: Recent experiences in accessing federal funds.* Statement of Cornelia M. Blanchette, Associate Director; Education and Employment Issues; Health, Education and Human Services Division. Washington, DC: Author.

U.S. General Accounting Office. (1998b, April). *Charter schools: Federal funding available but barriers exist.* Washington, DC: Author.

U.S. General Accounting Office. (2000, September). *Charter schools: Limited access to facility financing.* Washington, DC: Author.

Van Horn, C. E. (1991). The myths and realities of privatization. In W. T. Gormley (Ed.), *Privatization and its alternatives* (pp. 261–280). Madison: University of Wisconsin Press.

Vanourek, G., Manno, B. V., Finn, C. E., & Bierlein, L. A. (1997a, June). *Charter schools as seen by those who know them best: Students, teachers, and parents.* Washington, DC: Hudson Institute.

Vanourek, G., Manno, B. V., Finn, C. E., & Bierlein, L. A. (1997b). *The educational impact of charter schools.* Washington, DC: Hudson Institute.

Vickers, J., & Yarrow, G. (1988). *Privatization: An economic analysis.* Cambridge, MA: MIT Press.

Weick, K. E. (1976, March). Educational organizations as loosely coupled systems. *Administrative Science Quarterly, 21*(1), 1–19.

Weiss, A. R. (1994). Variations on a trend in public education: How schools are chartered in eleven states and in the Russian federation. *New Schools, New Communities, 11*(1), 10–20.

Weiss, A. R. (1997). *Going it alone: A study of Massachusetts charter schools.* Retrieved March 30, 1999 from: http://www.csus.edu/ier/charter/IRE_Report.html.

Wells, A. S., Grutzik, S. C., Carnochan, S., Slayton, J., & Vasudeva, A. (1999, Spring). Underlying policy assumptions of charter school reform: The multiple meanings of a movement. *Teachers College Record, 100*(3), 513–535.

Wells, A. S., Lopez, A., Scott, J., & Holme, J. J. (1999, Summer). Charter school as postmodern paradox: Rethinking social stratification in an age of deregulated school choice. *Harvard Educational Review, 69*(2), 172–204.

WestEd & U.S. Department of Education. (2000a, October). State and school information. Retrieved October 18, 2000 from: http://www.uscharterschools.org/pub/uscs_docs/gi/state_map.htm.

WestEd & U.S. Department of Education. (2000b, June 30). Tennessee charter school information. Retrieved September 28, 2000 from: http://www.uscharterschools.org/pub/sp/47.

WestEd & U.S. Department of Education. (2000c, August 4). Puerto Rico charter school information. Retrieved December 20, 2000 from: http://www.uscharterschools.org/pub/sp/31.

WestEd & U.S. Department of Education. (n.d.). Overview of charter schools. Retrieved November 9, 2000 from: http://www.uscharterschools.org/pub/uscs_docs/gi/overview.htm.

Whitty, G. (1984, April). The privatization of education. *Educational Leadership, 41*(7), 51–54.

Wilson, L. A. (1990). Rescuing politics from the economists: Privatizing the public sector. In R. C. Hula (Ed.), *Market-based public policy* (pp. 59–68). New York: St. Martin's Press.

Windler, W. (1996, September). Colorado's charter schools: A spark for change and a catalyst for reform. *Phi Delta Kappan, 78*(1), 66–69.

Wise, A. E. (1989). Professional teaching: A new paradigm for the management of education. In T. J. Sergiovanni & J. H. Moore (Eds.), *Schooling for tomorrow: Directing reforms to issues that count* (pp. 301–310). Boston: Allyn & Bacon.

Wohlstetter, P. (1990, April). *Experimenting with decentralization: The politics of change.* East Lansing, MI: National Center for Research on Teacher Learning. (ERIC Document Reproduction Service No. ED337861)

Wohlstetter, P., & Anderson, L. (1994, February). What can U.S. charter schools learn from England's grant-maintained schools? *Phi Delta Kappan, 75*(6), 486–491.

Wohlstetter, P., & Griffin, N. (1997a, March). *Creating and sustaining learning communities: Early lessons from charter schools.* Paper presented at the annual meeting of the American Educational Research Association, Chicago, IL.

Wohlstetter, P., & Griffin, N. C. (1997b, September). First lessons: Charter schools as learning communities. *CPRE Brief.* Philadelphia: Consortium for Policy Research in Education.

Wohlstetter, P., Wenning, R., & Briggs, K. L. (1995, December). Charter schools in the United States: The question of autonomy. *Educational Policy, 9*(4), 331–358.

Worsnop, R. L. (1992, November). Privatization. *Congressional Quarterly Researcher, 2*(42), 977–1000.

Wuthnow, R. (1983). The political rebirth of American evangelicals. In R. C. Liebman & R. Wuthnow (Eds.), *The New Christian Right: Mobilization and legitimation* (pp. 167–185). New York: Aldine.

Zollers, N. J., & Ramanathan, A. K. (1998, December). For-profit charter schools and students with disabilities: The sordid side of the business of schooling. *Phi Delta Kappan, 80*(4), 297–304.

Index

Accelerated Schools, 95
Accountability mechanism, 9, 134–136, 152
  charter schools and, 15, 134–135, 169–
    173, 190–194
  community and, 136
  freedom for accountability trade-off,
    52–53
  government contracts and, 135–136
  information on accountability systems,
    191–193
  information on consequences, 193–194
  macrolevel empirical backdrop, 190–191
  parents and, 136
Achievement of students, 186–190
  context for, 186–187
  data concerning, 188–190
Adams, J. E., 6
Adelmann, A., 28, 87
Administrators, opposition to charter
  schools, 37–38, 215
Allen, Jeanne, 172
Allocative efficiency, 154–155
Alternative schools, 23
American Association of School Administrators, 38
American Federation of Teachers (AFT),
  12, 15, 17, 20, 22, 24–25, 37, 39–41,
  56–57, 74, 111, 134, 138, 140, 147 n.
  3, 149, 162, 164, 165, 169, 171, 178,
  204
Americans with Disabilities Act (ADA), 69
Anderson, A. B., 62, 64
Anderson, L., 26, 71, 72, 77, 79–81, 86, 88,
  89
Anderson, R., 140

Archer, J., 135, 152, 186–187, 190, 191,
  194
Arsen, D., 19, 51–52, 72, 127, 129, 136–
  140, 142, 143, 148 n. 6, 151, 158–160,
  162–164, 176, 179–182, 196, 203, 209,
  210, 212, 214, 215
Assumptions about charter schools,
  125–136
  accountability, 134–136
  autonomy, 126–131
  competition, 131–134
Ausbrooks, C., 78–84, 88, 89–91, 94, 96,
  98, 99
Autonomy, 126–131
  of charter schools, 52–53, 129–131,
    137–141
  of choice for consumers, 8, 105, 111,
    128, 136
  of markets for suppliers, 127–128
  shared decision making and, 10, 130–131
  site-based management and, 8, 10,
    130–131
  in strengthening individual schools,
    137–141
  of teachers in charter schools, 80–81,
    166, 174–175

Baber, W. F., 113
Bailey, R. W., 113, 132, 154, 168
Barrett, E. J., 78–84, 88, 89–91, 94, 96, 98,
  99
Bateman, M., 2–3, 6, 36, 39, 41, 42, 56, 58,
  131, 135, 200
Bauman, P. C., 103, 105
Beck, L. G., 8, 129, 131, 163, 164, 215

Becker, H. J., 3, 162, 182, 197, 199, 202

Beers, D., 105, 117–118

Bell, P., 111–112, 156

Bennett, J. T., 120, 121, 153, 154

Bennion, J. W., 123

Berman, P., 12–13, 17–19, 29–32, 34, 40, 49, 51–53, 55–56, 58, 66, 67, 71–78, 82–83, 85–87, 92, 93, 128, 137, 141, 143, 145, 160, 174, 175, 183, 186, 187, 190, 192–194, 199, 201, 204

Bierlein, L. A., 2–3, 4, 6, 11, 36–42, 45, 52, 54, 55, 56, 58–64, 68, 69, 71, 73–84, 87, 92–94, 96, 97, 128, 130–132, 135, 136, 139–141, 158, 163, 166, 169, 171, 175–177, 181, 183–185, 187–190, 194, 200–201, 207

Bierwith, J., 162

Blackorby, J., 71, 72, 77, 79–81, 86, 88, 89

Block, M. K., 121, 127, 128, 134, 142, 143, 145, 146, 150, 154, 163, 181, 206, 207

Board of directors of charter school, 88–90
  composition of, 89–90
  member selection, 88–89
  responsibilities of, 88

Bomotti, S., 5–6, 17, 19, 77, 79, 80, 125, 166, 173–175, 177, 179, 180

Bonan, J., 123

Borwege, K., 207

Bowman, D. H., 172

Bowman, G. W., 105, 118

Boyd, W. L., 104

Braden, J. S., 73, 75, 97, 99, 170, 171, 178–179, 185, 189, 191, 201–202, 205, 207, 212

Bradley, A., 119

Branham, D., 78–84, 88–91, 94, 96, 98, 99

Brazer, H. E., 111

Briggs, K. L., 10, 15, 39, 43, 44, 46–47, 49, 55, 78–84, 88–91, 94, 96, 98, 99, 127–131, 136, 139, 140, 170, 193

Brown, B. W., 154

Brown, S., 133, 150, 151

Buchanan, J. M., 120, 131

Buckley, J., 142–146, 170, 188, 205, 206, 209–211, 213, 215

Budde, Ray, 2, 22, 23–25, 42, 130, 140, 143

Budde-Shanker charter model, 22, 23–25

Buechler, M., 2–4, 9–10, 16, 52, 56, 118, 138, 140, 142, 150, 153, 155, 161, 165, 166, 179–182, 187–189, 200, 209, 210

Bulkley, K. E., 3, 5, 9–15, 17–18, 22, 23, 42, 44–46, 115, 118–120, 126, 128–139, 143, 151, 153, 158

Burr, Sue, 19–20, 26

Business cooperatives, 52

Butler, S., 110, 150, 151

Campbell, R. F., 123

Capital costs of charter schools, 62–63

Carlos, L., 4, 18, 20, 67, 94, 98, 125, 126, 129, 130, 139–141, 151, 164, 173–176, 179, 180–185, 187, 189, 191, 193, 200

Carnegie Forum on Education and the Economy, 8, 124

Carnochan, S., 11, 13, 15–17, 25, 26, 105, 117, 153, 157

Carroll, B. J., 109

Categorical funding for charter schools, 59–61
  federal, 60–61
  state, 59–60

Caudell, L. S., 1–2, 16, 37, 52, 128, 135, 143, 157, 163, 178, 186

Center for Education Reform, 29–34, 37–38, 48–52, 56, 70–72, 85, 87, 89, 93, 95, 97, 129, 135, 136, 138, 150, 161–163, 166, 170, 183, 207, 209

Center for Market-Based Education, 90–91

Center for School Change, University of Minnesota, 70, 72–73, 78, 86, 90, 95

Certification of teachers, 56–57, 78

Chaisson, S., 78–84, 88–91, 94, 96, 98, 99

Charter-as-test kitchen approach, 145

Charter Friends Network, 70

Chartering process, 53–55
  caps on number of charter schools, 54–55
  chartering agencies and appeals, 53–54
  length of charter, 54

Charter schools
  acountability and, 15, 134–135, 169–173, 190–194

autonomy and, 52–53, 129–131, 137–141

concerns about effectiveness of schooling, 114–124

cost-benefit analyses of, 149–168

data on, 71–91

described, 3–5

dimensions of all, 48–70

educational program of, 91–99

effects of, 169–217

enrollment data, 32–34, 71–72, 201

history of, 22–47

in history of school reform, 5–9, 126–136

importance of, 1–3

metanarrative on, 16–20

nature of, 3–5

popularity of, 11–16, 29–36

reasons for studying, 1–3

reform dynamics for, 136–146

scaffolding of, 9–10, 101–114

shared assumptions of, 126–136

size of, 137

system-wide change and, 144–146, 205–215

types of, 50–51

Charter Schools Expansion Act of 1998, 34

Charter Schools in Action (Hudson Institute), 73–74, 79, 81–82, 84–85

Charter Schools Initiative Project (NEA), 40–41

Cheung, S., 151, 193

Choice
ideology of, 105, 111
school, 8, 105, 111, 128, 136

Cibulka, J. G., 107

Ciffolillo, K., 186

Citizens League, 27

Clark, C., 78–84, 88, 89–91, 94, 96, 98, 99

Clark, D. L., 123

Clark, S., 142–146, 170, 188, 205, 206, 209–211, 213, 215

Clarkson, K. W., 152

Clayton Foundation, 79, 81

Cleine, R., 79–81, 86, 94, 97, 99

Clinton, Bill, 34, 35

Cloke, P., 111–112, 156

Coalition of Essential Schools, 95

Cobb, B., 5–6, 17, 19, 77, 79, 80, 125, 166, 173–175, 177, 179

Cobb, C. D., 10, 20, 73, 75, 195, 201, 202

Cohen, D. K., 147 n. 2

Collins, T., 134, 137, 139, 161, 164

Committee for Economic Development, 115–117

Communication, within school districts, 213–214

Community
accountability and, 136
and organizational and professional culture, 175–176
in strengthening individual schools, 137–138, 163

Community Learning Centers, 95

Competition, 131–134
benefits of, 132–134, 150–151
cushioning effects and, 213, 215
negative consequences of monopolies, 131–132
in privatization, 9, 15–16, 110–114
system-wide change and, 143–144

Conant, R. W., 109

Condition of education, in states, 43–44

Consortium on Productivity in the Schools, 116–117

Contexts for charter schools, 169–173
importance of, 145–146
political, 46–47
student achievement, 186–187
varying, 17–19

Contreras, A. R., 13, 15, 25

Cookson, P. W., 115, 134, 150, 152, 163–164, 197, 213–215

Core Knowledge, 95, 140

Corwin, R. G., 3, 4, 20, 76, 78, 79, 141, 162, 174, 179, 182, 184, 185, 196, 197, 199, 202, 203

Crawford, M., 164, 215

Creaming hypothesis, 152, 161–163, 196–197

Cronin, T. E., 104–105

Cummings, L., 79–81, 86, 94, 97, 99

Curriculum, 94–96
  development of, 96
  focus on, 95–96
Cutter, M., 28–29

Dahrendorf, R., 102–104, 106
Data on charter schools, 71–91
  founders, 84–87
  leadership, 87–91
  parents, 81–84
  schools, 71–73
  students, 73–77
  teachers, 77–81
David, J. L., 123
De Alessi, L., 109, 110, 112, 120
Decentralization, 8, 10, 113, 130–131
DeHoog, R. H., 103, 152, 153, 156
Democracy
  loosening bonds of, 102
  recasting of, 104–105
Deregulation, 10, 130
DiLorenzo, T. J., 120
Dimensions of charter schools, 48–70
  financial, 57–65
  governmental relations, 65–69
  legal, 49–57
  private organization relations, 70
Directors of charter schools, 90–91
  professional and educational back-
    grounds of, 90–91
  responsibilities of, 90
Donahue, J. D., 103, 108, 167, 168
Dowdle, B., 110, 111
Downs, A., 121
Drown, R., 30, 32, 51, 54, 55, 57–60, 63–
  65, 71, 174
Drury, D. W., 170, 171, 178–179, 185,
  189, 191, 201–202, 205, 207, 212
Dudek & Company, 120, 165, 167
Dunkle, M., 34
Dunn, C., 34
Dykgraaaf, C. L., 60, 77, 195, 198–200

Easton, T. A., 109
Economic environment, 106–114. *See also*
  Financial dimensions of charter schools

budget maximization in, 120–122
critical analyses of public sector, 107–109
discontent and skepticism, 106–107
move from industrial to postindustrial
  economy, 106
perception of state overinvolvement, 107
privatization and, 9, 15–16, 111–114
recalibration of market-governmental
  provision of services, 109–114
Economic factors, state, 43
Economies of scale, 156
Educational administrators, opposition to
  charter schools, 37–38, 215
Educational Excellence Network, 127, 129,
  130, 134, 160
Educational philosophy of charter schools,
  92–93
  range of philosophies, 92–93
  as unifying force, 93
Educational productivity, 115–119
  disconnection with public, 119
  inability to reform successfully, 117–119
  outcome concerns, 115–117
  standards and, 116–117
Educational program of charter schools,
  91–99
  core education philosophy, 92–93
  parent involvement, 97–99
  target focus, 93–97
Educational reform
  of educational system, 141–146
  history of, 5–9, 117–119
  strengthening individual schools,
    137–141
Education by Charter (Budde), 23–24
Education Commission of the States, 31,
  64–65, 72–73, 78, 86, 90, 95
Education management organizations
  (EMOs), 51–52
Effectiveness of schooling, 114–124
  concerns about educational productivity,
    115–119
  questions about existing governance,
    119–124
  standards for charter school effective-
    ness, 170–173

Effects of charter schools, 169–217
  context and, 169–173
  individual school effects, 173–205
  system-wide impact, 141–146, 205–215
Efficacy, and charter schools, 176–177
Efficiency
  allocative, 154–155
  cost-benefit analysis of charter schools
    and, 153–155
  funding schemes for charter schools,
    164–165
  opposition to charter schools, 155–157
  productive, 155
Elementary and Secondary Education Act
  (ESEA), 34
Ellig, J., 105, 117–118
Elmore, R. F., 37, 105, 123, 124, 150, 158,
  160, 162, 195
Elshtain, J. B., 102
Employment conditions in charter schools,
  55–57, 166–168
  employee benefits, 55–56
  employers of teachers, 55
  teacher qualifications, 56–57
  union relations, 55–56
Empowerment of teachers, 173–174
Engler, John, 39
Enrollment data, 32–34, 71–72, 201
Environmental fit, 14
Epstein, J. L., 97
Equity and charter schools, 194–205
  cost-benefit analysis of charter schools
    and, 157–165
  creaming hypothesis, 152, 161–163,
    196–197
  patterning by disability, 197–200
  racial-ethnic composition, 73–75,
    200–204
  socioeconomic status, 60–61, 75–76,
    202–205
Ericson, J., 18, 19, 29–32, 34, 40, 49, 51–
  53, 55–56, 66, 67, 71–77, 82–83, 85–
  87, 92, 93, 128, 137, 141, 143, 145,
  160, 174, 175, 183, 186, 187, 192–194,
  201, 204
Evaluation Center, The, 78–80, 82, 83, 86,

  88, 89, 96, 98, 99, 139, 175, 178, 183,
    188
Expenditures of charter schools, 61–65
  capital costs, 62–63
  operational costs, 61
  start-up costs, 63–65

Facilities of charter schools, 72–73
Farber, P., 69, 189
Farrar, E., 147 n. 2
Federal government
  categorical funding for charter schools,
    60–61
  legislation concerning students with disa-
    bilities, 60–61, 69, 76
  relations with charter schools, 68–69
  role in charter school expansion, 34–36
Financial dimensions of charter schools,
    57–65. *See also* Economic environ-
    ment
  budget maximization in governance,
    120–122
  categorical funding, 59–61
  charter school expenditures, 61–65
  organizational identity and, 50–52
  other revenue sources, 65
  per-pupil base funding, 57–59, 63
  viability of funding schemes, 164–165
Fine, M., 26, 115
Finn, C. E., 2, 4, 10, 11, 18, 36–38, 40, 45,
  52, 54, 55, 58–62, 64, 65, 68, 69, 71,
  73–84, 87, 92–94, 96, 97, 104, 115,
  117, 122–123, 128, 130, 132–142, 145,
  148 n. 5, 148 n. 6, 151, 158, 160, 163,
  166, 169–178, 180, 181, 183–191, 194,
  196, 199, 200–201, 206–209, 211
Finnegan, K., 71, 72, 77, 79–81, 86, 88, 89
Fitzgerald, J., 88, 89, 91, 95, 98
Fitzgerald, R., 102–103, 113, 132
Fixler, F. L., 152
Fixler, P. E., 114
Flaherty, J. F., 76, 78, 79, 174, 179, 182,
  196, 197, 203
Fleming, T., 123
Flexibility, and charter schools, 31–32, 176
Florestano, P. S., 103, 107, 110

For-profit management of charter schools,
51–52
Founders of charter schools, 84–87
characteristics, 84–85
reasons for founding a charter school,
85–87
Fulford, N., 4, 12, 14, 142, 143, 145, 158,
205
Fuller, B., 37, 105, 123, 150, 158, 160, 162,
171, 188, 195
Fulton, M. F., 60, 63, 64
Funding for charter schools. *See* Financial
dimensions of charter schools
Fusarelli, L. D., 3, 58, 72, 98, 116, 154

Garcia, G. F., 123, 129, 133, 135, 160,
164–166, 170
Garcia, M., 123, 129, 133, 135, 160, 164–
166, 170
Gardner, H., 22
Garn, G. A., 6, 12, 17, 41, 70, 114, 123,
129, 132, 133, 136, 138–139, 166, 200
Geographic location of charter schools, 72
Gerber, M. M., 14, 16, 119, 135, 197–199
Gifford, M., 81–84, 96, 121, 127, 128, 132,
134, 142, 143, 145, 146, 150, 154, 163,
171, 181, 183–185, 192, 196–197, 200,
202, 203, 206, 207
Gilmer, S., 9
Ginsberg, R., 5–6, 17, 19, 77, 79, 80, 125,
166, 173–175, 177, 179
Glass, G. V., 10, 20, 73, 75, 195, 201, 202
Glickman, C. D., 123
Glover, R. W., 123
Goenner, J. N., 19, 40, 133, 151, 175, 183,
207–209
Goldring, E., 23
Good, T. L., 73, 75, 97, 99, 170, 171, 178–
179, 185, 189, 191, 201–202, 205, 207,
212
Gormley, W. T., 111, 156
Gottfried, P., 104, 105, 108
Governance in schools, 119–124
budget maximization, 120–122
empire building, 120–122

Government. *See also* Federal government;
School boards; States
accountability and contracts, 135–136
economic environment and, 106–114
sociopolitical environment and, 102–106
Government accountability, 192–193
Governmental relations of charter schools,
65–69
federal government, 68–69
school district, 65–67
state education agency, 67–68
Grade configurations in charter schools, 72
Great Britain grant-maintained schools, 26
Griffin, N., 11, 70, 96, 128, 135, 137, 140,
150, 166, 171, 173, 175–177, 179, 181,
186–188, 190–192, 194
Grutzik, S. C., 11, 13, 15–17, 25, 26, 105,
117, 153, 157
Guthrie, J. W., 1, 6, 16, 38, 59, 63, 116,
118, 122–124, 128, 131–133, 136, 138,
139, 142, 143, 150, 153, 157, 159, 162,
186, 187, 192, 208

Hadderman, M., 5, 15–16, 36, 207
Hakim, S., 105, 118
Handel, L., 69
Hanke, S. H., 110, 111, 121
Hanson, E. M., 124
Hardin, H., 110, 111, 113, 121, 131
Harrington-Lueker, D., 35, 38, 61, 94
Hart, G. K., 19–20, 26, 172
Hassel, B. C., 2, 5, 9–10, 15–17, 19, 26,
29, 36, 37, 43–46, 49–50, 53, 57, 62–
63, 65, 71, 84, 94, 95, 102, 105, 125–
126, 130, 131, 135, 139, 143–145, 147
n. 3, n. 4, 154, 156, 157, 159, 175–
176, 179, 181, 190, 196, 205, 206,
208–212, 214, 215
Hatry, H. P., 152
Healthy Start program, 95
Heinz, D., 104
Hemming, R., 107, 153, 154, 168
Henderson, K., 77, 95, 170, 184, 197–199
Henig, J. R., 173, 184, 186, 187, 194
Herdman, P., 194

Heubert, J. P., 15, 69, 73, 198, 205
Hilke, J. C., 120–122, 132–133, 154, 155
Hill, P. T., 1, 6, 16, 38, 59, 63, 105, 116,
 118, 122–124, 128, 131–133, 136, 138,
 139, 142, 143, 150, 153, 157, 159, 162,
 186, 187, 192, 208
Himmelstein, J. L., 103–104
Hirsch, Eric, 31
Hirsch, W. Z., 103, 107, 113, 121, 122,
 132, 153–156, 168
History of charter schools, 22–47
 development of concept, 22–26
 efforts to influence charter school movement, 38–42
 factors influencing state approaches to
  charter legislation, 43–47
 growth of charter schools, 29–36
 Minnesota as first charter school state,
  27–29
 opposition in, 36–38
 support in, 41–42
History of school reform
 charter schools in, 5–9, 126–136
 inability to reform successfully, 117–
  119
 intensification era (1980–1987), 6–7
 reformation era (1992–present), 8–9
 restructuring era (1986–1995), 7–8
Hodges, A., 164, 215
Hoff, D. J., 35
Holme, J. J., 12, 17–19, 41–42, 101, 104,
 138, 139, 148 n. 5, 157, 159, 163, 164,
 167, 186, 197
Holyoke, T. T., 173, 184, 186, 187, 194
Hood, C., 103, 104, 106–108, 114–115
Horn, J., 78, 80, 83, 86, 88, 89, 179, 181,
 189, 193, 195–200, 207, 213, 215
Hudson, Henry, 23
Hudson Institute, 60–61, 73–74, 75, 76,
 79, 81–82, 84–85, 173–174, 188–189,
 200, 201
Hula, R. C., 102–103, 109, 156

Immerwahr, J., 115
Individualized Education Plans (IEPs), 76

Individual school effects, 173–205
 accountability, 190–194
 customer satisfaction, 182–186
 equity, 194–205
 organizational health, 173–182, 212
 strengthening, 137–141
 student achievement, 186–190
Individuals with Disabilities Education Act
  (IDEA), 60–61, 69, 76
Innovation. *See also* Educational reform;
  History of school reform
 background on, 178–179
 as breakthrough change, 179–180
 defining, 140–141
 as institutional change, 182
 as meeting market needs, 181
 in school management, 143
 as shift from local practice, 180–181
 in strengthening individual schools, 138–
  141, 178–182
 as systemic activity, 181, 212
Innovative schools, 23
Instruction methods, 96–97, 140
Ismael, J. S., 110, 129
Izu, J. A., 18, 67, 94, 98, 125, 126, 129,
 130, 139–140, 151, 164, 173–176, 179,
 180–184, 187, 189, 191, 193, 200

Jasin, C., 3, 4, 16, 68, 118–119, 122, 125,
 128, 129, 131, 153–155, 166, 168, 182,
 208
Jehl, J., 69
Jennings, W., 28, 87
Johnson, M. H., 121, 153, 154

Kamprath, N., 12–13, 17, 18, 29, 31, 32,
 51, 66, 67, 71–78, 85–87, 92, 174,
 183, 190, 192–194, 199, 201, 204
Kane, P. R., 79, 86, 88–90, 98, 99
Katz, M. B., 102–105
Kaufman, J., 119
Keller, T., 82–84, 183, 196–197
Kemerer, F., 78–84, 88–91, 94, 96, 98, 99
Khouri, N., 79–81, 86, 94, 97, 99
Kirp, D. L., 8

Kolderie, Ted, 2, 5, 10, 13–16, 19, 25–28, 52, 112, 123, 127, 134, 141–142, 152, 171, 187

Lacireno-Paquet, N., 173, 184, 186, 187, 194
Lagomarsino, B., 4, 20, 141, 184, 185
Lane, B., 3, 4, 17, 18, 70, 94, 125–126, 128, 134, 139–142, 144–145, 146 n. 2, 158, 161–163, 190, 192
Lange, C., 86, 88, 89, 95, 98, 99
Lawton, M., 123
Leadership of charter schools, 87–91
  board of directors, 88–90
  school directors, 90–91
Learning Matters, Inc., 41, 66, 93
Legal foundations of charter schools, 49–57
  accountability trade-off, 52–53
  chartering process, 53–55
  employment conditions, 55–57
  organizational identity, 50–52
Lehr, C., 86, 88, 89, 95, 98, 99
Levine, M., 128, 143
Levy, F., 106, 116
Lewis, D. A., 106
Lewis, S. K., 60, 77, 195, 198–200
Lieber, R., 38, 123, 142
Lieberman, M., 118
Liebman, R. C., 104
Lighthouse effect, system-wide change and, 143, 144–145
Limited English Proficient (LEP) students, 77, 158, 200–201, 202
Limited-term contracts, 54
Lindelow, J., 123
Little Hoover Commission, 3, 14, 22, 66, 118, 123, 128, 130, 131, 133, 136, 142, 161, 171, 173, 177–179, 182, 183, 187, 194, 200, 205–206
Loan pools, 65
Localism, 14, 198–199
Local level. *See also* School boards
  varying contexts for charter schools, 18–19
Lopez, A., 12, 17–19, 41–42, 101, 104, 138, 139, 148 n. 5, 157, 159, 163, 164, 167, 186, 197

Loveless, T., 3, 4, 16, 68, 118–119, 122, 125, 128, 129, 131, 153–155, 166, 168, 182, 208
Low-income students, 60–61, 75–76, 202–205
Lugg, C. A., 104
Lutz, S. W. M., 93, 194

Magnet schools, 23
Mahtesian, C., 15, 51, 209
Manno, B. V., 2, 4, 10, 11, 18, 36–38, 40, 45, 52, 54, 55, 58–62, 64, 65, 68, 69, 71, 73–84, 87, 92–94, 96, 97, 104, 115, 117, 122–123, 128, 130, 132–142, 145, 148 n. 5, n. 6, 151, 158, 160, 163, 166, 169–178, 180, 181, 183–191, 194, 196, 199, 200–201, 206–209, 211
Mansoor, A. M., 107, 153, 154, 168
Market accountability, 191–192
Marsh, J., 71, 72, 77, 79–81, 86, 88, 89
Marshall, R., 106, 115–118
Martin, B., 107, 110–113, 152, 156, 167
Massachusetts Department of Education, 80–82
Mathews, D., 116, 118, 119
Mayberry, M., 104, 115
Mazzoni, T., 27
McCabe, B. C., 112, 127–128, 145, 149, 151, 154, 155, 157, 159, 161–164
McDonald, J. P., 116–117
McGaughy, C. L., 164, 215
McGree, K., 5, 10, 15, 18, 53, 66, 67, 101, 104, 118–119, 134–135, 137, 138, 141, 142, 149, 153, 158, 160, 162–165, 167
McKinney, J. R., 52, 77, 139, 140, 199
McLaughlin, M. J., 77, 95, 170, 184, 197–199
McQueen, A., 34
Medler, A., 96, 144, 145, 170
Meloy, L. M., 123
Metanarrative on charter schools, 16–20
  moving target problem, 19
  reliability problems, 19–20
  varying local context in, 18–19
  varying state context in, 17–18

Michigan Education Association (MEA), 39, 40, 45

Mickelsen, H. H., 19, 20, 161–163, 171, 206

Miller, J. R., 111

Minnesota, 27–29
early charter schools, 28–29
legislation for charter schools, 27–28

Mintrom, M., 42–45, 47

Miron, G., 78, 80, 83, 86, 88, 89, 178, 179, 181, 183, 189, 193, 195–200, 207, 213, 215

Mission of charter schools, 126–136, 163
accountability, 134–136
autonomy, 126–131
community and, 137–138
competition, 131–134
innovation and, 138–141

Molnar, A., 2, 11, 14–17, 20, 41–42, 101, 133, 147 n. 4, 152, 153, 155, 160, 165, 167, 188

Montessori method, 95

Morale, and charter schools, 176–177

Moser, M., 173, 184, 186, 187, 194

Muir, E., 30, 32, 34, 51, 54, 55, 57–60, 63–65, 71, 174

Mulholland, L. A., 2, 55, 79, 88, 90, 130, 134, 139, 162, 166, 185, 189, 191, 193–195

Murnane, R. J., 106, 116

Murphy, J., 6, 8–10, 14, 109, 129, 131, 147 n. 4, 163, 164, 175, 215

Murphy, M., 151, 193

Nakagawa, K., 3, 162, 182, 197, 199, 202

Nappi, C. R., 139, 154, 209

Nathan, Joe, 3, 6, 15, 23, 24, 26–28, 36, 37, 39, 40, 48, 52, 56, 69, 70, 100, 115, 122, 123, 127, 132–135, 141, 151, 157, 161, 166, 170, 189, 193, 200, 203, 207–209

National Assessment of Educational Progress (NAEP), 43–44

National Association of Elementary School Principals (NAESP), 38

National Association of Secondary School Principals (NASSP), 38

National Charter School Accountability Network, 70

National Charter School Finance Study, 57–59, 60

National Charter School Study, 66, 69, 98

National Commission on Excellence in Education, 6

National Conference of State Legislatures, 31–32

National Education Association (NEA), 3, 37, 39–41, 49–52, 164

National education groups, 40–41. *See also names of specific educational organizations*

National Opinion Research Center, 119

National School Boards Association (NSBA), 38

Nation at Risk, A (National Commission on Excellence in Education), 6

Nelson, B., 12–13, 17–19, 29–32, 34, 40, 49, 51–53, 55–56, 58, 66, 67, 71–78, 82–83, 85–87, 92, 93, 128, 137, 141, 143, 145, 160, 174, 175, 183, 186, 187, 190, 192–194, 199, 201, 204

Nelson, H. F., 30, 32, 34, 51, 54, 55, 57, 59, 60, 63–65, 71, 153, 155, 174

New American Schools Development Corporation, 70, 95

Newell, L., 123

Nielson, L., 78–84, 88–91, 94, 96, 98, 99

Niskanen, W. A., 120–122

Northeast and Islands Regional Educational Laboratory, 3, 14, 15, 56, 127, 161

Northwest Regional Educational Laboratory, 4, 116, 157, 158, 164

Ogle, M. L., 81, 83, 96, 132, 134, 171, 184, 185, 192, 200, 202

Operational costs of charter schools, 61

Opposition to charter schools, 36–41
customer satisfaction and, 185–186
educational administrators and, 37–38, 215
efficiency and, 155–157
equity and, 152, 159–165

Opposition to charter schools (*continued*)
  fear of clustering at-risk students, 163,
    164
  quality and, 152
  reasons for, 149–150
  school boards and, 37–38, 40
  state politics and, 45
  system-wide change and, 209–210
  teacher unions and, 37, 38–40, 45
Orfield, G., 37, 105, 123, 150
Organizational health, 173–182, 212
  innovation and, 178–182, 212
  organizational and professional culture,
    173–177
Organizational identity of charter schools,
  50–52
  for-profit management of charter
    schools, 51–52
  public, nonsectarian schools, 50
  types of charter schools, 50–51
Organizational theory, 12–13

Pack, J. R., 107, 109–111, 121, 150
Page, A., 9
Page, L., 128, 143
Paideia, 95
Parent involvement, 97–99
  amount of, 99
  parent involvement activities, 97–99
Parents and charter schools, 81–84
  accountability and, 136
  customer satisfaction and, 182–186
  demographic data on, 81–82
  learning about charter schools, 84
  parent involvement, 97–99
  parents' rights, 9
  reasons for choosing charter school,
    82–84
  school choice and, 8, 105, 111, 128, 136
Parents' rights, 9
Parker, A., 78–84, 88–91, 94, 96, 98, 99
Pedagogical techniques, 96–97, 140
Perpich, Rudy, 27–28
Per-pupil base funding, 57–59, 63
Perry, E., 128

Perry, R., 12–13, 17–19, 29–32, 34, 40, 49,
    51–53, 55–56, 66, 67, 71–78, 82–83,
    85–87, 92, 93, 128, 137, 141, 143, 145,
    160, 174, 175, 183, 186, 187, 190,
    192–194, 199, 201, 204
Peters, T., 151
Philadelphia Schools Collaborative, 26
Phillips, K., 81, 96
Picus, L., 18, 67, 94, 98, 125, 126, 129,
    130, 139–140, 151, 164, 173–176,
    179–184, 187, 189, 191, 193, 200
Pierce, L. C., 1, 6, 16, 38, 59, 63, 116, 118,
    122–124, 128, 131–133, 136, 138, 139,
    142, 143, 150, 153, 157, 159, 162, 186,
    187, 192, 208
Pines, B. Y., 111
Pioneer Institute, 70
Pipho, C., 133, 214
Pirie, M., 108, 110, 112, 114, 121, 132,
    136, 151, 165, 168
Pitsch, M., 34, 35
Plank, D., 19, 51–52, 72, 127, 129, 136–
    140, 142, 143, 148 n. 6, 151, 158–160,
    162–164, 176, 179–182, 196, 203, 209,
    210, 212, 214, 215
Poland, S. V., 38, 139–140, 166
Policy entrepreneurs, 42, 45
Poole, R. W., 152
Popularity of charter schools, 11–16, 29–36
  environmental fit and, 14
  explanations for, 12
  federal government role in expansion,
    34–36
  framework to attract diverse viewpoints,
    14–16
  in historical development process, 29–36
  increased flexibility of charter laws,
    31–32
  increasing enrollment of charter schools,
    32–34
  increasing number of charter schools,
    32–34
  multiple ends for, 13–14
  multiple meanings of, 12–13
  number of states with charter laws, 30–31

Postindustrialism, 14, 106, 163
Postmodernism, 163
Powell, A. G., 147 n. 2
Powell, J., 71, 72, 77, 79–81, 86, 88, 89
Powers, J. M., 115, 134, 150, 152, 163–164, 197, 213–215
Premack, E., 28, 87, 95, 97
President's Commission on Privatization, 107–108, 112, 113, 114, 152
Prielipp, L. A., 3
Private organizations
    as charter school funding source, 65
    charter school relations with, 70
Privatization, 9, 15–16, 110–114
    charter schools and, 110
    defined, 110
    free market and, 113–114
    objectives of, 110–111
    as political versus economic act, 111–114
Productive efficiency, 155
Professionalism, of teachers in charter schools, 105–106, 165–166, 175
Progressivism, 112, 122
Prudential Foundation, 65
Public Agenda, 19, 20, 115, 119, 128, 133, 134, 146 n. 2, 147 n. 4
Public Charter Schools Program, 34, 68–69
Public School Academies (PSAs), 52, 176, 180, 203, 214. *See also* Charter schools
Public schools
    charter schools compared with, 50, 81
    conversion to charter schools, 50–51, 71–72
    creaming by charter schools and, 152, 161–163, 196–197
Putnam, R. D., 102, 104

Quality, 118
    cost-benefit analysis of charter schools and, 150–152
    customer satisfaction and, 182–186

Raack, L., 14, 142, 143, 145, 158, 205
Ramanathan, A. K., 60, 162, 189, 199, 200
Ramsey, J. B., 122, 168

Reform dynamics in charter schools, 136–146
    reforming educational system, 141–146
    strengthening individual schools, 137–141
Regional factors, state, 43
Reichgott, Ember, 27–28
Reliability, in study of charter schools, 19–20
Rentner, D., 34, 69
Retirement benefits for teachers, 56
Reynolds, K., 178, 179, 181, 209
Richards, C. E., 108, 115, 118
Rofes, E. E., 1–2, 5, 6, 11, 12, 17, 20, 22–23, 38, 41–42, 67, 71, 92, 104, 116–117, 127, 129, 133, 134, 137, 138, 140, 142, 144–146, 147 n. 3, 151, 158–161, 163–165, 182, 197, 198, 201, 207–210, 212–215
Rosenblum Brigham Associates, 5, 17–20, 93, 133, 137–138, 143, 145, 173, 175–177, 181, 206, 208–210, 212–214
Ross, R. L., 104, 156
Rothstein, R., 16, 97, 145, 170, 186
RPP International, 17–19, 49, 50, 67, 73–77, 85, 93, 97–98, 133, 161, 201
Rungeling, B., 123

Salaries
    of directors of charter schools, 91
    of teachers in charter schools, 81, 166–167
Sarason, S. B., 1, 2, 53, 114, 116–118, 123, 124, 129, 139, 148 n. 6, 170, 171, 175–177, 203, 211, 212
Sautter, R. C., 2, 5, 27–29, 127, 133, 137, 139, 140, 143
Savas, E. S., 103, 109–114, 121, 122, 131–132, 136, 151
Sawicky, M. B., 108, 115
Scaffolding of charter schools, 9–10, 101–114
    economic environment, 106–114
    sociopolitical environment, 102–106
Scheerens, J., 155

Schnaiberg, Lynn, 15, 30–32, 43, 50, 66, 70
Schneider, M., 142–146, 170, 188, 205, 206, 209–211, 213, 215
Scholastic Aptitude Test (SAT), 44
School-based management. *See* Site-based management (SBM)
School boards
  charter school relationships with, 65–69
  efforts to influence charter school movement, 40
  opposition to charter schools, 37–38, 40
School choice, 8, 105, 111, 128, 136
School directors. *See* Directors of charter schools
School districts. *See also* School boards
  dynamics within, 213–215
  governmental relations, 65–67
Schwartz, W., 96, 154, 162–163
Scott, J., 12, 17–19, 41–42, 101, 104, 138, 139, 148 n. 5, 157, 159, 163, 164, 167, 186, 197
Scott, R., 4, 20, 141, 184, 185
Seader, D., 113
Seidenstat, P., 105, 118
Seldon, A., 111, 114
Sepannen, P., 86, 88, 89, 95, 98, 99
Shanker, Albert, 22, 24–26, 37, 42, 116, 123
Shared decision making, 10, 130–131
Shore, R., 108, 115
Silverman, D., 12–13, 17–19, 29–32, 34, 40, 49, 51–53, 55–56, 66, 67, 71–78, 82–83, 85–87, 92, 93, 128, 137, 141, 143, 145, 160, 174, 175, 183, 186, 187, 190, 192–194, 199, 201, 204
Sinclair, M., 86, 88, 89, 95, 98, 99
Site-based management (SBM), 8, 10, 130–131
Sizer, T. R., 123
Slayton, J., 11, 13, 15–17, 25, 26, 105, 117, 153, 157
Smith, F. L., 168
Smith, S., 138, 158
Smrekar, C., 23
Snauwaert, D. T., 122–123

Social factors, state, 43
Social market, 10
Sociopolitical environment, 102–106
  democratic professionalism and, 105–106
  empire building and, 120–122
  ideology of choice, 105, 111
  impairment of infrastructure, 102
  loosening bonds of democracy, 102
  plummeting support for government, 102–104
  privatization and, 111–114
  rebalancing control in favor of lay citizens, 105
  recalibration of locus of control, 104
  recasting of democracy, 104–105
Solmon, L. C., 121, 127, 128, 132, 134, 142, 143, 145, 146, 150, 154, 163, 181, 200, 202, 206, 207
Solomon, D., 12–13, 17, 28, 31, 32, 51, 67, 74, 75, 78, 85, 87, 174, 190, 192, 199
Solomon, O., 18, 29, 51, 66, 67, 71–73, 75–77, 85–87, 92, 183, 192–194, 201, 204
Southwestern Minnesota Initiative Fund, 70
SRI International, 75, 199, 202
Standards. *See also* Accountability mechanism
  for charter school effectiveness, 170–173
  educational, 9, 116–117
Starr, P., 103, 108, 110–114, 156
Start-up costs of charter schools, 63–65
States. *See also names of specific states*
  categorical funding of charter schools, 59–60
  factors influencing approaches to charter schools, 43–47
  increased flexibility of charter laws, 31–32
  legal foundations of charter schools, 49–57
  legislative compromises and, 211–212
  number with charter laws, 30–31
  partisan control of state government, 44–45
  per-pupil base funding of charter schools, 57–59, 63

policy entrepreneurs in, 42, 45
political context of, 46–47
state education agency relations with
    charter schools, 67–68
varying contexts for charter schools,
    17–18
Students in charter schools, 73–77
    clustering at-risk students, 163, 164
    creaming high-performing students, 152,
        161–163, 196–197
    customer satisfaction and, 182–186
    Limited English Proficient (LEP) stu-
        dents, 77, 158, 200–201, 202
    low-income, 60–61, 75–76, 202–205
    racial-ethnic composition, 73–75,
        200–204
    students with disabilities, 60–61, 69, 76–
        77, 158, 197–200
Students with disabilities
    in charter schools, 60–61, 76–77, 158,
        197–200
    legislation concerning, 60–61, 69
Sullivan, B., 27
Sund, C., 37
Sunderman, G., 14, 142, 143, 145, 158, 205
Support for charter schools, 41–42
    actions of supporters, 42
    customer satisfaction and, 182–185
    efficiency and, 153–155, 164–165
    equity and, 157–159
    groups and individuals, 42–43
    ideological frameworks, 42
    impact on employees, 165–168
    quality and, 150–151
    reasons for, 149
    system-wide change and, 207–209
Sustainability, and charter schools, 176
Sykes, G., 19, 51–52, 72, 127, 129, 136–
        140, 142, 143, 148 n. 6, 151, 158–160,
        162–164, 176, 179–182, 196, 203, 209,
        210, 212, 214, 215
System-wide change, 141–146, 205–215
    background of, 206–207
    definition of impact, 207
    explaining disappointing results, 210–215
    logic of, 141–142

opposition to charter schools and,
    209–210
pathways to, 142–144
response strategies in, 144
support for charter schools and, 207–209
viability of, 144–146
Szabo, J. M., 14, 16, 119, 135, 197–199

Taebel, D., 78–84, 88, 89–91, 94, 96, 98,
    99
Taylor, Ian, 113
Teachers in charter schools, 77–81
    autonomy of, 80–81, 166, 174–175
    certification, 56–57, 78
    demographic data on, 79–80
    education, 78–79
    employment conditions for, 55–57,
        166–168
    organizational and professional culture
        and, 173–175
    professional experience of, 79
    professionalism and, 105–106, 165–166,
        175
    reasons for working in charter schools,
        80–81
    salaries of, 81, 166–167
Teacher unions
    efforts to influence charter school move-
        ment, 38–40
    employment conditions in charter
        schools and, 55–56
    opposition to charter schools, 37, 38–40,
        45
    original model for charter schools, 22,
        23–25
Tedin, K., 78–84, 88–91, 94, 96, 98, 99
Tenure
    of directors of charter schools, 91
    of teachers in charter schools, 56,
        166–167
Teske, P., 142–146, 170, 188, 205, 206,
    209–211, 213, 215
Thayer, F. C., 111, 113, 152, 167
Thomas, D., 207
Thomas, K., 78–84, 88–91, 94, 96, 98, 99
Thompson, F., 154

Timar, T. B., 8

To, D., 30, 32, 34, 51, 54, 55, 57–60, 63–65, 71

Tomlinson, J., 102

Traub, J., 13, 70, 91, 129, 147 n. 4

Tucker, M., 106, 115–118

Tufts, C. R., 111

Tullock, G., 113, 114, 120–121, 131–133

Tushnet, N., 18, 67, 94, 98, 125, 126, 129, 130, 139–140, 151, 164, 173–176, 179–184, 187, 189, 191, 193, 200

Tyack, D., 105, 118, 122–124, 132, 133, 138, 158–160

UCLA Charter School Study, 11–12, 58–59, 66–67, 75, 77, 85, 90–92, 109, 125, 129, 130, 132, 134, 138, 139, 142–144, 147 n. 4, 151–153, 155, 158, 166, 169–171, 173–177, 179–181, 187, 190–192, 194, 195, 199, 210, 212, 213

Unions. *See* Teacher unions

U.S. Department of Education, 12–13, 18, 30–32, 35, 49, 51, 56, 63, 64, 67–69, 71, 73–76, 82–83, 85, 87, 92–94, 97

U.S. General Accounting Office, 16, 57, 60–63, 68–69, 118, 136, 171

University of Minnesota, 17, 49, 50, 67, 70, 73–77, 85, 93, 97–98, 133, 161, 201

Van Horn, C. E., 111, 112

Vanourek, G., 2, 4, 10, 11, 18, 36–38, 40, 45, 52, 54, 58–62, 64, 65, 69, 71, 73–84, 87, 94, 96, 97, 104, 115, 117, 122–123, 128, 130, 132–142, 145, 148 n. 5, n. 6, 151, 158, 160, 163, 166, 169–178, 180, 181, 183–191, 194, 196, 199, 200–201, 206–209, 211

Vasudeva, A., 11, 13, 15–17, 25, 26, 105, 117, 153, 157

Vergari, S., 42–45, 47

Vickers, J., 121, 156

Vinzant, J. C., 112, 127–128, 145, 149, 151, 154, 155, 157, 159, 161–164

Voluntary association, accountability through, 191

Waiting lists for charter schools, 183

Watkins, Tom, 41–42

Weick, K. E., 10

Weiher, G., 78–84, 88–91, 94, 96, 98, 99

Weise, R., 9

Weiss, A. R., 54, 129, 130, 140, 145, 175–177, 179, 180, 184, 206

Wells, A. S., 11–13, 15–19, 25, 26, 41–42, 101, 104, 105, 117, 138, 139, 148 n. 5, 153, 157, 159, 163, 164, 167, 186, 197

Wenning, R., 10, 15, 39, 43, 44, 46–47, 49, 55, 127–131, 136, 139, 140, 170, 193

WestEd, 30, 31, 32, 35

White, R., 79–81, 86, 94, 97, 99

Whitty, G., 115

Whole-school reform, 141

Wilson, L. A., 132

Windler, W., 128, 136, 186, 207

Wise, A. E., 123

Wohlstetter, P., 8, 10, 11, 15, 18, 26, 39, 43, 44, 46–47, 49, 55, 67, 70, 94, 96, 98, 125–131, 135–137, 139–140, 150, 151, 164, 166, 170, 171, 173–177, 179, 180–184, 186–194, 200

Wolf, R., 186

Worsnop, R. L., 110, 168

Wuthnow, R., 104

Yamashiro, K., 18, 67, 94, 98, 125, 126, 129, 130, 139–140, 151, 164, 173–176, 179, 180–184, 187, 189, 191, 193, 200

Yarrow, G., 121, 156

Zahorchak, G. L., 104

Zollers, N. J., 60, 162, 189, 199, 200

About the Authors

Joseph Murphy is the William Ray Flesher Professor of Education at The Ohio State University and the President of the Ohio Principals Leadership Academy. He is also the Chair of the Interstate School Leaders Licensure Consortium. Murphy is a former Vice President of the American Educational Research Association (Division A, Administration). He is co-editor (with Karen Seashore Louis) of the 1999 AERA *Handbook of Research on Education and Administration*.

Murphy's primary interest is in school improvement, with emphases in the areas of policy and leadership. He also works in the area of leadership preparation and training. He has written twelve books in these areas and edited another eleven. His most recent book, *The Productive High School: Creating Personalized Academic Communities*, was published in 2001. Murphy has also published more than 150 book chapters and articles for leading academic journals and professional outlets.

Catherine Dunn Shiffman is a Ph.D. candidate in the Department of Leadership and Organizations at Vanderbilt University. She holds an Ed.M. from the Harvard Graduate School of Education and a B.A. from Middlebury College. She taught as a Peace Corps Volunteer in Thailand, and has worked on education policy issues at the Institute for Educational Leadership in Washington, D.C. and the U.S.-Indochina Reconciliation Project in New York City.